Montaigne and the
Art of Free-Thinking

The Past in the Present

Montaigne and the Art of Free-Thinking

Richard Scholar

2010

Peter Lang Oxford

First published in 2010 by

Peter Lang Ltd
International Academic Publishers
Evenlode Court, Main Road, Long Hanborough, Witney
Oxfordshire OX29 8SZ
United Kingdom

www.peterlang.com

A catalogue record for this book is available from the British Library

ISBN 978-1-906165-21-5

COVER ILLUSTRATIONS:
Plates: *Reproduction en quadrichromie de l'Exemplaire de Bordeaux des* Essais *de Montaigne*,
ed. Philippe Desan (Fasano-Chicago: Schena Editore, Montaigne Studies, 2002).
Portrait: Philippe Desan, *Portraits à l'essai: Iconographie de Montaigne*
(Paris: H. Champion, 2007).

Printed in the United Kingdom
by the MPG Books Group

for Ita and Beatrice

Contents

Key to the Text

All references to the original text of Montaigne's *Essais*, unless otherwise specified, are to the edition of Pierre Villey and V.-L. Saulnier (Paris: Presses universitaires de France, 1992). All references to the original text of Montaigne's *Journal de Voyage* are to the edition of Fausta Garavini (Paris: Gallimard, 1983). All quotations in foreign languages are given along with, and preceded by, an English translation. For passages from Montaigne, I have used the translation by Donald M. Frame of *The Complete Works* (London: Everyman's Library, 2003), the only one to include the travel journal and the letters. I have, for reasons of consistency, made Frame's spelling conform to the practices of UK English. Any further modification of his translation is indicated. All other translations, unless otherwise stated, are my own.

First references to individual chapters of the *Essais* give book and chapter number, in the form 'I.26', as well as the chapter title in English and French. References to specific passages of the *Essais* give page numbers for the Frame translation and the Villey-Saulnier edition: they take the form 'F 135, VS 151'. The letters [A], [B], and [C] appear on occasions in quotations from the *Essais* and in my discussion of them. These letters are modern scholarly shorthand for the three main chronological strata of the text's composition: [A] refers to text that first appeared in the editions of 1580 or 1582; [B] to text that first appeared in the edition of 1588; [C] to the additions that Montaigne made after 1588 to the so-called 'Bordeaux copy'. Where I begin a quotation with no letter to indicate its date, it should be assumed that the text is from the A-stratum if it comes from Books I and II and from the B-stratum if it comes from Book III, and that it remains so until a different stratum is indicated. Post-1588 additions also appear in the 1595 edition of Montaigne's *Essais*, the first to appear after the author's death, and a rival text to the Bordeaux copy. When I describe an addition as having been made 'after 1588', I mean it appears in the text of the Bordeaux copy and of the 1595 edition alike, and I point out any differences between the two texts that matter to my argument. References to specific passages of the *Journal de Voyage* give page numbers for the Frame translation and then for the Garavini edition: they take the form 'F 1166, G 221'. Sources for all other quotations and references are provided in the Notes, along with a few suggestions of further reading. I have used, as much as possible, editions that are easily accessible, listing dates of first publication, where these are known.

Two illustrations appear in the book (pp. 82, 85). They show pages of the Bordeaux copy taken from the *Reproduction en quadrichromie de l'Exemplaire de Bordeaux des* Essais *de Montaigne*, ed. Philippe Desan (Fasano-Chicago: Schena Editore, Montaigne Studies, 2002), plates 253 and 254.

The Spirit of the Essais

Somewhere in the La Mancha region of Spain, in the last decades of the sixteenth century, there lived a gentleman who spent his times of leisure reading books of chivalry with such devotion that he almost completely forgot about the management of his estate. His name was Don Quixote de la Mancha. This man, his mind full of the chivalric adventures he devoured in his library at home, reached the strangest of resolutions: he would start a new life, accompanied by his faithful squire Sancho Panza, and set off on his steed, the long-suffering Rosinante, in quest of adventures, exposing himself to danger on many other occasions, but winning eternal renown for his pains. The rest is fictional history.

At around the same time, in the Périgord area of southwestern France, there lived another provincial gentleman of liberal education and independent means who might equally be said to have read more of the books in his library than was good for his estate. His name was Michel de Montaigne. This man, his mind full of the history, philosophy, and poetry he read, reached a strange resolution of his own: he would stay put, as much as he could, and embark instead upon adventures of thought in the pages of a book which he would go on writing as long as there was ink and paper in the world, his quest being to try out his mind on the questions that his experience of life and his reading raised for him and, where he could, to rescue and befriend the truth. The rest is literary and philosophical history.

There are some good reasons for thinking of Montaigne as a Don Quixote in the world of letters. The analogy between the Spanish knight errant and his French contemporary is, in certain respects, inexact: Montaigne's adventures happen in thought not deed, his steed is his mind, and his windmills are the Platos of this world at whom he tilts again and again in his search for a truth that he can recognize. It might be observed, too, that, whereas Don Quixote's decision was, as Cervantes tells us, one of the strangest conceits to enter the head of any madman, Montaigne's was the resolution of a luminously sane man. We should, however, be wary of concluding from this that all the sanity in the comparison belongs to the Seigneur de Montaigne, and all the madness to Don Quixote de la Mancha. Montaigne sees his mind running away from him at times, as we will see, and Don Quixote, Cervantes insists, spoke nonsense only when it came to chivalry: on all other topics of conversation he demonstrated clarity of mind and freedom of thought. Montaigne sets himself the formidable task of attempting to do the same. It is this, above all, that makes the analogy between the two figures revealing.

We know a great deal of what Montaigne thinks about all kinds of questions. We know, because he tells us, on page after page of his *Essais*. This is indeed, in an important sense, what his *Essais* are: written records of the author's thoughts on various matters of opinion, great and small, that preoccupy him. It might seem surprising, with this wealth of evidence at hand, that Montaigne could prove so elusive in his thinking. Yet elusive he proves. The problem for us lies not so much in knowing what he thinks as in understanding how he can think all the things he says he thinks. It arises, above all, because he appears to be as volatile in his opinions as he is voluble about them. In one place he reckons the truth of the matter to be green; in another place he calls it yellow. When he sees it as green, he counters those who declare it to be yellow and thinks aloud with those who see it the same way as he, but he puts forward his own opinion in a more tentative manner than most on either side: he invariably says only that it seems green to him, as if aware that on another occasion, he may see it as yellow. Sooner or later, of course, he does. There is something profoundly engaging about a figure so free and able to disagree with himself, as much as with everyone else, in the course of his thinking. Engaging, certainly, but also disconcerting. What, we are left wondering, does all that thinking amount to? What value might it have for us? In what spirit are the *Essais* to be read?

*   *   *

On 28 February 1571, his thirty-eighth birthday, Michel de Montaigne was reborn. In the course of the previous year he had resigned the legal office of magistrate he held in the Bordeaux *Parlement* and retired to the estate that had passed to him along with his title after the death of his father Pierre in 1568. He now announced his intention to start afresh. Weary of the burden of public affairs, he would spend what little time he had left on this earth far from all worldly cares, in the bosom of the Muses. We know that this was his intention because he says so in the official statement of his retirement that he had inscribed in Latin on the wall of the study next to his newly refurbished library. You can still visit the library today. It is – as it was then – on the third floor of a round tower at one corner of the hilltop château of Montaigne, near Saint-Emilion, some thirty miles east of Bordeaux; it offers – as it did then – unhampered views across the countryside in three directions. The books, which Montaigne had arranged around him in five rows of shelves on all sides, are no longer there. But the inscription, duly dated the last day of February 1571, has been restored. It ends with a declaration: Montaigne will consecrate this place he calls home, this sweet ancestral retreat, to his 'freedom, tranquillity, and leisure' ('libertati suae tranquillitatique et otio'). A new life had begun.

That new life lasted over two decades. By no means was all that time spent in the retirement Montaigne had envisaged. He was appointed Knight of the Order of Saint-Michel and made a gentleman-in-ordinary of the king's chamber by the three kings who in succession ruled France during that time; he travelled through Europe as far as Rome; he served two terms as Mayor of Bordeaux; he mediated on numerous occasions between Catholic France and Protestant Navarre in the Wars of Religion that had engulfed both kingdoms, receiving visits at Montaigne from the King of Navarre, the future Henri IV of France, and even finding himself, in 1588, briefly imprisoned in the Bastille for his pains. He hardly, in short, shuffled off all wordly cares.

But he did succeed in spending day after day in his book-lined tower, buried in the bosom of the Muses, and his intercourse with them changed literary and philosophical history. It produced an ever-expanding brain-child: two Books of *Essais* in 1580, then a third one in 1588, along with numerous additions to the existing chapters of Books I and II. After 1588, Montaigne wrote as much as ever, composing no new chapters but continuing to extend and revise the existing ones. A copy of the 1588 edition in which he recorded these new thoughts and rephrasings, scribbling between the lines, in the margins, and – where necessary – on loose pages, has been preserved: this is the famous 'Bordeaux copy' ('exemplaire de Bordeaux'). Montaigne had a further edition of his now successful work in mind. But he did not live to see it completed. He succumbed to a throat infection and died on 13 September 1592, aged fifty-nine, at home.

Three years after his death, in 1595, a new edition of the *Essais* appeared in print. Edited by two of its author's closest friends, Marie de Gournay (1565–1645) and Pierre de Brach (1548–1605), it was for centuries held to be the authoritative expression of Montaigne's final intentions. It suffered a serious challenge to its authority in the twentieth century from those who judged the Bordeaux copy to be more authentic, and though the argument has recently flowed back towards the 1595 edition, the debate continues between supporters of the two 'final' versions in which Montaigne's text still exists.

That debate bears witness to the continuing importance of the body of work that he produced in his tower. Had Montaigne not written as he did, he would be today a figure of minor interest to French historians of the period, a moderate Catholic and supporter of the monarchy who played his part in the pressing affairs of the day. But write he did, and in such a rich and strange way that the *Essais* remain – if you will excuse the pun – a towering achievement, one that puts Montaigne on a par with his European near-contemporaries Miguel de Cervantes (1547–1616) and William Shakespeare (1564–1616). No one before Montaigne had ever written a book quite like the *Essais*, and it remains one of a kind, despite its many admirers and imitators. The text, for all its uniqueness, has nonetheless played a part in all kinds of developments whose effects are still with us. It helped to bring the arguments of the ancient philosophical schools to the attention of a wider readership, for example, and to make modern secular forms of autobiographical writing possible. It created the conditions for a further, and major, shift in literature and philosophy alike: the invention of the essay. It has haunted generations of readers, including famous ones from Shakespeare to Orson Welles and beyond, and it continues to do so today.

Many of Montaigne's readers have been engaged and disconcerted in equal measure, as I suggested earlier, by the character of his thinking. This, too, is a source of continuing debate. A widespread response – especially among those with an interest in intellectual history – is to portray the thinking of the *Essais* as the expression of a particular doctrine or culture. Montaigne has appeared to many as a late Renaissance humanist, imbued with a deep admiration for the recently revived tradition of classical antiquity and humane learning (history, ethics, poetry, and rhetoric), and personally engaged in that tradition's study of what it is to be human. Sometimes he takes the guise of a civic humanist, committed to a life of political or ethical action rather than one of contemplation, at other times that of a Christian humanist who reconciles the wisdom of the ancients with the Catholic faith in which he was born, lived, and died. His interest in ancient wisdom has frequently been seen as an adherence to one or other of its philosophical traditions. He has been identified, in particular, with three of those traditions: stoicism, with its reasoned fortitude in the face of death and bereavement; scepticism, with its radical doubt and suspension of judgement on all matters of opinion; and Epicureanism, with its insistence on the role of chance and the importance of pleasures – those of the body and mind alike – in life. It is to scepticism that Montaigne's place in the history of thought has been most frequently assigned: it has become a matter of routine, nowadays, to identify Montaigne as a sceptic. The personal nature of his writing, meanwhile, appears to others as expressive not of his late Renaissance humanism, but of his early modern subjectivism, his interest in the inner workings of what we moderns have come to call 'the self'. All such identifications – of Montaigne as a humanist, civic, Catholic or otherwise, as a Stoic, sceptic, Epicurean, and more besides – are, to a certain degree, helpful and correct; which means, of course, that each of them, in itself, is an unhelpful distortion. The target never stops moving.

Not everyone feels the need to fasten Montaigne's thought to just one doctrine. Some fix it to several in turn. The early twentieth-century scholar Pierre Villey made the traditions of stoicism, scepticism, and Epicureanism central to an account of Montaigne's intellectual development in three phases, each of which, he considered, broadly corresponded to a Book of the *Essais*: Montaigne, Villey argued, wrote first (in Book I) under the impersonal influence of the Stoics, then (in Book II) under the grip of a sceptical crisis, and finally (in Book III and the late additions to the earlier two Books) from the position of an Epicurean philosophy of nature to which he had lent a personal twist. Villey's story of Montaigne's evolution remains influential one hundred years after it was first written. It is difficult to manage without historical narratives of this kind, and Villey's seems particularly plausible, not least because it encapsulates something of the intellectual atmosphere that surrounds each of the three Books in turn. That encapsulation comes, however, at the cost of what is most distinctive – and disconcerting – about Montaigne's contribution to the history of thought. As Terence Cave says, in a powerful formulation of the most important objection to Villey's work, 'Montaigne was never, and never aspired to be, a "thinker" who moved from one philosophical position to another in the course of his life.' Montaigne's quests of the mind are altogether more idiosyncratic, as well as volatile, than the intellectual-historical approach tends to suggest.

An alternative response to these qualities of Montaigne's thought as they work themselves out in his writing has been to examine, at close quarters, the writing itself. This has been and remains a widespread approach taken in literary studies of the *Essais*. Montaigne appears here as a writer who, imbued with the techniques of classical rhetoric and poetics, combines these in the *Essais* to produce his own distinctive literary style, characterized by contradictions, qualifications, and abundance of meaning. Where the intellectual-historical approach tends to produce overarching syntheses of Montaigne's thought, the literary approach eschews these, confining itself to one chapter of the *Essais* in isolation and tending to see the chapter as a reflection on its own textual processes and problems. It is impossible to read the *Essais* without noticing these features of their writing, and the literary approach sheds valuable light on them, but it does so, in turn, at a cost: it loses from view the positive trace of Montaigne's thinking and the patterns this forms across the *Essais* as a whole. As David Quint says, in arguing eloquently for a reading that assumes that what Montaigne chooses to discuss may be as important as the way in which he writes about it, 'for all its willed diversity, his book can be read as a book, and its individual [...] chapters should be related to a continuing argument.' There is more than one argument running through the *Essais*, of course, but Quint's point stands. To empty Montaigne's text of the questions it poses about the world beyond, of the arguments it sets running, would be seriously to diminish its ambitions.

Neither of the two approaches to Montaigne that I have sketched above – the intellectual-historical and the literary – is sufficient by itself, in my view, if one is to follow the author's train of thought through the pages of his book. If combined, however, they might serve the purpose. It is important to recognize that Montaigne's thought can be difficult to grasp, certainly, but it is never gratuitously so: its value lies in its volatility, its refusal to submit to the crystallizations of doctrine, its determination to remain on the move in the search for an elusive truth. There is nothing new about this view of Montaigne. Marie de Gournay offers an ardent as well as an early formulation, in her preface to the 1595 edition of the *Essais*, when answering those who complain that the text is wilfully obscure:

This book is no manual for beginners: it is the Koran of the masters; the quintessence of philosophy; a work not for tasting but for digesting and chylifying, the last book one should pick up and the last one should put down.

Ce n'est pas icy le rudiment des apprentifs, c'est l'Alcoran des maistres: la quinte essence de la philosophie: œuvre non à gouster, mais à digerer, et chylifier, le dernier livre qu'on doit prendre, et le dernier qu'on doit quicter.

Montaigne has produced the quintessence of philosophy, in Gournay's view, by making his own the ideas not of one particular philosophical school, or two, or three, but by appropriating – to borrow a phrase from the *Essais* to which we will return – I know not what quintessence of all this mercurial mixture. And this quintessence, Gournay says, Montaigne offers up for slow and lingering readerly rumination, digestion, and ultimately – once 'chylification' (the production of digestive juices) has taken place – absorption. The thoughts of the dead man will survive, modified, in the minds of the living. Gournay sees that the philosophic adventure of the *Essais* is also that of their diligent, thinking, reader.

* * *

I have had, in the writing of this book, three preoccupations: the first has been to offer an alternative – and a corrective – to the still widespread tendency to reduce Montaigne's thought to the expression of an '-ism'; the second has been to show that thinking and writing are intimately related in Montaigne, that he thinks as he does because of the way he writes and vice versa, so that understanding his thought means reading his text as he presents it to us; the third has been to ask how it is that a text so rooted in the time and place of its composition can also – indeed does – continue to speak to the present, to haunt its readers, to ask them the questions that matter.

My suggestion, in what follows, will be that Montaigne brings to his writing of the *Essais* the spirit of free-thinking. He possesses the classical learning that the European Renaissance prized, but he treats that learning with independence of judgement and a disarmingly light touch, and in his *Essais* he creates an experimental, anti-authoritarian, and above all profoundly thoughtful mode of writing that makes all questions accessible to his readers. Whether examining what it might be to die, the nature of friendship, or the use of horses in different times and places to relay messages, Montaigne always searches for that elusive thing called the truth. He rarely sticks to the question in hand and he almost never reaches any kind of conclusion. Instead, he keeps searching, commenting all the while on the obstacles that his mind encounters and the unexpected directions it takes in the course of its various adventures. Montaigne's compositions are the records of these adventures: they are writing trials of judgement that are always open to an afterthought, a change of mind, and a new flight from the errors of prejudice and habit. They are, in other words, the literary art he makes of free-thinking. By thinking aloud in this way on page after page of his book, he invites us, his readers, to follow the twists and turns of his mind, and challenges us to embark, in his company if we like, on our own search for the truth. That challenge and that offer of companionship explain why this 'freest, most energetic of spirits', as – for reasons we will explore later – the radical German philosopher Friedrich Nietzsche (1844–1900) called Montaigne, continues to haunt his readers today.

What, though, do I mean by 'free-thinking'? We should not assume that our understanding of the phrase is Montaigne's. The modern world has enshrined various freedoms as universal human rights and created international laws and institutions whose purpose, however difficult this may be to achieve, includes the protection of those rights. Article 19 of the 1948 United Nations Declaration of Human Rights speaks of 'the right to freedom of opinion and expression' and says that 'this right includes freedom to hold opinions without interference'. It is striking that the phrase 'freedom of thought' occurs not in article 19, but rather in the previous article, which deals with freedoms of conscience and religion. This fact reflects a decisive shift in the meaning of the phrase since the age of Montaigne, for it is now generally understood – in the Declaration as elsewhere – to refer primarily to the realm of religious belief, and to indicate the agnosticism or atheism of a secular worldview that maintains a principled independence from the dogmas of any church or creed. Whether it remains free from dogmas of its own making is open to question, but whatever view one takes of it, secularism is certainly well established enough by now to have produced an alternative worldview at a time when, in the so-called Western world at least, established religion is on the wane. Perhaps this explains the relative decline of the phrase 'free-thinking': we in the West no longer associate religious nonconformism with freedom because, in this sphere as in so many others, we take it for granted that we are free to pick and choose.

Montaigne belongs to a different world: one in which free-thinking was not exclusively or even primarily a matter of religious belief or disbelief but a much wider anti-authoritarian cast of mind that he and his contemporaries could bring to bear on all kinds of questions. That kind of free-thinking – and this is the kind I have in mind when I use the term – is an inheritance of the classical philosophical tradition: it is, for that reason, an exemplary instance of a moment in the history of European culture that is time and again characterized as one of Renaissance or 'rebirth'. It is expressed in formulations such as a proverbial phrase that starts life in the work of Aristotle (384–322 BCE), the great Athenian philosopher and pupil of Plato (427–347 BCE), and which is, as we will see, widely used across Renaissance Europe in its Latin version: 'Amicus Plato sed magis amica veritas' ('Plato is my friend but a greater friend is truth'). Free-thinking is, at root, the attempt to reflect upon any particular question across the field of human enquiry by asking not 'What does Plato say about the question?' – 'Plato' means here the dominant figure of authority in place – but 'What do I think about the question? Do I agree with what Plato says? Or am I obliged to reject his view in the search for truth?' To question received ideas in this way is to practise free-thinking: to infuse the life of the spirit with the energy of freedom.

Nietzsche was by no means the earliest of his readers to comment on Montaigne's free spirit. That distinction, as I hope to show in what follows, must go to Montaigne himself. Despite all the reasons we have for seeing things the author's way, however, he has not been the most influential person to comment on his own freedom of spirit. That accolade surely belongs to the polymath and ardent Christian writer Blaise Pascal (1623–62). Pascal reads Montaigne – with a unique combination of fascination and repulsion – in the context of the heated debate in seventeenth-century France about the challenge posed by free-thinking, or *libertinage* as it came to be known at that time, to religious orthodoxy. This debate resonated throughout Europe in that century and the next as the modes and moods of free-thinking became absorbed into the movement known as the Enlightenment, whose promotion of reason over authority was accompanied by scepticism about the articles of Christian faith, and even, in some extreme cases, by atheism. It is in the course of this debate, in other words, that a radicalized and specifically irreligious version of free-thinking comes to the fore: the version most familiar to us moderns. Pascal makes a major intervention in the early phase of the debate, for he attempts to bring the doubting and the indifferent of his age back to Christian belief through argument and persuasion, and he identifies Montaigne as the prototype of the out-and-out sceptic, the free-thinking *libertin*, he has in his sights. It is in this context, as we shall see in the closing pages of this book, that Pascal speaks of the 'thoroughly free spirit' that Montaigne brings to all questions. There has been no more influential reading of Montaigne than that of Pascal. His friends in the austere Jansenist movement of Port-Royal after his death adopted it; Voltaire (1694–1778) among others explicitly contested it in the age of Enlightenment; and Nietzsche's admiring remark about Montaigne's free spirit, quoted above, owes much to Pascal. I have already pointed out that Montaigne is commonly characterized as an out-and-out sceptic even today. There are other reasons why this is so, as I have already suggested, but, as many studies of Montaigne's scepticism amply confirm, the fact remains that the history of ideas is still conditioned by Pascal's seventeenth-century version of Montaigne and free-thinking.

I owe a debt of my own to Pascal. When I was working several years ago on the text in which he speaks of Montaigne's 'thoroughly free spirit', it struck me that this was a brilliant intuition at the heart of a misrepresentation. I wanted to prise out that intuition from its local time and place because I thought that it might help cast light back on to Montaigne's mode of thinking and writing in the *Essais*. I was reading at the same time the work of Ian Maclean and others, discussed in chapter 2 below, on the medieval and Renaissance pre-history of free-thinking in the learned disciplines. Montaigne, perhaps because he deliberately adopts the position, outside those disciplines, of an amateur and a gentleman, hardly figured in their work. I started to wonder whether he had a role to play in a broader pre-history of free-thinking, and if so what that role might be, and – last but not least – whether the answers to those questions might offer a context for understanding his 'thoroughly free spirit' on something more like its own terms. It seemed to me then, as it still does now, that Pascal was right to portray Montaigne as a free-thinker but that he fundamentally misrepresented the character of his free-thinking.

*   *   *

What, then, is its character? Montaigne is no straightforward hero of free-thinking, or rather, he is no hero of straightforward free-thinking. His adventures have none of the naïve idealism associated with Don Quixote's chivalric quests. He reflects upon and practises free-thinking with complexity and prudence, lucidity and dexterity, alike.

He is, as we will see, just as concerned with the limits to this form of intellectual engagement as he is with the form itself. Free-thinking appears time and again in his work to have been made possible – but, at the same time, to have been limited in its possibilities – by the prevailing cultural horizon of the time and place of its making. The limits to free-thinking may take the form of external constraints: the laws and customs of the society in question, for example, and the ways in which that society exercises control over the dissemination of thought. They may also take the form of inner constraints: these include the passions, self-interest, and over-zealous commitment to a cause, all of which are capable of prejudicing one's apprehension of the truth, or – more insidiously still – those characteristic ways of thinking and doing that are simply taken for granted. Free-thinking, for Montaigne, invariably exists in a state of tense interaction with its own limits.

Another way of putting the same point might be to say that, throughout the *Essais*, free-thinking is itself put to the test. Montaigne sees – and shows – how valuable it is: the central place it occupies in an underlying network of interrelated secular freedoms – including those of the body to travel and of the tongue to speak – needed to sustain a good life in an age as rotten as the civil-war-torn age in which he lived. For Montaigne, thinking is always embodied, and he claims to have used all his 'little prudence' ('petite prudence'), in his final chapter 'Of experience' (III.13: 'De l'expérience'), to remain free and unconstrained in his movements (F 999–1000, VS 1072). He simultaneously sees – and shows – how difficult free-thinking is, how fraught with risks, how subject to external and internal constraints alike. At times, as if to protect and sustain the freedom he craves, he prudently advocates the enforcement of external constraints. He critically analyses, at other times, the role played by various internal constraints in limiting the possibilities of free-thinking. This is not to say that Montaigne is omniscient in this respect: he knows full well that he, too, is curbed in his thinking by the things he takes for granted. But this very acknowledgement is the sign of an intelligence capable of probing its own limits and thus of seeing past the confines of its own cultural horizon to what he calls, in 'Of the education of children' (I.26: 'De l'institution des enfâns'), 'country beyond' (F 130, VS 146: 'du païs au delà').

The interaction in Montaigne's mind between free-thinking and its limits does not, in other words, end in paralysis. It results in lucidity about the difficulties involved and dexterity of execution as Montaigne twists and turns his way into the space between the extremes of freedom and constraint. It is in the borderland between these two extremes that the free-thinking of the *Essais* takes place.

Montaigne offers a powerful image for this place in 'Of solitude' (I.39: 'De la solitude'). He describes it as a 'back shop' of one's own:

> We should have wife, children, goods, and above all health, if we can; but we must not bind ourselves to them so strongly that our happiness depends on them. We must reserve a back shop all our own, entirely free, in which to establish our real liberty and our principal retreat and solitude.

> Il faut avoir femmes, enfans, biens, et sur tout de la santé, qui peut; mais non pas s'y attacher en maniere que nostre heur en depende. Il se faut reserver une arriereboutique toute nostre, toute franche, en laquelle nous establissons nostre vraye liberté et principale retraicte et solitude.   (F 214, VS 241)

So powerful is the image of the back shop that it is easy to take it literally and imagine that Montaigne is describing a private room somewhere in the tower on his estate or, indeed, the tower itself. The back shop of which he speaks is, in fact, an inner space that, he says, we should carry within ourselves and be able to retire to at all times and in all places. But there may nonetheless be, as John O'Brien has suggested, a deep connection in Montaigne's imagination between the estate, the tower, and the back shop: all are places of retreat that offer the mind the freedom from the pressing obligations of the world it needs and craves. Another such place, needless to add, is the ever-expanding text of the *Essais*.

It will be observed that the passage just quoted takes for granted who 'we' are. We have – or we should have, if we can – a wife, children, and possessions, as well as our health, suggesting that we are a wellborn adult male. And we have, too, it seems, a solid grounding in classical authors, familiar as we are with, among other things, the work of the Greek materialist philosopher Epicurus (341–271 BCE) and the Roman Stoic philosopher Seneca (4 BCE–65 CE), to whom Montaigne refers at the end of the chapter when advising us to people our solitude with great figures from the past and to conduct inner conversations with those exemplary dead in the privacy of our own back shop. 'Of solitude' thus exemplifies the point I made earlier about how the free-thinking of the *Essais* is manifestly created and conditioned by its environment: that of the French gentleman with humanist interests that Montaigne was. But it also enlarges that environment to include readers of the future, living in different times, different places. It does so through the use of the capacious pronoun 'we' ('nous'). In that pronoun, Montaigne certainly includes himself, but there is also room in it for the reader. We may judge that, by choosing to speak of 'us' in this way, the author is not only taking for granted, but attempting to inflict upon us, the coordinates of his own subjectivity; but we may equally judge that he is creating, with the resources at his disposal, a fragile and yet precious idea – the idea of free-thinking – that he expects us, in our turn, to digest, chylify, and make our own.

Montaigne's free-thinking is, then, complex and prudent, but also lucid and dexterous, in character. These qualities have a consequence that is worth spelling out as a further, defining characteristic of his free-thinking, which is that it appears in the *Essais* not only as a piece of subject-matter about which he writes but also as a manner in which he writes: as a mode of operation as well as a topic of reflection. Those two strands, while distinct for the purposes of analysis, are woven together time and again in the fabric of the text. Montaigne, in other words, inherits free-thinking as a theme from the ancients and turns it into an art of his own: the art of the *Essais*.

⋆ ⋆ ⋆

What this means is that free-thinking offers a precious opportunity to grasp the nature – as well as the detail – of Montaigne's venture. I realize that this claim might appear exorbitant. Free-thinking is, after all, by no means the only idea that permits this kind of approach: essaying might be another, and a much more prominent one at that, given the title that Montaigne chose for his text. It is clear, too, that free-thinking reaches certain parts of the *Essais* better than it does others: the early chapters of Books I and II that do little more than sew together examples from other authors in a miscellaneous compilation, for example, start to show signs of free-thinking only as Montaigne adds to them flashes of independent insight and judgement in later versions. Free-thinking can hardly be said, as a result, to offer some kind of interpretative 'key' to the *Essais*. This should come as little surprise, however, since a text as complex and many-sided as this one admits of no key. Free-thinking offers the most that any approach may hope to achieve: a way in and around the text; but one that nonetheless leads into the heart of its preoccupations and procedures.

My starting point is the observation that, on various occasions throughout the text, Montaigne draws upon a cluster of words and phrases belonging to the language of free-thinking in his search for truth. That cluster is a capacious one. At its heart are expressions linking the terms 'liberté' ('freedom', 'liberty') and its near-synonym 'licence' to the activity of thinking, the faculty of judgement or the mind itself, but it also includes antonyms belonging to the counter-languages of prejudice and constraint. This book examines such expressions at close quarters and in their wider context in an attempt to understand how free-thinking operates in the text as both a topic of reflection and a mode of operation. My working assumption throughout this book is that the character of Montaigne's free-thinking – as of his mind more generally – needs to be understood in its historical context but is to be found first and foremost in the fabric of his text. Making sense of the text means considering the topics it treats, the questions it asks of them, and the ideas it encounters and produces along the way. But it also means recognizing that those ideas are embedded in the words, phrases, sentences, chapters, and Books of the *Essais*, and that they are best understood in that setting.

The result is a literary companion to the thought of the *Essais* as it unfolds across the three Books. I explore Montaigne's free-thinking as both a matter and manner of his work and show how it works in its own right and in relation to neighbouring ideas and contexts. I start, in chapter 1, with a study of Montaigne's opening moves, his habit of constantly introducing his text to the reader, from one end of the *Essais* to the other. Taking Books I, II, and III of the *Essais* in turn, I then examine a pair of chapters from each, offering a close reading of a single passage from the chapter in question. Each of those exercises in close reading stands alone, and may be read in isolation from the others, but in each instance I suggest what place the chosen passage has in the unfolding story that Montaigne's text tells about itself.

This book alters, in several ways, the dominant picture we have of Montaigne. The overall linear framework of the book, which primarily treats the *Essais* as they are presented to the reader, may appear, on the face of it, an uncontroversial choice. But it is in fact a departure from the tradition, which has tended to examine the evolution of Montaigne's thought through the book's successive iterations, the so-called A- (1580–2), B- (1588), and C- (post-1588 additions to the Bordeaux copy) strata of composition. Of course, labelling those strata is something Montaigne never did or intended, whereas he most certainly decided upon – and stuck to – the order of his chapters. I consider that developments in Montaigne's free-thinking can be seen in the book's compositional strata and the order of presentation alike, and I examine both, but I ultimately privilege the second of the two. This is because I wish to restore to Montaigne's text its potential and its desire to tell a story about how its author, in the face of continuing difficulty, learned to think – and write – his way towards a kind of freedom. The first-person subject at the heart of the *Essais* appears, in this story, as a picaresque persona that the author invents in his questing search to rescue and befriend the truth. This perspective marks a significant revision of the widespread twentieth-century view of Montaigne's text as an early example of life-writing whose purpose is overwhelmingly psychological: to probe the inner workings of the 'self'. My book sees the first person of the *Essais*, the 'I', as instrumental to Montaigne's way of thinking as much as the object of his thinking. In this respect, the book not only combines the intellectual-historical and literary approaches sketched earlier, but also moves towards might be called a cognitive frame of reference: one that captures, as Terence Cave puts it, 'Montaigne's enduring preoccupation with thought as an experience to be studied and documented non-judgementally and non-didactically'. The story I have to tell of Montaigne's adventures of thought, as I have already intimated, directs the focus away from his adoption of philosophical positions and towards the sheer mercurial intelligence of the thinking he captures on the page: towards, that is, his use of the linguistic and literary resources at his disposal to record thought as it happens, as it encounters its limits, and as it peers beyond those limits into country beyond.

*   *   *

Who, then, is the Montaigne to emerge from this book? Neither the irreligious *libertin* nor the pious Catholic humanist, neither the sceptic nor the Stoic, neither the revolutionary nor the conservative, neither the modern writer nor the Renaissance sage that he has been portrayed to be at various moments in his various – and continuing – afterlife. He is, in each case, both – and therefore neither. He is a provincial gentleman of liberal education and independent means who, when presented with the chance to bury himself in the bosom of the Muses, produced a book the like of which the world has not seen before or since. He is, like Cervantes and Shakespeare, a literary mastermind of the European Renaissance who, over four centuries after his physical death, remains alive in the pages of his book and ready to serve as a companion to us on our own adventures of thought on this earth.

Too often, in the learned and popular imagination of France as much as of the English-speaking world, Montaigne is treated like the human equivalent of a world heritage site: as a monument to a past age, worthy of preservation, but hardly to be visited. He is less read and understood than Cervantes and Shakespeare, our taste for fictions and plays being keener than our taste for the thought-experiments he called essays, so the comparison with those two near-contemporaries of his often ends up being to the detriment of Montaigne. Act II, Scene i, of Shakespeare's late play *The Tempest* contains the only incontrovertible piece of textual evidence that its author read Montaigne (in John Florio's 1603 English translation): the verbal picture that Gonzalo paints of an ideal common-wealth, imagining that he and his shipwrecked companions have been washed up on the shores of an earthly Paradise, is based upon Montaigne's description of the New World society of the Brazilian Tupinambá in 'Of cannibals' (I.31: 'Des cannibales'). Montaigne often appears in literary history as a companion to Shakespeare, but usually – by an odd twist – in the guise of Gonzalo himself, the honest and venerable repository of Old World wisdom who, while rather opinionated, forgets the beginning of his opinion by the time he reaches the end. Passages culled from the *Essais* are frequently to be found, for example, in Shakespearean criticism, providing background information and local colour, but without being taken any more seriously than Gonzalo is by his companions.

In his last book, *Shakespeare the Thinker*, A. D. Nuttall says of his sub-ject that 'the fiery track of his thinking' can never be followed to a settled terminus because Shakespeare was 'simply too intelligent to be able to persuade himself that the problems were completely solved'. I would say the same of Montaigne, and that is why I prefer to think of Montaigne not as a Gonzalo, but as another Don Quixote.

Don Quixote not only embarks on quest after quest; he even talks the language of free-thinking. In Part II of the novel, his companion Sancho Panza, a man of ambition but very little brain, is finally, thanks to a practical joke played upon him by a duke and duchess, rewarded with the governorship of an island that his master had long promised him would one day be his. In Part II, chapter 42, Don Quixote gives Sancho advice as to how to conduct himself in his new role. This includes the need for him to keep his judgement free from passion or prejudice and attend to the truth of the question when the case of an enemy comes before him: a precept of free-thinking that, as we will see in chapter 7 below, Montaigne evokes and puts into practice. The advice also includes a warning to Sancho to lard his speech with fewer proverbs. However, Don Quixote fails to heed his own warning in the letter he sends to Sancho on his island in Part II, chapter 51, when, having revealed that he has all but fallen into disgrace with the duke and duchess, he produces by way of comment a famous free-thinking proverb:

> But, though it afflicts me much, it affects me nothing: for, in short, I must comply with the rules of my profession, rather than with their pleasure, according to the old saying, *Amicus Plato, sed magis amica veritas*. I write this in Latin; for I persuade myself, you have learned it since you have been a governor.

> Pero aunque se me da mucho, no se me da nada, pues, en fin en fin, tengo de cumplir antes con mi profesión que con su gusto, conforme a lo que suele decirse: 'Amicus Plato, sed magis amica veritas.' Dígote este latín porque me doy a entender que después que eres gobernador lo habrás aprendido.

There are no indications that Sancho has learned Latin since taking office, but thanks to Don Quixote, he has at least acquired a proverb befitting his new responsibilities.

Unlike Don Quixote, Montaigne never repeats that proverb verbatim, but he puts it into practice and reflects on its implications for free-thinking in page after page of the *Essais*. I have a final reason for thinking of Montaigne as a Don Quixote in the world of letters. In the course of his adventures, as we will see in the chapters that follow, Montaigne enlists the companionship and faithful service of his own Sancho Panza: the reader, who dreams one day of governing an island in the spirit of free-thinking, but is content for now to follow in the footsteps of the master.

1

Opening Moves

Let us begin at the beginning:

> This book was written in good faith, reader. It warns you from the outset that
> in it I have set myself no goal but a domestic and private one. I have had no
> thought of serving either you or my own glory. My powers are inadequate
> for such a purpose. I have dedicated it to the private convenience of my
> relatives and friends, so that when they have lost me (as soon they must),
> they may recover here some features of my habits and temperament, and
> by this means keep the knowledge they have had of me more complete and
> alive. If I had written to seek the world's favour, I should have bedecked
> myself better, and should present myself in a studied posture. I want to
> be seen here in my simple, natural, ordinary fashion, without straining or
> artifice; for it is myself that I portray. My defects will here be read to the
> life, and also my natural form, as far as respect for the public has allowed.
> Had I been placed among those nations which are said to live still in the
> sweet freedom of nature's first laws, I assure you I should very gladly have
> portrayed myself here entire and wholly naked. Thus, reader, I am myself
> the matter of my book: you would be unreasonable to spend your leisure
> on so frivolous and vain a subject. So farewell. Montaigne, this first day of
> March, fifteen hundred and eighty.

> C'est icy un livre de bonne foy, lecteur. Il t'advertit dès l'entrée, que je ne me
> suis proposé aucune fin, que domestique et privée. Je n'ay eu nulle consi-
> dération de ton service, ny de ma gloire. Mes forces ne sont pas capables
> d'un tel dessein. Je l'ay voué à la commodité particuliere de mes parens et
> amis: à ce que m'ayant perdu (ce qu'ils ont à faire bien tost) ils y puissent
> retrouver aucuns traits de mes conditions et humeurs, et que par ce moyen

ils nourissent plus entiere et plus vifve, la connoissance qu'ils ont eu de moy.
Si c'eust esté pour rechercher la faveur du monde, je me fusse mieux paré et
me presanterois en une marche estudiée. Je veus qu'on m'y voie en ma façon
simple, naturelle et ordinaire, sans contention et artifice: car c'est moy que je
peins. Mes defauts s'y liront au vif, et ma forme naïfve, autant que la reverence
publique me l'a permis. Que si j'eusse esté entre ces nations qu'on dict vivre
encore sous la douce liberté des premieres loix de nature, je t'asseure que je
m'y fusse tres-volontiers peint tout entier, et tout nud. Ainsi, lecteur, je suis
moy-mesmes la matiere de mon livre: ce n'est pas raison que tu employes
ton loisir en un subject si frivole et si vain. A Dieu donq, de Montaigne, ce
premier de Mars mille cinq cens quatre vingts.   (F 2, VS 3)

So runs the note, written by the author 'To the Reader' ('Au lecteur')
on the eve of the first publication of the *Essais* in 1580, which, preceding as it does the very first chapter of Book I, serves at the work's outset
as its preface. By preface, I mean the preamble to a work that sets out
its subject, aims, and means, and seeks, along the way, to capture the
reader's goodwill: an exercise in opening up the book to the reader and
the reader to the book. Such exercises are performed on the thresholds
of most books: they form an integral part of what publishers today call
the 'front matter'. Books written in the age of Montaigne tend to be lav-
ishly fitted out with prologues, dedicatory epistles, poems of praise, and
other prefatory materials, in a baroque architecture of interconnecting
antechambers through which the reader is to pass, collecting reassur-
ances about the author's credentials along the way, before being ushered
into the text. This brief note alone, however, awaits us on the threshold
of Montaigne's book. It thus appears to confer a unity of purpose upon
the project of the *Essais*.

Its first sentence confirms this impression of unity by addressing
directly, to a single reader, its pithy assertion of the book's essential good
faith. Adopting a modest, even self-deprecating tone, Montaigne goes
on to describe his book as a limited but sincere study in self-portraiture
designed to remember him to his family and friends after his (imminent)
departure from this world. The effect of this description is not to exclude
the reader from the circle of those who may be said to know Montaigne,
but to offer us a place within the circle of intimacy, assuming of course
that we recognize his book to be, indeed, written in good faith. The offer
of intimacy, moreover, includes readers who will come to the *Essais* long

after the author's demise because, as he emphatically concludes at the end of his letter to the reader, he is himself the matter of his book.

Between its initial assertion of good faith and its emphatic conclusion, however, there are moments when Montaigne's note to the reader seems much less certain about the book it is introducing. The second and third sentences quoted above find something to say of the book only by emphasizing what it 'merely' is or is not at all. In striking a depreciative tone, they serve of course a strategic function in the discourse of the preface, that of persuading the reader to show sympathy towards and understanding for the text on its own terms and despite its shortcomings. Renaissance handbooks on rhetoric – the art of persuasion – routinely analyse strategies such as *captatio benevolentiae*, the attempt to 'capture the goodwill' of the reader from the outset, and *preoccupatio*, the attempt to neutralize potential objections to the text by rehearsing (or 'occupying') them in advance. Montaigne, here as elsewhere, certainly deploys such strategies of persuasion. At the same time, however, these sentences seem to show and to cultivate a different kind of preoccupation with the limitations and inadequacies that they ascribe to the book: an absorption with possibilities that are set aside even as they are named. The idea, for example, that a book such as this might be designed to benefit the reader or to further the author's own glory, though governed by a 'not', is nonetheless opened up as a line of thought for further enquiry. The writing here marks a limit from which to peer into the uncertain country that lies beyond.

It does something similar towards the end of 'To the Reader' when Montaigne, having now positively described his aim in the book as unadorned self-portraiture, claims to have been constrained in its execution by a respect for public decency. Here, as before, the claim seems designed to capture the goodwill of the reader but also opens up a line of further thought, governed on this occasion by a past conditional, an 'if only'. The evocation of a literary gentleman who would have gladly portrayed himself in all his naked freedom, if only he had not been restrained from so doing by the rigid conventions of clothing, may be said to encapsulate both the immense seduction, for Montaigne, of freedom – including the freedom to think otherwise – and the regrettable necessity, given the time and place in which he lives, for that freedom to be tempered and restricted. The writing points exuberantly to the unfettered self-revelation that would have been possible outside the limit it has just marked. The indications are that Montaigne has in mind the far-flung nations of the

New World, but he does not say so, for neither their geographical location nor the veracity of what is reported about them matters here so much as the freedom that these nations are said to enjoy – and that would have made all the difference to his self-portrait. In conjuring up a freedom that is at once natural and political, sweet to the taste and yet available only elsewhere, this sentence raises questions about the actual constraints under which the self-portrait was written, the limiting effects these had on the writing, and the kind of freedom – if any – that it was able to find for itself. Pursuing these questions, like those raised by the spectre of authorial self-promotion and by reports from the New World, is a task to which Montaigne will turn in the text that is to follow.

'To the Reader' may therefore be said to open up the *Essais* in more ways than one. It introduces the text to the reader as animated by a single aim – authorial self-portraiture – but it does so in such a way as to admit of further development by setting in motion lines of enquiry that lead off in different directions through the text. It thereby captures, in a momentary vision of unity, the diversity that is to come, and it continues to do so in successive editions of the *Essais*, remaining substantially unchanged despite the continuing proliferation of the text. It establishes no eternal truth about that text: like any other letter, it is no more than a communication from one party to another, written at a particular place and time, and it is signed and dated as such. It leaves much else to be said about the nature of the enterprise that Montaigne undertakes in the pages of his book. What it continues to transmit, however, are an insatiable desire for communication across time and an ideal of mutual openness – the spirit in which Montaigne both expects to see his book treated and offers it to anyone wishing to read on.

A Second Preface in Book I

Those who read on soon encounter, in the short chapter 'Of idleness' (I.8: 'De l'oisiveté'), what appears, given its position early in Book I and its subject-matter, to be a second, belated, preface to the *Essais*. Like 'To the Reader', 'Of idleness' can be read as an exercise in capturing the goodwill of the reader that reveals other preoccupations. It offers an alternative image for the project of the *Essais* in recounting how Montaigne, having retreated from active life in early middle age, has come to find himself engaged in the process of writing something manifestly strange and new.

The chapter also offers a glimpse of how its author borrows material from his precursors and then takes that material in directions of his own. The title of the chapter, its opening critique of idleness, and the comparison through which that critique is first expressed – of idle minds to fertile fields left fallow – are all to be found in the same source, an encyclopaedic compilation by the Spanish historian Pedro Mexía (Pierre Messie) (1496?–1552?) which first appeared in Claude Gruget's influential French translation, *Various Lessons* (*Diverses leçons*), in 1552. Mexía proceeds in his treatment of the topic, 'The Excellence and Praise of Work, and the Damage that Idleness Causes' (I.29: 'L'excellence et les louanges du travail: et le dommage qu'engendre l'oisiveté'), by compiling the arguments of various authorities in support of his headline claim. Montaigne, by contrast, quickly shifts the perspective of his chapter onto his own troubled experience of living with an idle mind.

The passage in question, which ends the chapter, reads as follows:

Lately when I retired to my home, determined so far as possible to bother about nothing except spending the little life I have left in rest and seclusion, it seemed to me I could do my mind no greater favour than to let it entertain itself in full idleness and stay and settle in itself, which I hoped it might do more easily now, having become weightier and riper with time. But I find –

Ever idle hours breed wandering thoughts

– that, on the contrary, like a runaway horse, it gives itself a hundred times more trouble than it took for others, and gives birth to so many chimeras and fantastical monsters, one after another, without order or purpose, that in order to contemplate their ineptitude and strangeness at my pleasure, I have begun to put them in writing, hoping in time to make my mind ashamed of itself.

Dernierement que je me retiray chez moy, deliberé autant que je pourroy, ne me mesler d'autre chose que de passer en repos, et à part, ce peu qui me reste de vie: il me sembloit ne pouvoir faire plus grande faveur à mon esprit, que de le laisser en pleine oysiveté, s'entretenir soy mesmes, et s'arrester et

rasseoir en soy: ce que j'esperois qu'il peut meshuy faire plus aisément, devenu
avec le temps plus poisant, et plus meur. Mais je trouve,
>   *variam semper dant otia mentem,*
que au rebours, faisant le cheval eschappé, il se donne cent fois plus d'af-
faire à soy mesmes, qu'il n'en prenoit pour autruy; et m'enfante tant de
chimeres et monstres fantasques les uns sur les autres, sans ordre, et sans
propos, que pour en contempler à mon aise l'ineptie et l'estrangeté, j'ay
commancé de les mettre en rolle, esperant avec le temps luy en faire honte
à luy mesmes.   (F 25, VS 33)

This passage is structured around two instances of the verb 'to hope'
('espérer'), both applied to the first-person perspective of Montaigne,
and documents the change that takes place between them. It records the
author's initial hope that his mind will settle down and achieve wisdom
in retirement, the serene process envisaged by those who celebrate the
possibilities of a life devoted to leisure and learned study, the *otium* of the
classical moral tradition. It then shows him making the uncomfortable
discovery that *otium* merely produces, in a mind such as his, what are at
best idle fancies. This view has classical precedents of its own. Montaigne
makes this clear by introducing his change of perspective with a line of
verse quoted from the historical epic *The Civil War* (*De Bello Civili*, IV,
704) of the Latin poet Lucan (39–65 CE). He comes in the end to articulate
the altogether more limited and fragile hope that, by recording its excesses
in the pages of his book, he will succeed in subduing his runaway mind.
The passage does more, in the process, than describe a shift of position
on the theme of idleness: it dramatizes a fracturing of the author's identity
and of the intentions that animate the *Essais*.

Two characters, both internal to Montaigne, figure in this literary
psychodrama. The character referred to in the first person singular, as
'I' ('je'), starts centre-stage. It is he who takes the decision to live out his
few remaining days in the peaceful and carefree setting of home. It is he,
too, who judges that this is in the best interests of the second character in
the drama, 'the mind' ('l'esprit'). (In what follows, I shall call character 1
'the first person', and character 2 'the mind'.) Although the first person is
initially given the leading role, governing the main verbs throughout the
first sentence, he treats the mind even at this early stage with the circum-
spect indulgence inspired by a slightly obstreperous friend or relation.
He hopes that his mind will use the free time provided to settle down at

last, but this he can indeed only hope, since it is not in his power to bring about the desired change in his companion. The mind seems – such is the oddity behind this psychodrama – to have a mind of its own. At this point in the passage, however, that oddity is not felt in the writing. We are watching a domestic comedy.

The beginning of a more radical fracturing of the author's identity is signalled by the contrastive 'But I find' ('Mais je trouve') that introduces the short quotation from Lucan mentioned above. Montaigne's text is full of such quotations, taken chiefly from the poets, philosophers, and historians of the classical Latin tradition, but also from their ancient Greek and modern European counterparts. This feature of Montaigne's practice as a writer can prove disconcerting to modern readers who experience it as an obstacle to their understanding of the text: all those quotations in languages we ought to know better than we do or do not know at all, most of them taken from unfamiliar texts, mean so much time, spent away from the chapter we are trying to read, looking at the editorial notes at the bottom of the page or the back of the book ... This makes the quotations seem to us at once more remote – the product of a cultural memory we do not share – and more domesticated – framed by a reassuring modern editorial apparatus – than they would have to most sixteenth-century readers of the *Essais*. There is surely little to be done about this except to acknowledge the difference or, in the words of the London Underground, to 'mind the gap' and to begin the hard task of trying to understand on its own terms something of what the text has to say to us. Montaigne's practice of quotation not only differs from modern norms, but is in itself visibly complex, serving various purposes. Perhaps, indeed, the first thought to bear in mind upon coming across a quotation in the text is precisely that it serves a purpose there and is meant to have an effect. The quotation from Lucan that concerns us, for example, is taken from a soliloquy in which a Roman leader, Curio, explains his reasons for sending his army into battle without delay. But it appears here unmoored from its original context. A pithy formulation of universal applicability that contrasts markedly with the sentence it introduces, it plays a role akin to that of the chorus in a drama, interrupting the narrative told by the first person to comment lucidly on the unfolding action.

The sentence now launches into a freewheeling set of clauses that give the mind the reins. This equestrian metaphor might evoke Don Quixote's plodding steed. But Montaigne's mind, in this passage, is no second Rosinante: it is a horse that bolts hither and thither and takes the sentence with it through a troubled landscape of phrases and clauses filled with ever stranger beasts, all creatures of the mind, all lacking in order and purpose. This is a sentence filled with copulation: not just that of the mind with itself in idleness, but that of the writing too, which produces couples and copulatives in its pursuit of 'so many chimeras and fantastical monsters', those products of the 'ineptitude and strangeness' of the runaway mind.

That the writing is indeed tracking the mind in its helter-skelter course becomes clear at the end of the passage quoted above. Why it does so, however, remains less clear. The first person reappears at this point and explains that, faced with the continuing excesses of the mind, he has started, in Frame's rendering, 'to put them into writing'. A more faithful English translation of the phrase Montaigne uses, 'les mettre en rolle', would be 'to keep a record of them'. Fidelity is desirable here because it preserves the first instance of a metaphor to which the author will repeatedly turn in order to describe the writing of the *Essais*. This is the metaphor of the record or register, found in verbs such as 'to listen' ('écouter') and 'to record' ('enroller'), which are combined in one sentence of an important post-1588 addition to the chapter 'Of giving the lie' (II.18: 'Du démentir') dealing with this very subject: 'I listen to my reveries because I have to record them' ('J'escoute à mes resveries par ce que j'ay à les enroller'; F 613, VS 665). In 'Of idleness', the metaphor of the record offers an image for the *Essais* that differs from the static pictorial one of 'To the Reader' in that it makes of the text something always unfolding, an open-ended process. The image is a more uneasy one, too, implying less control of the process.

The literary psychodrama that is 'Of idleness' darkens when the first person offers, in the final clauses of the closing sentence, his motives for having started to record on paper the creatures of his mind. The first motive he offers, the pleasure of watching an inept and bizarre spectacle, suggests that he conceives of writing as a means of putting the disordered mind at a safe distance and reasserting his control over it. But it immediately becomes clear that no such control is possible when he offers, as a second and final motive, the mere hope that writing will make '[his] mind ashamed of itself'. The mind continues to have a mind of its own, in other words, and the dramatic interplay of divided forces within the identity of the author remains unresolved at the end of the chapter. So too do the motives behind a process of writing that nonetheless continues, unabated, in the pages ahead.

The two prefaces to be found early in Book I, the initial note 'To the Reader' and its non-identical twin 'Of idleness' (I.8), open up lines of enquiry that reappear in the seven short chapters on military and ethical themes that they frame. In their different ways, the first, fifth, sixth, and seventh chapters of Book I scrutinize, in the most difficult circumstances of confrontation and conflict, the ideal of openness that is formulated in 'To the Reader'. The very first chapter, 'By diverse means we arrive at the same end' (I.1: 'Par divers moyens on arrive à pareille fin'), stresses the peril and uncertainty that the ideal is bound to encounter. A series of contrasting military anecdotes, showing how an attitude of defiance as well as of submission may move the conqueror to spare the conquered, yields a reflection on the diversity of man and the difficulty of judging human actions. The example of the cruelty shown by Alexander the Great, added in 1588 and thereafter extended, ends this opening chapter in an image of startling carnage. The second, third, and fourth chapters of Book I, by contrast, record attempts to take pleasure from – or resist – the passions and the extravagances of the mind. The second chapter, 'Of sadness' (I.2: 'De la tristesse'), is a case in point. In opening and closing additions to the chapter, Montaigne declares first a natural insensitivity to extreme passions, then a resolution to strengthen his resistance to them by force of argument. The chapter thus appears, in retrospect, as an attempt at the resistance of which it speaks.

What 'To the Reader' and 'Of idleness' suggest, beyond their local context, is that a single preface to the *Essais* will not suffice. The process of introducing the book to its readers, of opening up perspectives on the text, is itself open-ended: it is not confined here – as is often the way – to the 'paratext', the space within the material book surrounding the main text, the realm of the preface. It extends on and on into the text.

Dedications and Apostrophes in Books I and II

The open-ended nature of the process just described may help to account for the fact that dedications and apostrophes are scattered throughout Books I and II. At important places in both Books, these materials appear above the surface of the writing, redirecting the attention of a privileged reader – an individual who is generally identified and directly addressed – to the text's subject, aims, and means as those are currently understood. They offer in this way privileged vantage points from which to glimpse Montaigne's evolving reflections on how his work was to be organized – and is to be read.

Dedications are the most visible form of prefatory material found in Books I and II. Three chapters carry a dedication in their titles, in each case to a wellborn woman in the author's circle of acquaintances, whom he also addresses in the text.

The first of these, 'Of the education of children' (I.26: 'De l'institution des enfans'), is couched as a letter of advice to an expectant mother, Diane de Foix (1542?–87), about how best to bring up the child soon to be born to her. The second of the three chapters, 'Of the affection of fathers for their children' (II.8: 'De l'affection des pères aux enfans'), carries on where 'Of the education of children' left off, in examining how parents should treat questions of succession once their children have reached an age of discretion. Montaigne presents the chapter's dedicatee, Madame d'Estissac (Louise de La Béraudière, born 1538), as a paragon of maternal affection towards her young son. Both chapters treat their subject-matter in such a way as to generate perspectives on the broader project that is the *Essais*: to sustain, in other words, the text's activity of reflecting on its own processes. 'Of the education of children', as we shall see in the next chapter, sketches through its educational precepts a model for the kind of thinking that characterizes the text as a whole. 'Of the affection of fathers for their children', in extending the subject of parental affection to what Montaigne calls 'the children of our mind' ('les enfantemens de notre esprit'; F 353, VS 400), produces important variations on the theme of the book as an exercise in authorial self-portraiture. These variations stress, at the outset, the unique oddity of the undertaking: 'It is the only book in the world of its kind, a book with a wild and eccentric plan' ('C'est le seul livre au monde de son espece, d'un dessein farouche et extravagant'; F 338, VS 385). But they assert equally emphatically, at the end of the chapter, the affection that Montaigne feels for his brain-child and the independence with which the child now goes into the world (F 355, VS 401–2). The self-reflective remarks of both chapters appear directly related to the dedications they carry: there is nothing more natural, after all, than the wish to offer somebody, along with a gift, some sense of what the gift is and why it matters. What Montaigne offers his dedicatee, in both cases, is his contribution to an ongoing conversation between them on a topic of shared interest, a conversation that he demonstrably values, since it also helps him to make sense of his own undertaking in the *Essais*.

The third chapter to carry a dedication, 'Twenty-nine sonnets of Etienne de La Boétie' (I.29: 'Vingt et neuf sonnets d'Estienne de la Boétie'), presents a more complicated profile. It needs to be understood in the context of the preceding chapter, 'Of friendship' (I.28: 'De l'amitié'), and of Montaigne's changing plans for the organization of Book I as a whole. Both chapters constitute prefaces to works by Etienne de La Boétie (1530–63), a legal colleague and fellow humanist writer with whom Montaigne experienced an intense if brief intimacy, and whose literary executor he became on his friend's sudden death. They are prefaces to works originally destined for inclusion in, but now conspicuous by their absence from, the *Essais*. Both, nevertheless, remain. They reinforce, as a result, the impression of a text that records the ebb and flow of time and circumstance, a text requiring many prefaces but exhausted by none, since these are caught in the same ebb and flow.

'Of friendship' (I.28) reveals Montaigne's intention to include La Boétie's early work of political theory, *On Voluntary Servitude* (*De la servitude volontaire*), in Book I of the *Essais*. The chapter starts in the mode of a preface to that work. Drawing on a further image from the visual arts to characterize the *Essais*, though a less flattering one than the metaphor of the self-portrait used in 'To the Reader' and elsewhere, Montaigne contrasts his work with that of a painter in his employment who places his masterpiece in the middle of the wall before filling the space around it with 'grotesques', portions of human and animal bodies arranged in fantastical combinations, a form of decoration that became fashionable throughout Renaissance Europe after it was discovered in excavations of ancient Roman houses. The burden of the contrast is that, unlike the painter, he is capable only of producing the grotesques; he has therefore decided to use La Boétie's discourse 'in honour of liberty against tyrants' ('à l'honneur de la liberté contre les tyrans'; F 164–5, VS 183–4) as his centrepiece, placed at the numerical middle of Book I, surrounded by his grotesques. These recall the runaway mind's self-begotten chimeras and fantastical monsters so vividly described in 'Of Idleness'. But in describing them here in terms of a pictorial metaphor, Montaigne quietly acknowledges them as his own creation, his contribution to a work of art by four hands. Weighing classical treatments of friendship against his intense experience with La

Boétie, whose loss he mourns, Montaigne both stresses the mysterious nature of the real thing – requiring the free choice of equals and yet, as we will see in chapter 6 below, born of an inexplicable force – and insists that it is, for all that, compatible with good citizenship. He illustrates that last point with reference to the virtue of La Boétie and his own decision, before 1580, to remove from Book I the treatise of his friend after it was published by French Protestants hostile to their king on two occasions in the mid-1570s, an initiative that he deplores, and from which he wishes to distance himself and the memory of his friend. Since this change of mind took place before 1580, when Books I and II first appeared in print, it is clear that he could have chosen to remove from the published work all traces of the initial design and the afterthought. He chooses to retain them, as if to mark by a kind of ellipsis the omission that he judged necessary, but which left an empty space at the middle of Book I.

'Twenty-nine sonnets of Etienne de La Boétie', the short chapter that follows 'Of friendship', introduces the sequence of love sonnets by La Boétie with which Montaigne filled that empty space in all the editions of the *Essais* published during his lifetime. It dedicates the sequence to Diane d'Andoins (1554–1621), Countess of Grammont and Guiche (or Guissen), then mistress of and counsellor to a king, Henri de Navarre (1553–1610), who will reappear later in our story. Like Don Quixote, Diane was a lover of the popular chivalric romance *Amadís of Gaul*, from which she took the name – Corisande – that Montaigne uses of her. The chapter thus places poems written by a man of controversial memory under the patronage of a lady who possesses literary tastes (about which Montaigne says much) and powerful connections (about which he maintains a discreet silence). This appeal to patronage is standard practice in literary works of the age. Altogether more surprising is the fact that Montaigne removes the poems from Book I in changes to his text made after 1588, adding nothing to the Bordeaux copy other than a brief note to the effect that they can be seen elsewhere, while retaining the chapter 'Twenty-nine sonnets of Etienne de La Boétie' as a trace of their earlier inclusion and dedication. Why he decided to do this is difficult to say. Montaigne's editors, building on the continuing work of literary historians on the question, offer different reasons – political, psychological, and literary – for his decision. Like nature, after all, scholarship abhors a vacuum. Montaigne, by contrast, could be said to have created one in his text. His dedicatory epistle, shorn of the sonnets it introduces, has at least one clear effect upon a reading of the text. In repeating the preceding chapter's gesture of omission, it confirms the absence of a centrepiece to Book I, leaving Montaigne's grotesques to proliferate around the unfilled space.

Dedications are not only the opening moves on offer in the *Essais*. On two instances in Book II, an apostrophe – as a moment of direct address, by way of an aside, is called in rhetoric – is offered to a lady in the middle of a chapter, unannounced. Both instances occupy significant positions, not only in their chapters, but also in the economy of the *Essais* as a whole.

The first instance, a complex one to which I will turn in chapter 4 below, comes in the middle of the 'Apology for Raymond Sebond' (II.12: 'Apologie de Raimond Sebond').

The second instance occurs in 'Of the resemblance of children to fathers' (II.37: 'De la ressemblance des enfans aux peres'). This is the final chapter of Book II and so, before the addition of Book III in 1588, brought the *Essais* as a whole to an end. A large part of the chapter is given up to a systematic critique of the medicine of Montaigne's age, its scientific pretensions, and its disastrous effects on individual patients. The apostrophe appears in the closing pages of the chapter as a casual afterthought and the fruit of circumstance. In so doing, it plays the role of a delayed dedicatory preface to 'Of the resemblance of children to fathers', one that also mirrors the opening moves of Book I.

Montaigne begins the chapter by looking back over the seven or eight years to have elapsed since he started writing his book. During this time, he says, he has fallen prey to the condition he feared the most: kidney stones. He describes how he has come to live with this most painful of conditions, and he rebukes philosophy for requiring one to display an external disdain for pain, when the challenge of simple endurance is hard enough to meet (F 696–701, VS 758–63). He guesses that he has inherited his predisposition to kidney stones from his father, who died of the condition, before declaring a second respect in which he resembles his father and indeed his forefathers: his dislike of medicine. While this dislike may also have started life as a mere inherited predisposition, Montaigne says, he has tried to make it his own considered opinion by bolstering it with arguments (F 701–3, VS 763–5). The critical survey of medicine that follows is thus presented as a thought-experiment designed to put those arguments to the test (F 704–22, VS 765–83). The survey is systematic, offering a brief history of controversy in medicine from

Hippocrates to the present day, and covering the various branches of the discipline as well as its dominant schools of thought. Montaigne takes an unremittingly contrarian approach to the medicine of his age, countering each of its hypotheses with one of equal and opposite force, and telling stories from his experience in order to illustrate its empty promises and mortal dangers. In a passage added to the text after 1588 he mourns once again, without mentioning him by name this time, La Boétie's death at the hands of his doctors (F 713, VS 774). He reserves his parting shot for the uses to which doctors put their experience when they legitimize their status, justify their prescription of habitual remedies, and make pseudo-scientific inferences. Since he has made it clear that he too is speaking from experience, he effectively brings the doctors' various claims for their art down to the same fragile epistemological level as his criticisms, the crucial difference being that he is not using his experience to claim any medical expertise or knowledge. He is only asking questions, and ask them he does, in wave after interrogative wave.

It is at this point in the chapter – as if all those questions had sum-moned an interlocutor – that Montaigne addresses another wellborn lady in his circle of acquaintances, Madame de Duras (Marguerite d'Aure-Gramont, 1549?–1586), as if by way of an afterthought. He claims that he had reached this very point in his composition of the chapter when she recently called on him: the abrupt apostrophe to Madame de Duras therefore imitates, at a textual level, the pleasurable interruption that her visit afforded him. The apostrophe's opening repeats the principal claims of Montaigne's initial note 'To the Reader'. This book of his, he says, is a self-portrait that he has undertaken in order that his family and friends – among whom he counts Madame de Duras – will remember him after his imminent demise, not as he ought to have been, but as he was. He sets no other store and seeks no glory from it: 'I do not at all seek to be better loved and esteemed dead than alive' ('Je ne cherche aucunement qu'on m'ayme et estime mieux mort que vivant'; F 723, VS 783). The implica-tion here is that the book ought to be approached in the same spirit of sincerity and openness as the one in which it was written. The mirroring effect here is remarkable: it appears to bring the author's understanding of his project full circle by recalling the opening of Book I at the end of Book II. In its end, it would seem, is its beginning.

That, however, would be to forget the very point from which 'Of the resemblance of children to fathers' starts and which it now repeats: the recognition that its ageing author and his text are caught in the onward flow of time. The circle cannot be closed. The letter addressed to Madame de Duras, in looking back to the opening of Book I, moves beyond it and brings Book II not so much to an end as to an opening of its own. It adds to the images of the self-portrait and the register a way of introducing the text present neither in 'To the Reader' nor in 'Of idleness': the image of Montaigne's text as an exercise in countering received wisdom.

The figure of Madame de Duras is crucial to this development. Medicine is an art by which, Montaigne intimates, she sets great store: this intimation allows him momentarily to present his chapter as a written contribution to an ongoing conversation, a form of presentation we have also seen him adopt in 'Of the education of children' and 'Of the affection of fathers for their children', with the difference being that on this occasion he is clearly addressing, in Madame de Duras, someone who thinks otherwise than he about the topic. If he has dared to shake the mysteries of medicine so boldly, he says, this is because the ancient authors on medicine, Pliny and Celsus, do the same, indeed, 'They speak far more roughly to their art than I do' ('Ils parlent bien plus rudement à leur art que je ne fay'; F 724, VS 784). The conversational metaphor, suggested by the sudden arrival of Madame de Duras in the middle of composition, spreads here to include written exchanges, letters, and controversies, as well as oral ones: Pliny and Celsus 'speak' to medicine in their books, as in turn does Montaigne, who, having interrupted it to address Madame de Duras, now proposes to continue the written conversation with medicine that he is dedicating to her. The apostrophe ends in these terms: 'Madame, that is enough. Surely you give me leave to resume the thread of my argument, from which I had turned aside to talk with you' ('Madame, en voylà assez: vous me donnez bien congé de reprendre le fil de mon propos, duquel je m'estoy destourné pour vous entretenir'; F 724, VS 784). Conversation is the medium through which one comes to form one's own thoughts: thinking about something requires thinking with others. The letter to Madame de Duras appears as a figure for the broader conversation – and the argument – to which it belongs and to which Montaigne returns in the closing pages of the chapter.

Those closing pages pursue the idea of the text as an exercise in shaking up received wisdom. They present the chapter as an attempt to lend form to the author's hostility to medicine: the form of a thought. Such an attempt requires a greater measure of control than the register described

in 'Of idleness'. Montaigne says that while he may yet weaken in his atavistic opposition to the medicine of his age, when – that is – illness finally
succeeds in unhinging his judgement, in the meantime he has at least
managed to put that opposition into better shape:

> I have taken the trouble to plead this cause, which I understand rather poorly,
> to support a little and strengthen the natural aversion to drugs and to the
> practice of our medicine which I have derived from my ancestors, so that it
> should not be merely a stupid and thoughtless inclination and should have
> a little more form.

> J'ay pris [la] peine de plaider cette cause, que j'entens assez mal, pour appuyer
> un peu et conforter la propension naturelle contre les drogues et pratique
> de nostre medecine, qui s'est dérivée en moy par mes ancestres, afin que ce
> ne fust pas seulement une inclination stupide et temeraire, et qu'elle eust un
> peu plus de forme.   (F 724–5, VS 785)

This sentence surrounds its claim with the modesty that accompanies
so many of Montaigne's opening moves. Once again, the modesty is in
part a strategy for capturing goodwill, but only in part. It reveals other
preoccupations, too, in this case with the sheer difficulty of freeing your
mind from the snare of prejudice and stupidity. Faced with the difficulty
of the exercise, and with the lure of vanity to which he refers a few lines
later on, Montaigne says merely that his intention has been to lend his
atavistic opposition to medicine 'a little more form'. The definitive formation of a thought remains a distant prospect, but the runaway mind
encountered in 'Of idleness' is now under some kind of control, and the
attempt has begun.

In making that attempt, the text is bound to encounter differences of
opinion among its readers, and Montaigne ends Book II by opening his
text up to that possibility. Those who love our medicine may well disagree
with his views, he says, and doubtless for good reasons. Such disagreement
was soon to be recorded in at least one quarter: we know that a report
on the *Essais*, prepared in 1581, as we shall see in chapter 7 below, for the
censors of the Roman Index, takes issue with Montaigne's decision in
this chapter to criticize medicine, no doubt because, as one of the three
faculties of higher learning in medieval and early modern universities,
medicine was associated with the other faculties of law and especially

theology, which the Vatican readers were concerned to defend. Those readers were, of course, merely confirming a prediction that Montaigne had made in the very text that they scrutinized. In the same edition of the chapter, published in 1580, he explains why he expects most of his readers to disagree with him and accepts such disagreement as an inevitable consequence of his way of writing and thinking. Madame de Duras is the immediate example, included and addressed within the text, of those who defend medicine, but the apostrophe to her is now over, and the plural is deliberately chosen: Montaigne is indirectly addressing his readers in general. The diversity that characterizes thought is not only a condition of its coming into being; it is the way the world goes; so it is to diversity that Montaigne offers the last word of Book II:

> I am so far from being vexed to see discord between my judgements and others', and from making myself incompatible with the society of men because they are of a different sentiment and party from mine, that on the contrary, since variety is the most general fashion that nature has followed, [...] I find it much rarer to see our humours and plans agree. And there were never in the world two opinions alike, any more than two hairs or two grains. Their most universal quality is diversity.

> Il s'en faut tant que je m'effarouche de voir de la discordance de mes jugemens à ceux d'autruy, et que je me rende incompatible à la societé des hommes pour estre d'autre sens et party que le mien, qu'au rebours, comme c'est la plus generale façon que nature aye suivy que la varieté, [...] je trouve bien plus rare de voir convenir nos humeurs et nos desseins. Et ne fut jamais au monde deux opinions pareilles, non plus que deux poils ou deux grains. Leur plus universelle qualité, c'est la diversité. (F 725, VS 785–6)

The Changing Picture in Book III

Let us recapitulate. We have seen how various of the elements – preambles, letters of dedication, and reflections on the nature of the text to come – that usually combine to form the preface to a work, neatly confined to its threshold, spill over into the text of the *Essais* at various points in Books I and II. We have seen how they interrupt the ordinary course of the text to redefine its aims, justify its methods, and disarm potential objections: to initiate once more, in other words, the process of opening up the book to the reader and the reader to the book. Such opening moves are no longer distinct from the rest of the text: they have become part of its fabric. The line between text and paratext, between the centre and the margins, is often blurred in Books I and II. One has only to consider 'Of idleness' (I.8), a chapter that certainly looks and feels like a preface but appears within the text proper, or the relationship between the absent centrepiece and the proliferating grotesques in 'Of friendship' (I.28). Prefatory discourse, once it has spilled over the threshold of the text, spreads across Books I and II.

Book III may be seen as an extension of that process. It presents an immediate contrast to the two earlier Books in that the visible apparatus of prefatory discourse – the prologues to works by other hands, the apostrophes to named individual readers, and the letters of dedication – has entirely disappeared. That contrast appears superficial on a closer look inside Book III, however, which reveals that the modes and moods of prefatory discourse have spread in varying degrees of intensity throughout the text. On occasions, indeed, they seem to have been so thoroughly absorbed into the fabric of the writing as to make Book III look like one giant preface. Seen in that way, Book III not only extends the spread of the prefatory started in Books I and II, but completes the process of its dissolution and absorption.

Once prefatory discourse has been dissolved into its constituent parts, these appear to take on a life of their own in the text, a life it turns out that they had all along. Techniques such as letter-writing, the dialogue mode, and self-reference combine in many a preface in order to perform its vital functions. This means that the notion of prefatory discourse helps to focus attention on these techniques and their interactions. Each of these techniques, however, can be seen playing a distinct role throughout the three Books of the *Essais*.

The letter form is a case in point, for the intimate, open-ended prose with which it has been associated since classical antiquity makes it an important model for Montaigne's entire style of writing. He suggests as much when, in 'A consideration upon Cicero' (I.40: 'Considération sur Cicéron'), he expresses his admiration for the letters that Epicurus and Seneca wrote to their friends, and then claims in a late addition that he too would have adopted the letter form if only he had had someone worth talking to (F 225, VS 252). The implication he goes on to offer – that only the best of friends would have made a suitable recipient of his thoughts – brings irresistibly to mind La Boétie, even though he is not named, and the *Essais* have been read as their author's written contribution to an imagined conversation or correspondence with the friend he mourns. The question of what Montaigne means by his choice of title is one to which we will turn in chapter 3 below. Suffice it to say for now that there are those in the period who perceive a connection between the epistles of the ancients, particularly Seneca's letters to Lucilius, and the modern compositions Montaigne gathers under the title *Essais*. One of the earliest and most influential essayists, the English polymath and politician Sir Francis Bacon (1561–1626), draws the parallel when, in the dedicatory epistle to the Prince of Wales intended for the 1612 edition of his own *Essays* (first published in 1597), he explains in the following terms the meaning of the title he has borrowed from Montaigne: 'Seneca's epistles to Lucilius, if one marks them well, are but *Essays*, that is, dispersed meditations, though conveyed in the form of epistles.'

The dialogue is a second informal and open-ended literary model with classical antecedents whose traces can be detected in the style of the *Essais*. Montaigne's use of dialogue is generally fleeting and rhetorical: he switches for a moment into direct speech to emphasize a point. He has, at other times, more sustained recourse to dialogue, and not merely for rhetorical effect, but as an instrument of thought. The dialogues that Plato wrote about his teacher Socrates (469–399 BCE) in ancient Athens provide Montaigne with his model. Where many later dialogue-writers use the form for dogmatic purposes, staging the learning of a lesson so as to transmit its content more effectively, Plato does the opposite. Like Socrates before him, says Montaigne in the 'Apology for Raymond Sebond', Plato sees teaching as an exercise in asking questions and provoking discussion from a position that is itself incorrigibly shifting and plural. Hence his manner of writing dialogues: 'Plato seems to me to have favoured this form of philosophizing in dialogues deliberately, to put more fittingly into diverse mouths the diversity and variation of his own ideas' ('Platon me semble avoir aymé cette forme de philosopher par dialogues, à escient, pour loger plus decemment en diverses bouches la diversité et variation de ses propres fantasies'; F 458, VS 509). Montaigne articulates here with reference to Plato what he practises at various points in the *Essais*: the use of dialogue to represent the diversity that inhabits his own thinking. A sustained example is to be found in the closing chapter of Book III, 'Of experience' (III.13), when Montaigne – returning to the medical preoccupations already discussed, as we have seen, in the corresponding chapter of Book II – stages a dialogue between his mind and his imagination in which the former attempts, by arguments weak and strong, to persuade the latter that it is for his own good that he suffers from kidney stones (F 1018–23, VS 1090–5). There is no more vivid illustration of Montaigne's diversity of thought.

Last but not least, the various metaphors that are used of the book in its prefaces also form part of the text's wider technique of self-reference, and they reappear when it pauses to redirect its attention to itself and its own workings. We have already seen the metaphors of the authorial self-portrait and the record recur in different places. If one were attempting to build a full picture, however, there are further important metaphors for the *Essais* that would need to be drawn in here – those, in particular, that describe the work as a form of confession, as a compilation, and, of course, as a process of essaying – and then analysed alongside the text's other procedures of self-reference: the repeated use of the adverb 'here' ('icy'), for example, as in the opening sentence of Montaigne's note 'To the Reader' with which we began. There is no shortage of examples. On the contrary, once one starts to track this set of procedures beyond the confines of the various prefaces, one finds an example on every other page of this consistently self-referential work. These examples bear out the suggestion made earlier: that once prefatory discourse has been dissolved into its constituent parts, each of these parts takes on a life it turns out to have had all along, the life of the text.

Let us end by looking at one of the many passages that might be described as extensions of prefatory discourse in Book III. The celebrated lines that open 'Of repentance' (III.2: 'Du repentir') fit this description because they deploy the techniques of the preface to open up new perspectives on the chapter to come and on the project of the *Essais* as a whole:

> Others form man; I tell of him, and portray a particular one, very ill-formed, whom I should really make different from what he is if I had to fashion him over again. But now it is done. Now the lines of my painting do not go astray, though they change and vary. [...] I cannot keep my subject still. It goes along befuddled and staggering, with a natural drunkenness. I take it

in this condition, just as it is at the moment I give my attention to it. I do not portray being: I portray passing. Not the passing from one age to another, or, as the people say, from seven years to seven years, but from day to day, from minute to minute. My history needs to be adapted to the moment. I may presently change, not only by chance, but also by intention. This is a record of various and changeable occurrences, and of irresolute and, when it so befalls, contradictory ideas: whether I am different myself, or whether I take hold of my subjects in different circumstances and aspects. So, all in all, I may indeed contradict myself now and then; but truth, as Demades said, I do not contradict. If my mind could gain a firm footing, I would not make essays, I would make decisions; but it is always in apprenticeship and on trial.

Les autres forment l'homme; je le recite et en represente un particulier bien mal formé, et lequel, si j'avoy à façonner de nouveau, je ferois vrayement bien autre qu'il n'est. Meshuy c'est fait. Or les traits de ma peinture ne forvoyent point, quoy qu'ils se changent et diversifient. [...] Je ne puis asseurer mon object. Il va trouble et chancelant, d'une yvresse naturelle. Je le prens en ce point, comme il est, en l'instant que je m'amuse à luy. Je ne peints pas l'estre. Je peints le passage: non un passage d'aage en autre, ou, comme dict le peuple, de sept en sept ans, mais de jour en jour, de minute en minute. Il faut accommoder mon histoire à l'heure. Je pourray tantost changer, non de fortune seulement, mais aussi d'intention. C'est un contrerolle de divers et muables accidens et d'imaginations irresolües et, quand il y eschet, contraires: soit que je sois autre moy-mesme, soit que je saisisse les subjects par autres circonstances et considerations. Tant y a que je me contredits bien à l'adventure, mais la vérité, comme disoit Demades, je ne la contredy point. Si mon ame pouvoit prendre pied, je ne m'essaierois pas, je me resoudrois: elle est tousjours en apprentissage et en espreuve.   (F 740, VS 804–5)

The genius of the passage lies in its combination of two images for the *Essais* which appeared antithetical in the opening pages of Book I: that of the self-portrait, implying artful execution and the stasis of a finished product, and that of the register or record, implying artless execution and the fluidity of a never-ending process. The manner in which Montaigne reconciles those two images here allows him to portray – with an unrepentant lucidity – the experimental manner in which he lives and writes.

The opening sentences sketch out how the chapter is to treat the question of repentance even as they fix the reader's attention, preface-style, on the nature of the work. Montaigne's first move is to distinguish his undertaking from that of those – moral philosophers and theologians, doubtless, though they remain unidentified – who 'form man', who define and instruct humankind in general, whereas he recounts and represents one particular – and ill-formed – man: Montaigne himself. We are already being led towards the image of the self-portrait in the third sentence. Before we reach that point, however, our attention is momentarily diverted from the nature of the undertaking towards the kind of man the author is, and would make himself, if he had the chance to start afresh. In pointing out the discrepancy between the real man and the man that might have been, the end of the first sentence entertains the possibility of repentance, if that term is understood to imply a disavowal of those past thoughts and deeds that produced the botched article. No sooner has the possibility of repentance been entertained, however, than the second sentence curtly dismisses it. What is done is done. The first two sentences thus offer a first glimpse both of what Montaigne means by repentance and of the suspicion with which he will come to treat it when, at the end of the preamble to the chapter, he makes it known – in a declaration that runs counter to the orthodox Catholic position of his day – that he rarely repents (F 742, VS 806).

It is only a glimpse at this stage, however, a momentary digression from the preamble in hand. The third sentence uses the emphatic 'Now' ('Or') to refocus attention on the nature of the work on which Montaigne is engaged – and to reveal a surprise and a puzzle: this is a painting that keeps changing and yet never ceases to be a faithful representation. The metaphor of the self-portrait is applied here to a situation of Heraclitean flux, a flux in which all things are caught, including the painter and his subject. As if under the influence of the ontological drunkenness they describe, the sentences stagger from the incapacitated painter to the reeling subject, and back again. Then they find their feet. It is neither Montaigne's task to settle his subject nor that of his subject to settle. A different kind of painting is under way. Montaigne clinches his point in a manner as memorable as it is pithy: 'I do not portray being: I portray passing' ('Je ne peins pas l'estre. Je peins le passage'). That formula – one of its author's most famous – tends to be reduced, by being quoted out of context, to the banal statement that Montaigne paints the passing of time into his self-portrait. However, you will notice that the formula speaks not of a self who passes, but only of a disquietingly subjectless 'passing': the flood of all-transforming time. The sentences that follow first qualify what that flood is – not the stately progression from age to age but the rushing of the hands around the clock – and then, as if in recognition that it was incapable of depicting such a flood, they drop the metaphor of the portrait.

They turn instead, first, to the image of a history – a history of the moment that charts minute reversals of chance and intention – and then to the notion of the book as a 'record' ('contrerolle'). That notion best allows Montaigne to depict the radical alterations that his book witnesses. The record is seen here as made up of a scattered sequence of moments, in each of which not only the circumstances of the thinking are different, but so too is the person doing the thinking: 'I am different myself.' The repetition of the adjective 'different' ('autre') in this sentence serves to emphasize the alterations of individual identity and situation through time. The notion of the record takes us back to its first appearance, in 'Of idleness', and to the ever-stranger creations of the runaway mind to which, in that chapter, it was conceived as a corrective. Yet things are different in 'Of repentance', for where 'Of idleness' described a psychodrama of errancy and flight in which the mind and the first person played antagonistic roles, here the two are reconciled to a shared life.

That way of life, which is also a way of writing, is described in the closing sentences of the passage. It may be seen as the product here of the tension between the self-portrait and the record: between the representation of a self that somehow always remains the same, a stable centre of core attributes and dispositions, and the record of what happens to a mind that is forever taking off in different directions. Those two metaphors for the project of the *Essais*, far from presenting alternatives, exist in a state of symbiosis. They support, between them, a manner of operating that is caught between the pull of the centre and that of the margins. The mind is perpetually beginning a new journey from one towards the other in order to put its capacities for thought-formation to the test: it is always, as he says in the last sentence, 'in apprenticeship and on trial'. Its manner is intrinsically experimental and initiatory. Montaigne describes this manner without complacency – he would prefer to be decisive – but also without repentance: things run that way for him in life, and in his book, which is a part of life.

This explains, no doubt, why his book is full of openings.

2

An Education in Free-Thinking

We saw, at the end of the previous chapter, how productively Montaigne's way of writing and thinking is caught between what might be called the pull of home – a stable centre of core dispositions – and the lure of away in the form of an endless departure upon new quests, at the margins of the familiar, for the adventuring mind. How, though, are those quests to be undertaken? Under what conditions? In whose company? And to what end?

Montaigne's free-thinking, as I shall suggest in what follows, offers us a context for understanding the particular turn of mind that he reveals in the *Essais*. It does so because it allows him to define an educational principle that he not only advocates but puts into practice. My example is taken from the first chapter of the *Essais* in which free-thinking appears as a topic: 'Of the education of children' (I.26: 'De l'institution des enfans'). This chapter directly follows 'Of pedantry' (I.25: 'Du pedantisme') and forms with it a diptych on the uses and abuses of learning. In using the stock arguments of textual authorities to lampoon the learning of the age for its reliance on those very arguments, 'Of pedantry' risks being hoist with its own petard, an irony which Montaigne sharpens by describing his book as a mere repository of commonplaces. Modest and lucid, such a remark not only befits the gentleman amateur that Montaigne consciously plays in the closing pages of the chapter, preferring arms to letters; it also implies in him the capacity for judgement whose absence in professional scholars he bemoans. Presented as an offshoot of the previous chapter and couched as a letter to an expectant mother, Diane de Foix, about how her son should be brought up, 'Of the education of children' is Montaigne's contribution to the sixteenth-century debate about education. It explicitly runs counter to the 'common usage' by portraying the ideal tutor as someone who, by listening instead of lecturing, develops the pupil's capacity to exercise judgement and think freely in pursuit of truth. It is hardly surprising that free-thinking should first appear in this context, since if you think it is an important thing for people to do, you are likely to advocate it as a principle central to their upbringing and education. What I want to argue, however, is that the chapter does not merely advocate the principle: it sets itself the task of practising the freedom of thought it preaches.

Defining Terms

Expanding upon my headline suggestion, that free-thinking offers a context for understanding the turn of mind that Montaigne reveals in the *Essais*, will require me to define with some care two key terms: 'free-thinking' and 'context'.

I shall start with 'free-thinking', and I propose to linger on its place in the history of medieval and early modern Europe, given its importance to this book as a whole. The phrase, as I said in the opening pages of this book, is generally taken to refer to the agnosticism or atheism of a secular humanist worldview that maintains a principled independence from the dogmas of any church or creed. This sense comes to us from the seventeenth and eighteenth centuries. The phrase comes, in that period, to be associated with deists and other nonconformists in Christian Europe who refused to submit their reason to the authority of established religion in matters of belief. The defenders of religious orthodoxy in France invent terms like *libertin* and *libertinage* to characterize their opponents and the loose morals with which they associate them. These are terms of abuse, in the first instance, but they come eventually, in a process that is familiar today, to be appropriated and valorized by the people to whom they are applied. Since *libertin* and *libertinage* are derived from *libre*, meaning 'free', the etymological link between these people and their notorious freedom of thought, *liberté de penser* or *liberté de philosopher*, is preserved in French as it is in the corresponding English terms and phrases ('free-thinking', 'free-thinker', etc). These still carry with them a whiff of their seventeenth-century association with religious heterodoxy.

But free-thinking has a much longer history than that, and a broader one too, even in the seventeenth century. Historians have shown that it appears as a commonplace anti-authoritarian gesture, derived from the ancients, in a wide range of medieval and early modern debates across the field of human enquiry. M. A. Stewart and Ian Maclean have between them provided the most comprehensive survey to date in tracing the long history of the Latin phrase *libertas philosophandi* and its cognates, including 'free-thinking', the standard English version. What this long history shows is that free-thinking is nothing like a school of philosophy, with a set of principles and a group of adherents, though it does tend to be associated with various such schools and not others. It is something at once more fragile and more flexible: a set of attitudes, expressed in a cluster of phrases, which are available for use at different times and places and whose uses vary accordingly. It needs always, therefore, to be seen in relation to specific conflicts or constraints – external and internal – that operate in a given situation to obstruct the free movement of thought. The history of free-thinking is always a contextual history.

That history is one of four interrelated intellectual contexts. The first of these is the debate within medieval and early modern science (or 'natural philosophy', as it was known) about the continuing legacy in this area of Aristotle, Plato's pupil and tutor to Alexander the Great, the ancient Greek philosopher whose many-sided works, as interpreted within a Christian framework, were placed, in the European Middle Ages, at the centre of all higher teaching and learning – the intellectual tradition known as 'scholasticism' because it was rooted in the universities or 'schools'. One instance of this debate is the stir that the Bolognese philosopher Pietro Pomponazzi (1462–1525) caused among his fellow natural philosophers by publishing in 1516 a treatise, entitled *On the Immortality of the Soul* (*De immortalitate animae*), in which he rehearses at length a materialist interpretation of Aristotle's account of the soul. This interpretation seemed to many to put Aristotle at odds with the Christian framework in which scholastic philosophers had so carefully placed him. The second of the four contexts mentioned above is the conflict between natural philosophy and theology that is reawakened each time the investigation of nature encroaches on or calls into question the revealed truths of religion. Pomponazzi's text, as Maclean points out, sparked conflict along this disciplinary borderline. So – notoriously – did the dissemination and defence of Copernican cosmology in the early seventeenth century by the

Tuscan astronomer and mathematician Galileo Galilei (1564–1642) and his followers, leading in 1633 to Galileo's trial and condemnation by the Inquisition in Rome to life imprisonment for suspected heresy.

The third context for free-thinking is the entire field of philosophy, which was understood to cover secular human enquiry in the broadest sense, not just natural or physical but metaphysical, moral, political, and so on. This sense of the term philosophy explains the ease with which the phrase *libertas philosophandi* and its vernacular equivalents cover freedom of thought in general. The most controversial example of a broader use of the phrase is to be found in the work of the Dutch-Jewish philosopher Benedict de Spinoza (1632–77). His *Theologico-Political Treatise* (*Tractatus theologico-politicus*) of 1670 sets out to show, as its subtitle states, 'that freedom of thought is not only compatible with piety and the peace of the commonwealth, but that to take away this freedom is to endanger the peace of the commonwealth and even piety itself' ('libertatem philosophandem non tantum salva pietate, et reipublicae pace posse concedi: sed eandem nisi cum pace reipublicae, ipsaque petate tolli non posse'). Spinoza's radical thesis, that the state should fix as its main purpose the preservation of the individual's freedom of thought, effectively subordinates the theological authority of the Church to the political power of the State. Its theological implications were immediately and widely perceived to be heterodox, which means that the reception of Spinoza is also a major episode in our fourth context for free-thinking, that of seventeenth- and eighteenth-century debates about secular challenges to religious orthodoxy. That fourth context overlaps, to some degree, with the second – the border wars between natural philosophy and theology – the difference being that the debate is now conducted in broader terms and outside the institutional setting of the universities.

The various intellectual contexts sketched above are, of course, in no sense watertight or permanent: they are blurred at the edges, liable to overlap, and each – if space permitted – would repay further contextualization. They nonetheless show something of the breadth and depth of the history of free-thinking in which I want to suggest that Montaigne has a place.

How that history evolves over the centuries on either side of his work is difficult to say with precision. Stewart tells a largely seventeenth-century story of definite transition as free-thinking ceases to be uniquely associated with the natural philosophy of the post-Copernican period and starts spreading across the entire field of philosophy: the conflict about the work of the anti-scholastic 'new' French philosopher René Descartes (1596–1650) that raged within Dutch universities during the middle decades of the seventeenth century serves, in Stewart's story, as the moment of transition. Maclean charts an earlier history, and a less linear one, which he nonetheless offers as part of a complex narrative about the origins of modern science. He argues that the tradition of free philosophizing within medieval and Renaissance universities – what we might call academic freedom – provides an institutional and educational context for the emergence of sceptical doubt in the period. Maclean's argument, as we shall see, has implications for our understanding of Montaigne's relationship with scepticism in general and, in particular, his ideas concerning the education of children.

At each moment in the long and complex history of free-thinking, the intellectual issues need to be seen in relation to two further contexts, the institutional and the literary.

The institutional dimension is a more or less permanent feature of the tradition. Questions of intellectual freedom and constraint were not only debated within universities in Protestant and Catholic Europe, but also between universities and the theological authorities who intervened at critical moments in their affairs, and similar issues mark the history of the book. In 1559, the Council of Trent started to censor books before publication and to compile an Index of forbidden books, a practice that spread across Catholic Europe. The policing of thought was a serious matter, and those who fell foul of the authorities often faced dire consequences, as is illustrated by the notorious cases of the Spanish physician and theologian Miguel Serveto (1511–53), executed in Calvinist Geneva for having questioned the doctrine of the Trinity, of the Italian philosopher Giordano Bruno (1548–1600), burnt alive at the stake in Catholic Rome for heresy, and of Galileo.

In the face of institutional constraints and in some cases the threat of the severest penalties for transgression, free-thinkers across Europe all adapt to the needs of their particular situation the same stock of anti-authoritarian phrases, and these phrases constitute the immediate literary context in which free-thinking is embedded. They form a kind of subterranean network of commonplaces linking its practitioners from the ancient past to those of the present. Uses of the phrase *libertas philosophandi* are at the centre of this network and appear regularly in a variety of forms. Related phrases are often associated with one of the great philosophers of the ancient world and their followers before being adapted and appropriated for general use. The formula 'The person who would be a philosopher must also be of a free mind' ('Opportet praeterea liberali animo philosophum esse'), for example, is initially transmitted by the followers of Plato in late antiquity: starting life as a sentence in the late Greek Platonist Alcinous' *Handbook of Platonism*, it is then translated by the great Florentine reviver of Plato, Marsilio Ficino (1433–99), in the Latin version quoted above. It appears in that version as an epigraph to the first exposition of Copernican cosmology, by Rheticus in 1541, and thereafter by Kepler and Galileo.

The adage 'Plato is my friend but a greater friend is truth' ('Amicus Plato sed magis amica veritas') fits the same pattern. It appears in a variety of guises and settings throughout its long history, as a number of scholars have pointed out, and is closely related to another formula: 'Truth is dear to us, and so is Plato, but truth is rightly the dearer' ('Et veritatem diligimus et Platonem, sed rectius est diligere veritatem'). The ultimate source for both sayings, as Leonardo Tarán has shown in an exhaustive study of the philological evidence, is a passage in Aristotle's *Nicomachean Ethics* (I. 6). Before coming to his discussion of the universal good, Aristotle claims that his investigation in this area is made more difficult by 'our friendship for the authors' of the ideas he wishes to criticize, but reflects that, in the final instance, the truth must matter more: 'Both are dear to us, yet it is our duty to prefer the truth' (1096a16–17). The particular friend he has in mind, though he mentions no names, is his former teacher Plato. Here, then, friendship is synonymous with the authority of a revered teacher. It so happens that Plato, at the beginning of the tenth book of the *Republic*, has his former teacher Socrates say of Homer, in similar terms, that 'we must not honour a man above the truth' (595c3) before he explains why poets are to be banished from the ideal state. So it seems that Aristotle is quietly returning his teacher and friend the backhanded compliment that Plato himself, via Socrates, paid Homer. Even at its ancient source, it seems, the free-thinking expression already takes the form of an adaptation.

When 'Amicus Plato' first emerged as a proverb is not clear, but what is known is that it was preserved for posterity in a Latin translation of a lost Greek Neoplatonic biography of Aristotle, and that in this biography – and throughout the European Middle Ages – Socrates takes the place of Plato as the friend to whom truth is preferred. Plato was restored to his rightful place in the proverb as early as 1490, by the physician Nicolò Leoniceno (1428–1524) in his correspondence with the humanist scholar and poet Angelo Poliziano (1454–94), and from 1574 onwards the proverb in its canonical form appears in posthumous editions of the *Adages* (*Adagia*), a treasure-house of ancient sayings with commentaries compiled by the great northern European humanist Desiderius Erasmus (1466?–1535), which grew to include the supplements of other humanists. As we saw earlier, it is in that very form that in 1615 Don Quixote cites the proverb in a letter he writes to the new governor of the island of Barataria, Sancho Panza. Throughout the sixteenth and seventeenth centuries, however, the proverb continues to take various forms and to include various friends beside Plato. Martin Luther (1483–1546), the architect of the Reformation in Germany, puts Plato together with Plato's teacher Socrates when, in 1525, he uses the proverb in his debate about free will with Erasmus. Plato appears alongside his pupil Aristotle in the version found in a notebook kept by Isaac Newton (1642–1727) during his student days in Cambridge during the 1660s: 'Plato is my friend, Aristotle is my friend, a greater friend is truth' ('Amicus Plato amicus Aristoteles magis amica veritas'). Newton, whose fundamental discoveries in physics lay ahead of him, had every reason to include Aristotle the natural philosopher of the scholastic tradition among those friends of his that needed to be put in their place, and there is a nice irony to Aristotle's appearance alongside Plato, given the origins of the phrase.

The variety of forms that the proverb takes throughout this period sometimes reflects simple philological confusion: it shows, at other times, the precious ability of 'Amicus Plato' and other free-thinking sayings to adapt to the particular circumstances in which they are reused. In his dialogue on painting *L'Aretino* (1557), the art theorist Lodovico Dolce (1508–68) prefaces his comparison of the two great artists of the Italian Renaissance, Michelangelo (1475–1564) and Raphael (1483–1520), by having Aretino say that both are his friends but a greater friend is truth. He thereby reveals the processes of adaptation and appropriation that free-thinking phrases undergo in vernacular writing as well as in the Latin works of the period.

Those processes – of adaptation and appropriation – need to be understood in the wider literary and rhetorical context of Renaissance free-thinking. The humanist practice of imitation, as we will see, is the principal literary framework within which writers of the period adapt the sayings of others to their own purposes. We saw in the previous chapter that the development of informal and open-ended literary genres such as the letter and the dialogue – the genre chosen by Dolce in the example just given – is a feature of the age. These have distinct potential to support and structure thinking against the grain. So does argumentation *in utramque partem* ('on both sides of a question'), the classroom-originating rhetorical exercise that consists of inventing persuasive arguments for and against a philosophical or political position taken from history, as for example why Brutus was right to kill Caesar and why he was wrong. The sixteenth century sees the reinvention, in and outside the academy, of the practice of 'paradox'. Renaissance paradox is not to be confused with its modern equivalent of 'contradiction in terms', since it refers in that period, following its etymology, to a proposition that runs counter to common opinion, often causing surprise in the process. Paradox becomes increasingly associated with sceptical and other anti-dogmatic modes of thought in the late sixteenth and early seventeenth centuries. It is therefore one of the literary and rhetorical practices of the period that provide both a home and a model for free-thinking as it was practised in the Renaissance.

Montaigne has a distinctive place in the history of Renaissance free-thinking. But he hardly figures in that history as it is currently told. Various aspects of the historiographical tradition may explain why he has been overlooked in this way. He comes a little too early for the narrower seventeenth-century version of the story, and when the focus is on the emergence of the new science at the exclusion of the broader tradition, his contribution appears marginal. He is equally difficult to assimilate into the institutional framework of the history of academic freedom. A gentleman-scholar from a legal background who holds no position in the university world, which he tends to denigrate along with his own learning, he is subject to none of the constraints that professional scholars of his age faced within their faculties or from the theological authorities who regulated teaching and learning in the universities. The position of distinct institutional autonomy from which he writes – and the literary artfulness with which he writes – make him appear as marginal to the history of academic freedom as he does to the history of science.

But there is more to Renaissance free-thinking than the history of academic or scientific anti-authoritarianism: it flourishes wherever a thinker encounters an obstacle in the search for truth. Montaigne's autonomy should not be exaggerated. He knew of people throughout Europe who had opposed the authorities and suffered the consequences. In 'Of a lack in our administrations' (I.35: 'D'un defaut de nos polices'), he refers to the case of Sebastian Castellio (1515–63), the liberal Reformer best known for having advocated religious toleration of heretics in a published response of 1554 to the execution, already mentioned, of Miguel Serveto in Geneva. Montaigne praises Castellio's scholarship and laments his death in needless penury. That is a courageous act in itself. We will encounter other acts of similar courage in the course of this book. The Wars of Religion in France exerted extraordinary pressures on publishing as on many other public activities, and Montaigne's plans for the *Essais* seem to have been affected by those pressures, as his shifting intentions surrounding the inclusion of La Boétie's work at the heart of Book I, examined in chapter 1 above, strongly suggest. Once published, of course, his books were subject to the same processes of censorship and prohibition as all others in Catholic Europe in the period following the Council of Trent. During his stay in Rome in the winter of 1580–1, as we shall see in chapter 7 below, a copy of the recently published *Essais* was scrutinized by the censors of the Roman Index. Montaigne was no stranger to the policing of published thought.

He was no stranger, either, to the Renaissance current of free-thinking. A free unconstrained mind was, as he says in 'Of the education of children', one of the chief aims of the upbringing and education that his father designed for him: 'For among other things he had been advised [...] to educate my mind in all gentleness and freedom, without rigour and constraint' ('Car, entre autre choses, il avoit esté conseillé [...] d'eslever mon ame en toute douceur et liberté, sans rigueur et contrainte'; F 157, VS 174). Montaigne goes on to say here that his father pursued this aim so religiously that, for fear of snatching the child from sleep, he had him wake each morning, as if of his own accord, to the gentle sound of the harpsichord. Later in life Montaigne read figures central to the philosophical tradition of free-thinking from the ancient past – Socrates, Plato, Aristotle, Seneca, and company – and, unlike many humanists of his age, learnt from the ancients to consider that the ancients were not authoritative. The *Essais* record him pursuing truth on a variety of topics in the company of Plato and other friends. Some time after 1588 he read the *Nicomachean Ethics*, the source of the 'Amicus Plato' proverb and other free-thinking phrases, and he draws on Erasmus's *Adages* in various places in the *Essais*, though it is not clear from what edition. He reflects upon and practises free-thinking in sentence after sentence of the *Essais*, starting with several in 'Of the education of children', to which we will turn shortly.

Further examples are scattered across the three Books. One such, in the 'Apology for Raymond Sebond' (II.12), is framed as a gloss on Aristotle's practice of showing how his opinions differ from – and improve on – those of others: 'For truth is not judged by the authority and on the testimony of another' ('Car la verité ne se juge point par authorité et tesmoignage d'autruy'; F 456, VS 507). A second example occurs when, at the opening of his chapter 'Of the art of discussion' (III.8: 'De l'art de conférer'), Montaigne sets out his conception of conversation as a kind of mental jousting for the truth between two interlocutors: 'The cause of truth should be the common cause for both' ('La cause de la verité devrait être la cause commune à l'un et à l'autre'; F 856, VS 924). A third and final example comes from 'Of experience', the final chapter of the *Essais*, and concerns Montaigne's practice of self-study: 'I would rather be an authority on myself than on Cicero. In the experience I have of myself I find enough to make me wise, if I were a good scholar' ('J'aymerois mieux m'entendre bien en moy, qu'en Ciceron. De l'experience que j'ai de moy, je trouve assez dequoy me faire sage, si j'estoy bon escholier'; F 856, VS 924). The naming of Cicero here is a late alteration to the text: the 1588 edition referred to Plato.

Notice that Montaigne's sentences never correspond exactly to the free-thinking phrases mentioned earlier. This might appear to weaken the case for saying that he has a place in the history of those phrases and the tradition of free-thinking in which they are embedded. On the contrary, I think it should encourage us to recognize Montaigne's contribution to the Renaissance tradition of free-thinking as distinctively literary as well as anti-institutional, and to see evidence for this view in his habit of rewriting free-thinking commonplaces according to the literary processes of adaptation and appropriation.

This means that to understand what place Montaigne deserves in the history of free-thinking, and what cast of mind he brings to the questions he treats in the *Essais*, we need to keep turning to the text itself, to the twists and turns of its sentences.

Before we do so once again, let me explain briefly why I describe free-thinking as a 'context' for the *Essais*. By context, I mean an element that surrounds a particular passage of text and helps to clarify its meaning, to reveal what purposes it serves. If the element in question is a further passage of the same text, the context is internal, and it is in this sense that one might describe 'Of pedantry' (I.25) as a context for 'Of the education of children' (I.26), for example, or 'Of idleness' (I.8) for 'To the Reader'. As the latter example suggests, internal contexts need not be contiguous to the text, especially in a predominantly miscellaneous work like Montaigne's. Some are local; others act at a distance: in chapter 6 below, for example, I will argue that 'Of friendship' (I.28) offers a context for Montaigne's discussion of friendship in 'Of vanity' (III.9: 'De la vanité'). The contextual element in question may equally be external to the text. Some of these elements are themselves texts, while others are manifestations or practices of the surrounding culture: the writings of La Boétie may be considered an external context for the *Essais*, for example, as may the Wars of Religion. Some contexts are at once external and internal: they belong to the practices of the wider culture and to those of the text. Free-thinking falls into this in-between category: it is to be found outside the text as a topic and a mode of Renaissance thinking, but it can also be seen at work within the *Essais*, and in both guises helps to clarify the text's meaning and purpose.

It should already be clear just how fragile a thing any context is. It is always only one of a number, so if it is accorded too much attention or prominence, it risks distorting the meaning it was intended to illuminate. The best response to this risk is to situate the chosen contextual element by reference to others surrounding the text: to put it in its place, as it were, on a map of the landscape. But this response carries risks of its own. The number of contextual elements one might choose is of course indefinite, and each of these elements is itself likely to be a complex text or cultural practice, therefore requiring a contextualization of its own. There is no end, in short, to the making of contexts: we are faced with an infinite regress ... Such problems dog all contextual work, of course, but they are made particularly acute by a text as complex and elusive as the *Essais*. Its ability to make connections between discrete elements of the surrounding culture increases the number of features that must be included for the work of contextualization to be adequate. And since the text not only connects these elements, but combines them in unique ways, its meaning always exceeds the contexts it causes to proliferate.

A Tale of Three Contexts

The passage from 'Of the education of children' to which I would now like to turn offers a powerful illustration of the same point:

> Let the tutor make his charge pass everything through a sieve and lodge nothing in his head on mere authority and trust: let not Aristotle's principles be to him any more than those of the Stoics or Epicureans. Let this variety of ideas be set before him; he will choose if he can; if not, he will remain in doubt. [C] Only fools are certain and assured.
>   [A] For doubting pleases me no less than knowing.
> For if he embraces Xenophon's and Plato's opinions by his own reasoning, they will no longer be theirs, they will be his. [C] He who follows another follows nothing. He finds nothing; indeed he seeks nothing. *We are not under a king; let each one claim his freedom.* Let him know that he knows, at least. [A] He must imbibe their ways of thinking, not learn their precepts. And let him boldly forget, if he wants, where he got them, but let him know how to make them his own. Truth and reason are common to everyone, and no more belong to the man who first spoke them than to the man who says them later. [C] It is no more according to Plato than according to me, since he and I understand and see it in the same way. [A] The bees plunder their flowers here and there, but afterward they make of them honey, which is all theirs; it is no longer thyme or marjoram. Even so with the pieces borrowed from others; he will transform and blend them to make a work that is all his own, to wit, his judgement. His education, work, and study aim only at forming this.

> Qu'il luy face tout passer par l'estamine et ne loge rien en sa teste par simple authorité et à credit: les principes d'Aristote ne luy soyent principes, non plus que ceux des Stoiciens ou Epicuriens. Qu'on luy propose cette diversité de jugemens: il choisira s'il peut, sinon il demeurera en doubte. [C] Il n'y a que les fols certains et resolus.
>   [A] *Che non men che saper dubbiar m'aggrada.*
> Car s'il embrasse les opinions de Xenophon et de Platon par son propre discours, ce ne seront plus les leurs, ce seront les siennes. [C] Qui suit un autre, il ne suit rien. Il ne trouve rien, voire il ne cerche rien. *Non sumus sub rege; sibi quisque se vindicet.* Qu'il sache qu'il sçait, au moins. [A] Il faut qu'il

emboive leurs humeurs, non qu'il aprenne leurs preceptes. Et qu'il oublie
hardiment, s'il veut, d'où il les tient, mais qu'il se les sçache approprier. La
verité et la raison sont communes à un chacun, et ne sont non plus à qui
les a dites premierement, qu'à qui les dict après. [C] Ce n'est non plus selon
Platon que selon moy, puis que luy et moi l'entendons et voyons de mesme.
[A] Les abeilles pillotent deçà delà les fleurs, mais elles en font apres le miel,
qui est tout leur; ce n'est plus thin ny marjolaine: ainsi les pieces empruntées
d'autruy, il les transformera et confondera, pour en faire un ouvrage tout sien:
à sçavoir son jugement. Son institution, son travail et estude ne vise qu'à le
former.   (F 135, VS 151–2)

This passage is taken from the early part of the main section of the chapter in which Montaigne sets out his views on the upbringing of children.
His main target throughout is the assumption that education essentially
involves the transmission of a lesson by someone who knows it to someone who does not. He considers that assumption to be a widespread
one of the age, as he shows at the outset of the chapter, when he tells
Madame de Foix that what he is offering her, on the subject of education, is a paradox in the Renaissance sense of the term: 'a single fancy of
mine […] which is contrary to common usage' ('une seule fantasie que
j'ay contraire au commun usage'; F 133, VS 150). This is no mere exercise,
then, in promoting a change of curriculum. We are accustomed to think
of the sixteenth century as the period in which humanism, the movement
of educational and cultural reform based on study of the Greek and Latin
literature of pagan classical antiquity, comes to challenge the dominance
of scholasticism. We might therefore be tempted to assume that in 'Of
the education of children' Montaigne is siding with the humanists; and
he certainly repeats his criticism, already made in 'Of pedantry', of the
monarchic authority accorded to Aristotle in the schools. That criticism is
implicit in the first sentence of our passage. But all the indications in that
sentence – and in 'Of the education of children' as a whole – are that he
is targeting a misuse of authority in education found among scholastics
and humanists alike: the one that arises every time a teacher dictates a
lesson to be learnt by rote instead of attempting to nurture in the pupil the
precious ability to exercise personal judgement and, in time, to espouse
the lesson that has been learnt.

Most of the passage is given up to a series of practical suggestions as
to how that nurturing is to be understood and approached. Montaigne

argues for the independence of reason from authority, the legitimacy of doubt, and the importance of personal appropriation. Perhaps one of the most surprising stylistic features of his writing in the passage, given these arguments, is its constant recourse to other people's sayings. This might seem to leave Montaigne in a state of contradiction – never more beholden to authority than when he claims we ought to shake it off! But that would be to forget the literary context of imitation that I have already mentioned and to which I shall return. The passage is, in fact, a tale of three contexts – free-thinking, scepticism, and imitation – and of the interactions between them.

Free-thinking provides the immediate internal context to our passage, which is surrounded by references to the loss of intellectual freedom that education commonly entails, as two examples will show. In the first, taken from the development directly preceding the passage, Montaigne asserts that the excessive respect for our teachers we have had drummed into us has robbed us of our freedom:

> Our mind moves only on faith, being bound and constrained to the whim of others' fancies, a slave and a captive under the authority of their teaching. We have been so well accustomed to leading strings that we have no free motion left; our vigour and liberty are extinct.

> Nostre ame ne branle qu'à credit, liée et contrainte à l'appétit des fantasies d'autruy, serve et captivée soubs l'authorité de leur leçon. On nous a tant assubjectis aux cordes que nous n'avons plus de franches allures. Nostre vigueur et liberté est esteinte.   (F 134, VS 151)

Physical metaphors of movement and its constraint are powerfully at work here. They are applied to the mind, to a mind kept in shackles, meaning that the freedom Montaigne declares extinct is a particular one: the freedom to think otherwise. But when the word 'liberté' appears in the text, it refers not just to the freedom of the mind but to freedom itself, as if the general condition of being free amounted to – or depended upon – having the freedom to think. Notice, too, that it is 'our' freedom whose death knell Montaigne sounds. The first person plural pronoun implicates more than just the pupils of the age: it includes the writer and the reader too. These sentences are part of a development, added in 1588, which seems designed to pose the problem in all its seriousness: this is the state we are in and that we need to think our way out of, and yet to do so, we would need of course to recover the very freedom of thought we have lost. The lucidity that comes simply from recognizing the predicament is the first step.

In the second example, taken from the sentences directly following our passage, Montaigne emphatically repeats the underlying problem using the language of freedom and constraint:

> It is the understanding, Epicharmus used to say, [...] that makes profit of everything, that arranges everything, that acts, dominates, and reigns; all other things are blind, deaf, and soulless. Truly we make it servile and cowardly, by leaving it no freedom to do anything by itself.

> C'est, disoit Epicharmus, l'entendement [...] qui approfite tout, qui dispose tout, qui agit, qui domine et qui regne: toutes autres choses sont aveugles, sourdes et sans ame. Certes nous le rendons servile et coüard, pour ne luy laisser la liberté de rien faire de soy. (F 135, VS 152)

The first sentence recapitulates the argument of the preceding passage by quoting a saying from the fifth-century BCE poet Epicharmus as reported by the late Greek writer Plutarch (46?–127? CE), whose moral discourses and parallel biographies ('Lives') of famous Greeks and Romans Montaigne read in the 1572 French translation of Jacques Amyot (1513–83), and which he refers to or borrows from on hundreds of occasions in the *Essais*. The second sentence renews the claim, made before our chosen passage begins, that our understanding is enslaved once we take away its freedom. Once again, the all-implicating first person plural ('we') is used, although here it acts as a kind of hinge to include not only all those who are or have been pupils but also the teachers: the perpetrators as well as the all-too willing victims of that intellectual servitude which commonly passes for education.

Free-thinking does not just frame our text as a context: it also provides the text – to which we now return – with its opening move and its dominant theme. The first sentence's suggestion that the tutor's task is to make the pupil sift every principle he is taught through the judgement, rather than take it on trust and embed it as a doctrinal certainty in the mind, reveals the anti-authoritarian stance fundamental to free-thinking. Authorities there are aplenty in this sentence, too, and in those that follow:

Socrates's pupils Xenophon and Plato are named, along with Plato's pupil Aristotle and the Epicurean and Stoic schools of later antiquity, in a veritable roll-call of the philosophies of ancient Greece and Rome. That roll-call serves not to emphasize the monolithic weight of ancient thought, but to show its diversity, and this has the effect of removing from any one of the august names listed the unique unchallenged authority it might enjoy in the schools or among the humanists. Diane de Foix's son should learn to think for himself by having the ideas of Aristotle and other friends set before him; he will choose if he can; otherwise he will remain in doubt. Ancient thought is thus broken down into materials that are ready to be sifted and weighed in the balance of individual judgement – into instruments with which to think freely.

Two observations need to be made about the way in which the process of free-thinking is described in these sentences and those that follow. Each observation, as will be seen, suggests a further context for the passage.

The first observation is that, as has just been said, free-thinking may lead its practitioner to doubt rather than certainty. This thought inevitably calls to mind the Greek philosophical school of later antiquity that is missing from the roll-call, the school of radical scepticism, which practises the strange art of perpetual doubt on all topics and is the subject of a detailed presentation in the 'Apology for Raymond Sebond' (II.12), to which we will turn in chapter 4 below. Historians relate the early modern history of free-thinking to the transmission of sceptical thought in the period, as was noted earlier, and Montaigne's text is a major vehicle of that transmission. Free-thinking and radical scepticism need to be understood as interrelated contexts for the *Essais*, then, and this passage may be said to offer one local instance of their interaction. That instance needs to be handled delicately, however, since Montaigne does not mention the sceptics by name here, as he could have easily chosen to do, and he even seems to lead us off their trail by quoting a reflection on doubt from an unrelated source, a line from the *Inferno* (XI.93) of the Italian medieval poet Dante Alighieri (1265–1321), in which the poet congratulates himself for having expressed his confusion at the answers his guide has given him on his journey through Hell: 'For doubting pleases me no less than knowing' ('Che non men che saper dubbiar m'aggrada'). We are not dealing here with some resounding clash of intellectual contexts, then, but with a sentence-level shift of emphasis whereby Montaigne first mentions doubt as one of the two possible results of free-thinking and then, as if anticipating a particular objection to doubt in his reader, stresses via Dante that he accepts knowledge and doubt with an equal mind. It is true that in the preceding sentence, added after 1588, he appears to go a step further in mocking the certainty of fools: 'Only fools are certain and assured' ('Il n'y a que les fols certains et resolus'). But the quotation from Dante restores the passage to its balancing act. What matters in free-thinking is not the result – whether this is dogmatic certainty or sceptical doubt – but the process itself: the present participle in the English phrase is, in this sense, peculiarly appropriate.

The second observation to be made is that the free-thinking child is encouraged to proceed in his pursuit of the truth not by clearing away the past and starting from the scratch of a *tabula rasa*, as Descartes will do a generation later in his *Discourse on the Method* (*Discours de la méthode*) of 1637, but by making certain ideas from the past his own. This recommendation, with its interest in the personal appropriation of ideas and sayings, evokes a third context: that of literary imitation, a much studied feature of Renaissance humanist writing. Imitation, as developed in northern Europe by Erasmus, is anything but slavish: it requires the budding writer to collect admired excerpts from authors of the past, inwardly digest them, and then reproduce them in the service of self-expression. Students of the period were encouraged to gather excerpts under subject headings in a 'commonplace book' so as to provide themselves with the necessary literary materials for their own compositions. Anthologies of excerpts – printed commonplace books, *florilegia*, containing (as the name suggests) 'flowers' of ancient rhetoric from many sources, and the like – became a recognized genre in their own right, with Erasmus's *Adages*, already mentioned, providing a celebrated and ever-expanding example and a major resource for writers. Encylopaedic compilations such as those of Pedro Mexía and others provide a similar resource. Like Angelo Poliziano before him, whom we last saw swapping versions of the 'Amicus Plato' phrase with his correspondent Nicolò Leoniceno, Erasmus took part in the Ciceronian debate of the late fifteenth and early sixteenth centuries. That debate pitted those who thought that the work of the Roman politician, orator, and writer Marcus Tullius Cicero (102–43 BCE) was to be imitated as the single and supreme model of classical prose against those, like Poliziano and Erasmus, who favoured eclectic imitation in the service of self-expression. The verb 'to express oneself' (*seipsum exprimere*) was, indeed, coined in Latin by Poliziano in the course of this debate. Erasmus

justifies his theory of eclectic imitation by adapting to his purposes the
age-old network of metaphors that sees other people's sayings as flowers
and writers as bees. He uses it to pose a rhetorical question: 'Do bees collect the substance for making honey from just one shrub?' ('Apes num ex
uno frutice colligunt mellificii materiam?')

Literary imitation offers a wider context for the *Essais* that is of
equal importance to the two – free-thinking and scepticism – already
discussed. There are echoes of the Ciceronian debate in 'Of pedantry'
(I.25) and 'A consideration upon Cicero' (I.40): Montaigne's position
and literary sensibility in both chapters are resolutely pro-Erasmian.
So engrained in the text of the *Essais* is Montaigne's habit of silently
rewriting the sayings of others, indeed, that the entire enterprise could
be seen as a commonplace book in the Erasmian style. He says as much
in 'Of physiognomy' (III.12: 'De la phisionomie'): 'Even so someone
might say of me that I have here only made a bunch of other people's
flowers, having furnished nothing of my own but the thread to tie them'
('Comme quelqu'un pourroit dire de moy que j'ay seulement faict icy
un amas de fleurs estrangeres, n'y ayant fourny du mien que le filet à
les lier'; F 984, VS 1055). But he goes on in the same passage to stress, in
true Erasmian fashion, that in each and every of his many borrowings
he aims to express himself. The thread, at the very least, is his. In 'Of
the education of children' he discusses his practice of literary imitation
in similar fashion. Early in the chapter (F 130–1, VS 146–8) he acknowledges his bottomless debt to Plutarch and Seneca before criticizing the
humanist writers of his day who botch their imitations by larding their
texts with undigested chunks from the ancients. He concedes that his
criticisms might be turned against him and complains of his weak faculties, but claims that he is at least aware of his inferiority to Plutarch
and the others, and insists – explicitly distinguishing himself now from
the authors of printed anthologies – that he has an equal share in the
thoughts he borrows from others. In 'Of physiognomy' he goes still
further in claiming that, if he had taken his own advice instead of following the fashion of the age, he would have spoken his mind all by
himself (F 984, VS 1055). What Montaigne imagines here amounts to
a severance of the Erasmian link between eclectic imitation and self-
expression. Notice how at moments such as these, the text no longer fits
within the pre-established literary context of humanist imitation, but
takes that context in a new direction.

Something similar could be said of our chosen passage of text, which entwines the themes and practices of literary imitation together with those of free-thinking so closely that they can no longer be disentangled, but understood only in their dynamic interaction. Diane de Foix's son will learn to think freely if he applies the techniques of imitation to his speaking and writing; and he will learn to produce sentences that are masterpieces of imitation if he thinks in this way: for Montaigne, then, free-thinking thrives on imitation as much as imitation thrives on free-thinking. The rhetorical figure of chiasmus, whereby the order of words in one of two parallel clauses finds itself inverted in the second, comes to mind: we might say that imitation and free-thinking exist here in a chiasmus of interaction. This degree of interaction should not surprise us: the processes by which thinking and writing take place are bound to appear inextricably linked, as Montaigne shows them to be in this passage, if one believes, as he does, that language is the substance of which thought is made.

The gradual intertwining of free-thinking and imitation takes place throughout the second half of the passage. The two sentences in which the process starts bear repeating:

> Truth and reason are common to everyone, and no more belong to the man who first spoke them than to the man who says them later. [C] It is no more according to Plato than according to me, since he and I understand and see it in the same way.

> La verité et la raison sont communes à un chacun, et ne sont non plus à qui les a dites premierement, qu'à qui les dict après. [C] Ce n'est non plus selon Platon que selon moy, puis que luy et moi l'entendons et voyons de mesme.

Montaigne pictures a conversation between Plato and himself, undertaken in the pursuit of a truth that neither monopolizes, in which the two participants, 'he' and 'I', are given equal importance by the balancing syntactic structures of the sentences. Montaigne's decision after 1588 to imagine himself sharing an idea with Plato in particular make these sentences look for all the world like a hidden reworking of the free-thinking adage 'Plato is my friend but a greater friend is truth'. What is most striking, if this is the case, is the difference between the saying and its reworking. The saying implicitly sees Plato as an obstacle to the free-thinker's pursuit of the truth as well as a friend. But Montaigne, having said earlier that Diane de Foix's son will on occasions need to reject the ideas of past thinkers, now imagines a less confrontational situation in which he and I see things the same way. Both situations arise, as far as Montaigne is concerned, when your judgement is truly free. Whether the effect is a divergence or a convergence of views, it is always as a result of thinking with a privileged interlocutor – not a master but a friend – that you learn to think for yourself, and this kind of thinking requires you to appropriate ideas from the friend that match your own sense of where the truth lies. Free-thinking as Montaigne conceives it is inflected here, in other words, by the process of imitation that it requires. The terms of the discussion are already moving onto the terrain of imitation in the second half of the truth-and-reason sentence, with its interest in the ownership of particular sayings, and this shift is emphasized by the addition after 1588 of the sentence about Plato. But imitation, as Montaigne conceives of it in this passage, is itself already inflected by the free-thinking aim it serves. This aim is clearly restated at the end of the penultimate sentence in which Montaigne draws on the commonplace metaphor of bees visiting flowers, used by Erasmus to argue that literary imitation should be eclectic, and appropriates it to his own argument about the need to cultivate independence of judgement. The work done by the child that is to be 'all his', says Montaigne in that sentence, is none other than that: the formation of 'his judgement'.

The passage ends in a sequence of sentences about free-thinking and the imitation it involves that are themselves masterpieces of free-thinking imitation. Beneath the passage and its surrounding sentences there lies a submerged network of passages from Seneca and Plutarch. This bears witness to Montaigne's praise of those two writers, at the beginning of the chapter, as his chief precursors. His borrowing from Plutarch in the sentences that follow the passage has already been mentioned. His particular debts to Seneca are to the philosopher's letters to Lucilius. Seneca's thirty-third letter provides Montaigne with the raw materials for the second of the three additions to the passage made after 1588. Seneca in that letter explains that Lucilius should not call upon him to provide pithy sayings of the chief Stoic philosophers because unlike the Epicureans, who submit themselves to the authority of the leader of their school, the Stoics live under no despot: 'We are not under a king: each lays claim to his own'

('Non sumus sub rege; sibi quisque se vindicat'). Montaigne quotes this sentence directly but silently changes the mood of the second verb from the indicative ('vindicat') to the subjunctive ('vindicet'), thus transforming Seneca's description of how the Stoics conduct their affairs into an imperative and a call to liberation of the mind from despotic authority. The rest of that second post-1588 addition is made up of hidden reworkings of passages from the same letter. The borrowings continue thereafter, but the main source is now the eighty-fourth letter, in which Seneca sets out his views on literary imitation by making extended use of the apian metaphor in a self-consciously imitative manner: 'We should follow, men say, the example of the bees' ('Apes, ut aiunt, debemus imitari'). The sentence in which Montaigne claims equal share in a thought with Plato is also a hidden remake of a Senecan sentence, as Terence Cave has pointed out, although from a different source: the text *On Anger* (*De ira*) (I.vi.5). Montaigne does not inherit this network of references: he constructs it by gathering passages from different texts and he reworks these borrowings in such a way as to argue for and exemplify, in a manner peculiar to him, the interrelation of intellectual freedom and literary imitation – of rewriting and free-thinking. In so doing, he offers in this passage one instance of what I called earlier the excess of the *Essais*, the ability of the text to exceed its contexts by connecting and combining them in unique ways. He imitates the roaming bee, certainly, but in his case it is a bee without a keeper.

The Sting in the Tail

Montaigne's adaptation of the sentence that he quotes directly from Seneca, as we have seen, produces a call to each of us to lay claim to the freedom that is rightfully ours. We may, indeed we should, think in the company of privileged interlocutors – with Plato and other friends – but we should never forget that the greater friend is the truth we seek. Montaigne thinks and writes by this principle, but in 'Of the education of children' he also formulates it, and this confronts him with some formidable questions. Is it ever really possible to think freely? Is it even desirable in the first place? Can everyone do it, or only a select few? Can people be taught to think freely, and if so, how? These questions recur throughout the *Essais*, as we will see, provoking complex and often contradictory responses.

The third of the questions posed above appears fraught with implications for 'Of the education of children' itself. That the pupil of whom Montaigne speaks in the chapter is a male of noble birth might lead one to conclude that he silently limits the possibility of free-thinking to those in that social group. That conclusion would be hardly surprising, if it were true, for he belongs to a society that commonly restricted possibilities of learning for women of all social conditions, as well as for men and women of lowly birth, and singled out wellborn males for privileged treatment in educational theory and practice alike. It is important to recognize that the prevalent attitudes of the society to which he belongs do condition Montaigne's approach to the questions that preoccupy him. This conditioning may well help to explain his decision to consider in 'Of the education of children' the upbringing of a wellborn boy. But it would be misleading to assume in general that the prevalent attitudes of the age wholly determine his approach, as I shall argue in chapter 4 below, and in this particular case it would be contrary to the paradoxical spirit of the chapter itself. Montaigne's advocacy of free-thinking in 'Of the education of children' goes beyond the limits of a contribution to a pedagogical theory restricted to boys of a social elite: it offers itself to be read as part of a wider reflection on the unconstrained turn of mind that children of all ages and of both sexes should cultivate; for among these children, Montaigne counts himself and his circle of readers, and in that circle he explicitly includes women, starting of course with Diane de Foix, to whom he dedicates 'Of the education of children'.

The final question posed above – can free-thinking be taught? – appears equally fraught with implications for the same chapter. This is because the chapter's paradoxical advocacy of an education in free-thinking risks installing Montaigne as the new authority on education – the poacher turned gamekeeper or, if you will, the wild bee turned bee-keeper – and thereby making of the chapter an authoritative statement of intellectual anti-authoritarianism. Montaigne takes care to avoid this situation by dismantling his authority on the topic even as he writes about it. The middle part of the chapter is framed by sustained expressions of authorial self-depreciation that go beyond the rhetorical demands of a *captatio benevolentiae*. We saw earlier how, at the beginning of the chapter, Montaigne compares unfavourably his weak faculties to those of the best ancient minds, but he also understates his own learning, claiming that any child halfway through school already knows more than he. All of this, he makes clear from the outset, compromises the position from which he presents his ideas in the chapter: 'These are nothing but reveries of a man who has tasted only the outer crust of sciences in his childhood, and has retained only a vague general picture of them' ('Ce ne sont icy que resveries d'un homme qui n'a gousté des sciences que la crouste premiere, en son enfance, et n'en a retenu qu'un general et informe visage'; F 129, VS 146). By 'sciences' he means learning in general. He reiterates his own failure to acquire such learning during childhood at the end of the chapter. His father's plan was, as we saw earlier, to have him brought up to think with a free unconstrained mind (hence the deployment of a harpsichord for the boy's daily wake-up call). But Montaigne goes on to say that this plan largely failed for two reasons: his own grindingly slow mind, which would have sent the best-laid plan awry, and the fact that his father did not see his plan through, sending him instead to the Collège de Guyenne in Bordeaux, which despite being the best school in France at the time and a flourishing example of Erasmian humanist education, was for all that, Montaigne says, still school. 'Of the education of children' presents its author, then, as the product of an educational experiment in free-thinking that yielded decidedly mixed fruits. In so doing, the chapter effectively calls its own authority on the topic into question, and asks to be judged with the freedom it advocates.

This posture has obvious implications for the relationship that Montaigne creates with his readers. If we, Montaigne's readers, are to learn from his example and, as he hopes we will, make the free-thinking adage about Plato and other friends our own, then our privileged interlocutor – and the friend to be discarded as and when the truth demands it – will on occasion be neither Plato nor Aristotle but Montaigne himself. This is a situation that he imagines and even prepares for on various occasions, though not in 'Of the education of children', where the inference remains to be drawn. Fourteen short chapters later, in 'A consideration upon Cicero' (I.40), he claims, in a passage added after 1588, that he has left room in his book for the minds of the future to produce from its subject-matter what he describes as 'numberless essays' ('infinis essais'; F 224, VS 251). This claim needs to be understood in context, once again, and in this case the immediate local context is provided by the preceding chapter, 'Of solitude' (I.39: 'De la solitude'), in which Montaigne issues a sharp critique of those who, like Cicero, vaingloriously seek future renown through their literary eloquence. 'A consideration upon Cicero' then extends the previous chapter's reflection on the search for renown. Its gesture towards the numberless essays of the future appears, in this context, as an anticipated reply to anyone who might choose to reflect Montaigne's criticism of Cicero's desire for literary renown back onto his own reasons for writing. Those of his readers who dwell on its eloquence, he suggests, undervalue his book's rich subject-matter. That subject-matter is rich, indeed infinitely so, because it invites any reader with an ounce of ingenuity to become a companion in the activity of the text. The suggestion in 'A Consideration upon Cicero' seems to act not only as a reply to an anticipated objection, then, but also as a message sent to the future: an invitation to Montaigne's readers to start thinking for themselves by essaying their own judgements on the matter of his text. What essaying is – and involves – is the subject of the next chapter.

3

An Introduction to Essaying

We have just seen how, in 'Of the education of children' (I.26), Montaigne uses free-thinking to define an educational principle that he not only advocates but practises in his book. He calls upon the cluster of words around 'essay' (the noun 'essai' and the verbs 'essayer' and 's'essayer') to put into practice the principle whereby you distance yourself from an unquestioning acceptance of authority on a matter of opinion and put your judgement, instead, to the test. The noun 'essai' occurs, as it happens, in 'Of the education of children'. Montaigne, before offering his word of advice to the chapter's addressee, denigrates his own capacities in the following terms: 'As for the natural faculties that are in me, of which this book is the essay, I feel them bending under the load' ('Quant aux facultez naturelles qui sont en moy, dequoy c'est icy l'essay, je les sens flechir sous la charge'; F 130, VS 146). And as we saw at the end of the previous chapter, the same word appears in an addition to 'A consideration upon Cicero' (I.40) made after 1588, in which he imagines his readers of the future undertaking an activity parallel to his own. It figures too, of course, in the title of his book. What exactly does Montaigne mean, though, by 'essay'? Does that meaning change over time? And why did he choose that word for his title?

Answering those questions will mean stripping away the familiarity we feel towards the word and travelling back to the period before it acquired the predominant meaning it has for us: to the time, that is, when Montaigne was writing a miscellany of thoughts he decided to publish under the title *Essais*, a decision without precedent, and one that was to have consequences for the future histories of philosophy and literature that he could have never foreseen. It will mean looking at his uses of the word at close quarters and in context. What these uses reveal is that, for Montaigne, essaying is a method of experimentation that he puts into practice in life and in the pages of his book. To the network of self-referential images discussed in chapter 1 above, then, essaying must now be added.

My example is a passage, in 'Of Democritus and Heraclitus' (I.50: 'De Democritus et Heraclitus'), where essaying is brought to the fore. The chapter is a short masterpiece in the style of Books I and II. It falls into two interconnected parts. The first offers an introduction to essaying as a mode and to the subject-matters, weighty and trivial, that it treats. Added to and much reworked towards the end of Montaigne's life, it offers one of the most revealing glimpses of what he takes essaying to be, and it also shows how essaying continues as a writing process throughout the compositional and early editorial history of the *Essais*. The second part of the chapter completes the masterpiece by offering a concrete example of and exercise in the essaying of Montaigne's judgement. It takes as its subject-matter the comparison, exploited by Seneca and others in classical antiquity and much revisited in the Renaissance, between the ancient Greek philosopher Democritus of Abdera (*c.* 460–370 BCE), who laughed at the folly of humankind as soon as he stepped beyond his own threshold, and his predecessor, Heraclitus of Ephesus (*c.* 540–480 BCE), who wept. The result is a thought-experiment that accepts the accidental as a condition of its being, privileges the mode of operation over the subject-matter in hand, and claims the freedom to proceed in doubt and ignorance. 'Of Democritus and Heraclitus', for these reasons, sets the tone for the *Essais* that surround it.

Essaying the Judgement

The chapter starts as follows:

> Judgement is a tool to use on all subjects, and comes in everywhere. Therefore in the tests that I make of it here, I use every sort of occasion. If it is a subject I do not understand at all, even on that I essay my judgement, sounding the ford from a good distance; and then, finding it too deep for my height, I stick to the bank. And this acknowledgement that I cannot cross over is a

token of its action, indeed one of those that it is most proud of. Sometimes in a vain and nonexistent subject I try to see if it will find the wherewithal to give it body, prop it up, and support it. Sometimes I lead it to a noble and well-worn subject in which it has nothing original to discover, the road being so beaten that it can walk only in others' footsteps. There it plays its part by choosing the way that seems best to it, and of a thousand paths it says that this one or that was the most wisely chosen. I take the first subject that chance offers. They are all equally good to me. And I never plan to develop them completely. [C] For I do not see the whole of anything; nor do those who promise to show it to us. Of a hundred members and faces that each thing has, I take one, sometimes only to lick it, sometimes to brush the surface, sometimes to pinch it to the bone. I give it a stab, not as wide but as deep as I know how. And most often I like to take them from some unaccustomed point of view. I would venture to treat some matter thoroughly, if I knew myself less well. Scattering a word here, there another, samples separated from their context, dispersed, without a plan and without a promise, I am not bound to make something of them or to adhere to them myself without varying when I please and giving myself up to doubt and uncertainty and my ruling quality, which is ignorance. Every movement reveals us.

Le jugement est un util à tous subjects, et se mesle par tout. A cette cause, aux essais que j'en fay ici, j'y employe toute sorte d'occasion. Si c'est un subject que je n'entende point, à cela mesme je l'essaye, sondant le gué de bien loing; et puis, le trouvant trop profond pour ma taille, je me tiens à la rive: et cette reconnoissance de ne pouvoir passer outre, c'est un trait de son effect, voire de ceux dequoy il se vante le plus. Tantost, à un subject vain et de neant, j'essaye voir s'il trouvera dequoy lui donner corps, et dequoy l'appuyer et estançonner. Tantost je le promene à un subject noble et tracassé, auquel il n'a rien à trouver de soy, le chemin en estant si frayé qu'il ne peut marcher que sur la piste d'autruy. Là il fait son jeu à eslire la route qui luy semble la meilleure, et, de mille sentiers, il dict que cettuy-cy, ou celuy-là, a esté le mieux choisi. Je prends de la fortune le premier argument. Ils me sont également bons. Et ne desseigne jamais de les produire entiers. [C] Car je ne voy le tout de rien: Ne font pas, ceux qui promettent de nous le faire veoir. De cent membres et visages qu'a chaque chose, j'en prens un tantost à lecher seulement, tantost à effleurer; et par fois à pincer jusqu'à l'os. J'y donne une poincte, non pas le plus largement, mais le plus profondement que je sçay. Et aime plus souvent à les saisir par quelque lustre inusité. Je me

hazarderoy de traitter à fons quelque matière, si je me connoissoy moins.
Semant icy un mot, icy un autre, eschantillons depris de leur piece, escartez,
sans dessein et sans promesse, je ne suis pas tenu d'en faire bon, ny de m'y
tenir moy mesme, sans varier quand il me plaist; et me rendre au doubte et
incertitude, et à ma maistresse forme, qui est l'ignorance. Tout mouvement
nous descouvre.   (F 266, VS 301–2)

This passage serves a prefatory function in 'Of Democritus and
Heraclitus' by introducing the process of essaying to which Montaigne
later subjects his material. That process is described throughout in richly
metaphorical terms. It is mainly seen, in the A-text that makes up the first
half of the passage, as a journey on which two characters have embarked:
the first person, 'I' ('je'), and his judgement. We might be reminded here
of an earlier chapter, 'Of idleness' (I.8), which also stages a psychodrama
involving two characters internal to Montaigne. 'Of idleness', as we saw in
chapter 1 above, has the first person set off in hot pursuit of his runaway
mind. In 'Of Democritus and Heraclitus', the judgement has replaced the
mind in the lead role alongside the first person, and the balance of power
is different: the first person does not pursue so much as accompany his
judgement on a journey; and he sets his judgement tests along the way.
The journey is different, too, from the one described in 'Of idleness': it
leads through a landscape filled with subjects of discourse, some of which
are to be explored vertically by going into depth, others horizontally by
taking a broad sweep. In the C-text that makes up the second half of the
passage, the judgement disappears along with the metaphor of the journey, leaving the first person to encounter subjects alone. These are still
seen in physical terms, but now as objects rather than places, and it is the
way in which the first person handles them that comes under scrutiny.
The last sentence states a kind of provisional finding: it is the manner of
essaying that counts, not the matter, since 'every movement reveals us'
('tout mouvement nous descouvre').

At the same time, that sentence leads into the rest of the chapter,
changing the pronoun to the first person plural 'us' ('nous') in such a
way as to give the point about essaying a universal reach. The examples
of Caesar, whose mind shows itself as much in the way he makes love as
war, and finally of Alexander the Great, as absorbed by a game of chess
as by his expedition to India, confirm the initial finding: 'Each particle,
each occupation, of a man betrays him and reveals him just as well as

any other' ('Chasque parcelle, chasque occupation de l'homme l'accuse et le montre également qu'un' autre'; F 267, VS 303). Actions are no longer seen simply as a neutral revelation of character, but also as an accusation, and the stage is set for the closing comparison of how Democritus and Heraclitus react to the human condition.

The idea that Montaigne's text is the place in which he makes essays is likely to seem familiar, at first sight, to readers of our age. We all know, after all, what an 'essay' is: it is a piece of prose writing on any subject, usually short in length and informal in style, the kind of composition that arts subjects in schools and universities thrive on. When Montaigne uses it in his title – and he is the first writer ever to do so – the word 'essai' means something quite different. Its principal sense, in sixteenth-century French, has to do with the idea of experimentation, and it is in that sense that he uses the word, although – as we shall see – in a quite specific way.

The passage from 'Of Democritus and Heraclitus' quoted above is a case in point. The 'essais' of which it speaks are undertaken 'here', in the book, but they are not understood to be co-extensive with its chapters: there are not fifty-seven of them, for example, in Book I. The shift of perspective may seem subtle, but it is far-reaching in its consequences, requiring us to abandon any false sense of familiarity we may feel towards essaying and its place in the work of Montaigne. The noun 'essai' has a number of possible meanings in sixteenth-century French: its dominant senses of 'trial', 'test', 'attempt', 'sounding', and 'sample' associate it strongly with the idea of experimentation; others like 'temptation' and 'risk' refer to the implications with which such experimentation is fraught; others still such as 'apprenticeship', 'exercise', 'prelude', and 'beginning' stress the sheer effort and the tentative process of initiation involved. Related to this third set of senses is the phrase 'coup d'essai', meaning the testing or trial-ling of one's powers, a first attempt or specimen sample. The verb 'essayer' has, as might be expected, related meanings including 'try' in the strong sense of 'endeavour', 'undertake', 'sample' and therefore 'taste', 'weigh up', 'run a risk', and 'start off'. Montaigne draws on the noun and verb in all these various guises and meanings in the course of his book. He uses the reflexive form of the verb with particular vigour: this reflects his strong sense that essaying is a self-directed activity in which the first person puts himself to the test, starts himself off, and so on. We saw, at the end of chapter 1 above, one instance of precisely this usage in 'Of repentance' (III.2): 'If my mind could gain a firm footing, I would not make essays [literally: I would not try myself out], I would make decisions; but it is always in apprenticeship and on trial' ('Si mon ame pouvoit prendre pied, je ne m'essaierois pas, je me resoudrois: elle est toujours en apprentissage et en espreuve'; F 740, VS 805). The intrinsically initiatory and experimental method that Montaigne here acknowledges as his own was noted earlier, but not his use of the reflexive verb 's'essayer', which immediately summons the related ideas of apprenticeship and trial. The 'essais' of which Montaigne speaks in the passage that opens 'Of Democritus and Heraclitus' are similarly in keeping with sixteenth-century usage of that term: they are tests to which the first person puts his judgement. They are, in a word, thought-experiments.

In the rest of that passage Montaigne draws on several of the meanings of 'essai' current in sixteenth-century French to describe how he conducts his thought-experiments. These meanings, and the metaphors with which they are associated, run throughout the passage. The A-text has the first person trying out his judgement on their journey through different subjects by making essays in the sense of tests and samples. Three situations are imagined. In the first, the subject is as deep as a river, an ideal opportunity to take a sounding – the verb used in French is precisely 'sonder' – and for the judgement to prove its worth to the first person by declaring the crossing to be beyond its powers. Montaigne pauses here to insist that its recognition of its own limitations is not just an intrinsic part of the work that the judgement performs but one of its proudest achievements – a point to which he will return later in the passage. In the second situation, the subject encountered is as superficial as the earlier one was deep, stimulating the attempt to lend it substance or, as the saying goes, to put flesh and bones on it. In the third and final situation, framed as an alternative to the second one by the repetition of 'sometimes' ('tantost'), the subject is a kind of monument, a place of secular pilgrimage, to which a thousand well-trodden paths lead: we are reminded here of the kind of subject-heading under which notable arguments and sayings – by Plato and other friends – are gathered in commonplace books of the period. In this situation, the judgement recognizes that it is playing a different game, one that requires it to choose what it takes to be the best and truest of the existing paths in order to demonstrate its independence: to show that it is capable of thinking freely in the company of others. These three situations are presented unsystematically and in no particular order, and the first person seeks none in particular in the course of his travels with his judgement, stressing that it is all grist to his mill. In this way the A-text pithily spells out the element of chance in all the various processes of essaying it has so far described.

In both the A-text and the C-text that follows it, the writing is remarkable for the physicality with which it describes abstract processes, an effect it achieves by restoring, to the metaphors it uses, their literal sense. The C-text has the first person, now presented as indistinguishable from his judgement, not so much taking soundings as tasting subjects and weighing them up. Montaigne describes these processes and the unusual results they produce by shifting between the visual and the tactile. His use of sensual and increasingly violent metaphors to describe his licking, brushing, pinching, or stabbing of subjects contrasts in its physicality with the earlier sequence in which the judgement is imagined giving body to a subject. The emphasis is not on manipulation and support here but on penetration and surprise as he thrusts into subjects as deep as he can and – in a marriage of visual and tactile metaphors – says that he likes to 'take' them, most often, 'from some unaccustomed point of view' ('par quelque lustre inusité'). This phrase calls to mind the Renaissance practice of paradox which, as we saw in chapter 2 above, consists of taking a stance on a particular subject that goes against customary ways of thinking. Always singular and usually paradoxical, Montaigne's essaying of subjects leaves both them and itself in a fragmented state, a fact that he accepts from the position of hard-won self-knowledge: 'I would venture to treat some matter thoroughly, if I knew myself less well' ('Je me hazarderoy de traitter à fons quelque matière, si je me connoissoy moins').

In the penultimate sentence of the C-text, essaying is viewed most explicitly as a method that the writer uses, and which has consequences for his text as a whole. The 'samples' ('eschantillons') of which he speaks, another metaphor related to that of the essay, are at once borrowings from other compositions, separated from their original contexts, and the host text in which these are dispersed. The writer stands back from these samples, asserting his independence from them and his right to treat them with the free play of his judgement, a treatment likely to be variable and to lead him to the temptation of doubt as well as to the self-aware ignorance that he describes here as his 'ruling quality' or, literally, 'mistress-form' ('maistresse forme'). The passage in 'Of the education of children' examined in the previous chapter comes to mind at this point. Montaigne suggests there that the child should weigh ancient arguments in the balance of his personal judgement and choose where he can but otherwise remain in doubt. Here in a post-1588 addition to 'Of Democritus and Heraclitus', the same process is described, and it is now acknowledged by the writer to be integral to his own haphazard method.

Essaying through Time

This brings us to our author's title for his book and to the passage through time of title and book alike. Essays, as Montaigne understands the term, are always essays of something: of his judgement, his natural faculties, himself. He uses the term 'essai' chiefly to refer to his method of putting those things to the test. The term best serves that purpose because it captures, through the rich semantic possibilities of its various forms and associated phrases, multiple aspects of the method: the initiatory and tentative mode of its enquiries are brought together with the risks and temptations of its free-thinking procedures in a word that stresses the experimental character of the method in all its aspects. Experimentation of this kind is an adventure of the mind, but an adventure in perpetual apprenticeship and uninsured vagrancy, and this too is captured by the connotations of the language of essaying. All of these meanings and connotations need to be read into Montaigne's use of the word in his title. He had settled on his title by 1580, but it seems likely to have been a recent decision, since the very few passages in which he refers to his book by its title appear only in the 1588 edition or in revisions made after 1588. The writing of his book becomes the privileged medium through which he conducts essays. But it is not the only one – inner reflection and conversation with others provide further possibilities for essaying – and, while Montaigne clearly considers that his book contains essays, he does not use that term to refer to the individual pieces of which the book is composed. He usually calls them 'chapters' ('chapitres'). His plural title refers to multiple instances, not of a literary genre, but of the method whereby he tries himself and his thoughts out on paper.

His contemporaries and early successors, as Hugo Friedrich pointed out in his 1949 study of Montaigne, understood his title in precisely these terms. This is borne out by their translations or glosses of it in various languages: in Latin, using 'gustus' ('tasting', 'foretaste') and 'conatus' ('endeavour', but also 'sketch'), both offered as classical equivalents of the late Latin word 'exagium' ('weighing') from which 'essai' in French is derived; 'saggi' in Italian, 'essays' in English (both also from the Latin 'exagium'), and 'experiencias' ('experiments', 'trials') in Spanish, all three combined with 'discourses' or its cognates; 'Gedanken' ('thoughts') together with 'Meinungen' ('notions' or 'opinions') in German. These variants all express something of the experimental, informal, and open-ended character of the essaying through life that Montaigne describes in 'Of Democritus and Heraclitus'.

In time, of course, several of these terms – 'saggio' in Italian and 'essay' in English as well as 'essai' in French – have come primarily to designate the literary genre of that name. This development starts in the years following Montaigne's death when writers such as Francis Bacon, as was noted in chapter 1 above, and Sir William Cornwallis (*c.* 1579–1614) pick up Montaigne's title and adapt it to their own philosophical or literary purposes. Seventeenth-century philosophers working in a range of fields – including Descartes, the austere Jansenist *moraliste* Pierre Nicole (1625–95), and the German metaphysician and mathematician Gottfried Wilhelm Leibniz (1646–1716), writing in French, and, in English, the virtuoso thinker and Fellow of the Royal Society Robert Boyle (1627–91) and the empiricist philosopher John Locke (1632–1704) – all practise, in Boyle's words, 'that form of writing which (in imitation of the French) we call essays'. The essay still remains available to philosophers as a generic alternative to more formal exercises in logic or high abstraction. As a literary genre, the essay has been most developed by English-language writers, including the Romantic essayist and critic Charles Lamb (1775–1834), the New England writer and thinker Ralph Waldo Emerson (1803–82), and the Bloomsbury novelist Virginia Woolf (1882–1941). Montaigne is traditionally seen as the creator of the essay, philosophical and literary, and later practitioners acknowledge his influence: Bacon quotes him in the first of his 1625 *Essays* ('Of Truth'), Emerson includes him among his *Representative Men* (1849), and Woolf devotes a short essay to him (1924). But his writing is of a different character from that of later practitioners: it is less sententious than Bacon's, for example, less systematic than Descartes's, less mannered than Lamb's, and less lofty than Emerson's; and, while it appears keenly aware of its own generic antecedents, the crucial point to make is that these do not, as they do for Montaigne's successors, include the genre of the essay itself. The essayistic tradition, in some ways, acts as an obstacle to our reading of the *Essais* because it creates in us a set of expectations that the text, when encountered at close quarters, upsets.

What this means is that, by a twist of linguistic history, *Essays* has now become a mistranslation of Montaigne's title. In its place Terence Cave suggests *Trials* or *Soundings*, and M. A. Screech *Assays of Michel de Montaigne*, although he, like all of Montaigne's English translators, retains the canonical *Essays* in his title. English translators struggle with the term inside the text as well as in its title. Frame renders 'essais' as 'tests' in the second sentence of the passage in 'Of Democritus and Heraclitus' quoted above, a translation that keeps the sense and prevents the danger of false familiarity, but he loses the direct semantic connection between 'essais' and the verb 'essayer' in the following sentence of the original by translating the verb as 'essay'. Screech uses 'assay' in both cases, which maintains the connection between the two, but at the price of an archaism that is absent from Montaigne's choice of lexis. Though their solutions differ, both Frame and Screech recognize that the noun 'essay' can rarely be used in modern English as if it remained innocent of the later, literary sense that has come to dominate it.

Essaying, like all processes, is caught in the flow of time. Montaigne makes this clear by using temporal markers such as 'sometimes' ('tantost') to designate variations in the tests he sets his judgement and by describing essaying as a kind of movement. He makes it clear, too, by revising and adding to the account he gives of essaying in 'Of Democritus and Heraclitus' throughout the nearly two decades during which he was writing his book: the passing of time is woven into the fabric of the passage. The genesis of the *Essais* is of exceptional interest not just to historians of the book, but to all of Montaigne's readers, because it crystallizes the open-ended temporal process of essaying that the text initiates. As Richard Sayce puts it, 'textual variants throw interesting lights on any author, but in Montaigne they touch the very substance of his being'.

Our passage exemplifies the temporal flux of the *Essais* in that it was composed in successive layers and remains to this day unfinished. The unfinished character of the passage raises specific problems for its readers. The first of these is the fundamental one of where Montaigne wanted his sentences to begin and end. A second problem has to do with what he really means when he uses the word 'essai' in this passage. These problems are instances of a larger debate about whether, to borrow John O'Brien's phrase, we are actually reading what Montaigne wrote. The main point of contention in this debate is the final authentic state in which the text survives and on which an edition respecting the author's intentions should be based. In what follows I shall sketch the history and the arguments, commenting on currently available critical editions of the *Essais* along the way, and then show how the text's evolution and the ways in which it has been edited affect an understanding of our passage. My contention will be that, by a happy accident of history, the essaying of which the passage speaks continues to this day.

The early history of the *Essais* is complicated as well as enriched by Montaigne's practice of writing by accretion, in other words, by adding layers of text to existing chapters from edition to edition. The first edition of the text was published in 1580, by Simon Millanges in Bordeaux, under the title *Essais de Michel de Montaigne*. That first edition comprised Books I and II, written over the previous nine years or so. In 1582, a second edition appeared in Bordeaux, carrying no more than a few minor additions and corrections to the two Books. The next important edition, published by the Parisian publisher Abel L'Angelier in 1588, added a third Book of *Essais* along with interpolations in Books I and II amounting to over 600 additions and nearly 550 new quotations. The only change to the title was the addition of Montaigne's nobiliary title: it now read *Essais de Michel Seigneur de Montaigne*.

The text's accretion continued apace between 1588 and Montaigne's death in 1592. The writer wrote no new chapters during this period but significantly revised the text with a view to a new edition of his work: he interpolated a thousand or so new passages, thereby increasing the length of the 1588 edition by about a third (quite enough text to have made a fourth Book, had he been so inclined), while also making somewhere in the region of 9000 revisions to the punctuation. A copy of the 1588 edition in which Montaigne recorded these changes in his own hand, known as the 'Bordeaux copy' ('exemplaire de Bordeaux') because it is now held at the Bibliothèque Municipale of that town, still exists. The Bordeaux copy is a fascinating document and the most precious witness we have to the processes of thinking and writing that produced the late style of the *Essais*. Reproductions of various kinds, now widely available in print and online, show the scribbled additions and deletions as they are to be found *in situ* on each page. The Bordeaux copy bears the scars of its passage through history – a book-binder in the seventeenth or eighteenth century trimmed the edges off its margins and marginalia alike when preparing it for rebinding – but it is now treated with the veneration it deserves. While Montaigne did not live to see a new edition of his work go to press, his publisher Abel L'Angelier published one three years after the author's death, in 1595. The main title carried the important addition of a definite article – *Essais* had become *Les Essais* – and the subtitle claimed this to be a new edition, found after the death of the author, which he had personally revised and expanded by a third. Prepared by his adoptive daughter Marie de Gournay in collaboration with the poet Pierre de Brach, it includes many but by no means all of the additions and corrections found in the Bordeaux copy, together with many thousands of others – some of them significant – whose provenance is less clear.

What this means is that the genesis of the *Essais* has left posterity with a text in two states, one of them in the author's hand but manifestly work in progress, the other a printed text whose authority remains disputed.

The argument as to which of these – the Bordeaux copy or the 1595 edition – represents the text in its final authentic state has ebbed and flowed ever since. Marie de Gournay's text, which itself remained in a state of flux (she was dissatisfied with her 1595 edition and went on revising it for the next forty years), was considered the most complete and authentic for over three centuries: hers is the text in which Descartes, Pascal, and Jean-Jacques Rousseau, among many others, read the *Essais*. It would be of interest for that reason alone.

By the early twentieth century, Gournay's edition had lost its authority, and the Bordeaux copy, which bore the indisputable marks of authorial intervention, had supplanted it. The Bordeaux copy was the source-text for the twentieth century's three most important editions: the five-volume *Édition municipale* (1906–33) of Fortunat Strowski, François Gébelin, and Pierre Villey; the 1934 Pléiade edition of Albert Thibaudet, re-edited in 1962 by Maurice Rat; and the 1922–3 Alcan edition of Villey, re-edited in 1965 by V.-L. Saulnier with the Presses universitaires de France (PUF). The translations of Frame and Screech are based on these three editions. Those of Villey (PUF) and Thibaudet and Rat (in the Pléiade), scholarly yet reasonably priced and portable, became the standard editions for students and general readers as well as specialists. Both integrate the manuscript additions of the Bordeaux copy, but adapt its spelling to match those of the 1588 or 1595 editions, and use readings from the 1595 edition to restore passages that are missing from the Bordeaux copy as a result of the binder's knife or some other accident of history. Both indicate the chronological layer of composition to which each passage belongs, prefacing it with an A, B or C (Villey) or with one, two or three forward slashes (Thibaudet and Rat) to refer respectively to the text of 1580–2, that of 1588, and Montaigne's post-1588 additions to the Bordeaux copy. Both, in the interests of accessibility, offer translations of and sources for the many foreign quotations, modernize the punctuation, and introduce paragraph breaks within the chapters. In the editorial history of the *Essais*, then, the twentieth century belongs to the Bordeaux copy.

The century ended with André Tournon's 1998 Imprimerie nationale edition. Tournon pointed out that all previous printed editions of the *Essais*, even those based upon the Bordeaux copy, had failed to respect the fact that in it Montaigne systematically revises his punctuation, segmenting the longer, ambling sentences of 1588 into a succession of clipped phrases bristling with capital letters, full stops, colons, commas, and the like. Tournon restores the surprising effects of segmentation in his edition, but not in its entirety the original punctuation, taking the eyebrow-raising step of introducing two marks – the high stop and the dash – to clarify the functions of the many colons that Montaigne uses in ways foreign to the present-day reader. With the same reader in mind, Tournon modernizes the spelling and retains paragraph breaks as well as repeating Villey's labelling of compositional layers, though the As, Bs, and Cs are now discreetly relegated to the margins. Tournon's edition, like those of his twentieth-century predecessors, is caught between the competing demands of fidelity to Montaigne's intentions, as recorded in the text of the Bordeaux copy, and present-day accessibility.

The same is true of the two most recent printed versions of the *Essais*, the difference being that they consider as final and authentic not the Bordeaux copy, but the 1595 edition. The new Pléiade edition, which began life under the general editorship of the late Michel Simonin, was finally published in 2007; it replaced – in a sign of the times – the one by Thibaudet based on the Bordeaux copy. It followed into print the 2001 Pochothèque edition, prepared by a team working under Jean Céard, whose introduction is dedicated to the memory of Simonin. Simonin, building on detective work done in the 1970s by Richard Sayce and David Maskell, had argued against the definitive status accorded to the Bordeaux copy and proposed an alternative history rehabilitating the editorial work of Marie de Gournay. It is now generally agreed that Montaigne did not record solely in the Bordeaux copy the changes he decided to make after 1588, but that he possessed a second copy, now lost, which Gournay refers to in her preface and used when preparing the 1595 edition. That second copy was more complete in its revisions than the Bordeaux copy, it is claimed, and its presence behind the 1595 text – combined with the now restored faith in Montaigne's indefatigable literary executor and her editorial collaborator – argues powerfully for the authenticity of that text. The 2001 Pochothèque and 2007 Pléiade editions are put together on that basis. They promote a certain kind of historical authenticity in other ways, too, removing some of the innovations of modern editions, notably the paragraph breaks but also the labelling of textual strata, and restoring earlier innovations such as Gournay's 1595 preface and the index introduced in the L'Angelier edition of 1602. The underlying idea, congenial to our age of historical reconstructions and period musical instruments, is that we should have before us not only what Montaigne wanted us to read but also the text in which early readers encountered the *Essais*. The authenticity of any such reconstruction is compromised by the fact that we are its irredeemably belated consumers, of course, and, just like its twentieth-century predecessors, the Pochothèque and Pléiade editions intervene in various ways to cater for the needs and expectations of present-day readers.

This leaves twenty-first-century readers in the enviable position of having both texts – that of the Bordeaux copy and that of the first edition of the *Essais* to have appeared immediately after the author's death – widely accessible once more.

One might assume that the return to the 1595 edition has rendered the Bordeaux copy marginal to the textual tradition of the *Essais*. Nothing could be further from the truth. The debate, once heated between Tournon and Simonin, rumbles on. Partisans of the Bordeaux copy have to answer the strong case made for the central place of Marie de Gournay's edition in the textual tradition. Partisans of that edition have to concede that some of its readings need to be treated with particular caution. One example is its relocation of the chapter 'That the taste of good and evil depends in large part on the opinion we have of them' (I.14: 'Que le goust des biens et des maux depend en bonne partie de l'opinion que nous en avons') between 'A consideration upon Cicero' (I.40) and 'Of not communicating one's glory' (I.41: 'De ne communiquer sa gloire'); this alteration to the order of the chapters from that given in all editions published during

Montaigne's lifetime is unprecedented, unsupported by the Bordeaux copy, and anything but self-evident. A second example is the absence from the 1595 edition of around one half of the systematic revisions made in the Bordeaux copy to the punctuation of the 1588 text. It seems unlikely that Montaigne changed his mind so radically on this issue when working on the second copy, therefore likely that this is not just an absence, but an editorial omission. What this suggests in turn is that, while the good faith of Marie de Gournay and her collaborators need not be called into question, the exact fidelity of their transcriptions should. This should come as no surprise when one considers that, just like their present-day successors, they needed to weigh that principle against the expectations of their readers. Editing the *Essais*, it seems, always involves compromise.

Where next, then, for editions of Montaigne? While the debate rumbles on, and the jury remains out, Villey's PUF edition (now available in a handy single-volume format), though superseded in various ways by Tournon on the one hand and Simonin and Céard on the other, remains the first choice of most. Some prefer reading Montaigne in contemporary French, and such adaptations of the *Essais* are readily available, though they inevitably come at some cost to the specificities of Montaigne's historical situation and to his detailed linguistic and stylistic choices for his compositions. A diplomatic solution for the more historically minded would be to make available, in the same publication, the four most important states of the text – those of 1580–2, 1588, the Bordeaux copy, and 1595 – and allow people to navigate between them as they wished. Claude Blum's CD-ROM, *Le Corpus Montaigne* (1998), published in Paris by Bibliopolis, provides those texts and a wealth of others in what is an indispensable resource of the computer age. It is not suitable, however, for those of us who want to read the *Essais* in a printed edition, combining authenticity and accessibility, which can be lifted off the shelf at no risk of a sprain or torsion and does not cost an arm and a leg. One obvious next move would be a composite text, based on the 1595 edition, but leaving 'That the taste of good and evil depends in large part on the opinion we have of them' (I.14) in its original place and incorporating the punctuation of the Bordeaux copy. I for one hope that, if and when it comes, it will discreetly reintroduce the labelling of textual strata, which is certainly inauthentic, but always enlightening. Montaigne's text, whatever its editorial future, will continue to require its editors to face uncertainty and to exercise good judgement in weighing up the conflicting evidence of

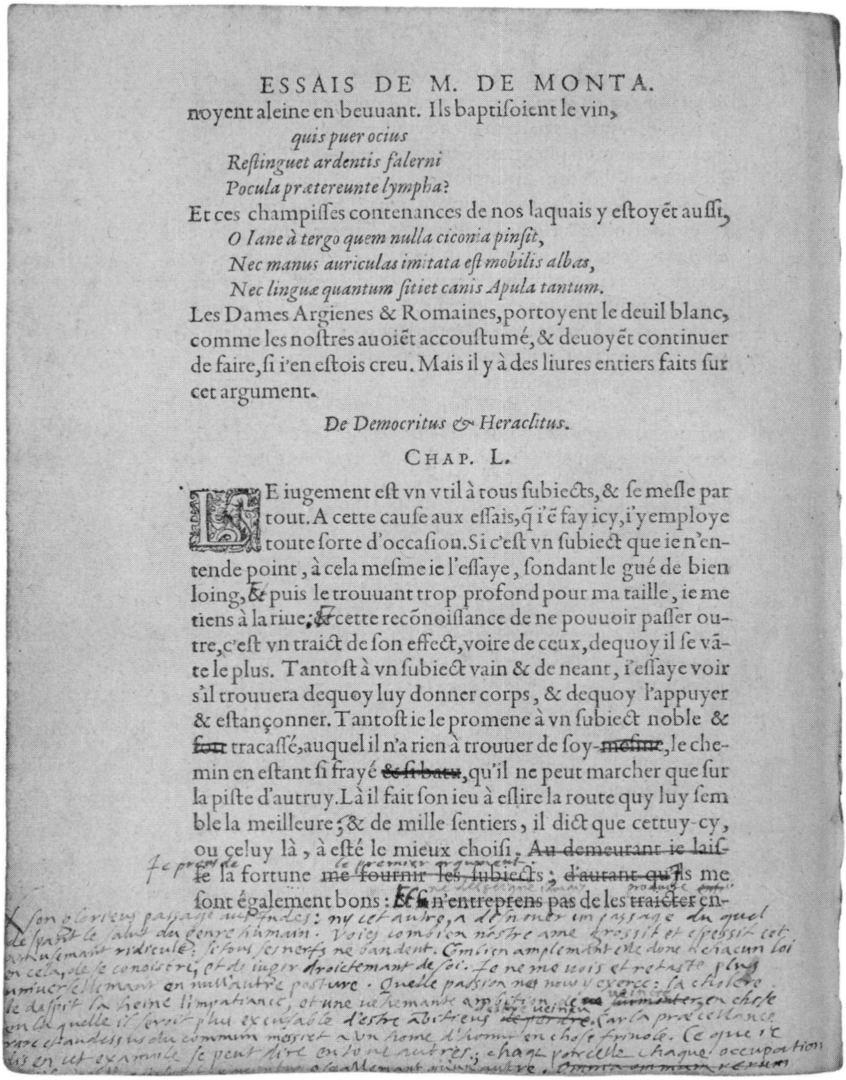

ESSAIS DE M. DE MONTA.

noyent aleine en beuuant. Ils baptisoient le vin,

quis puer ocius
Restinguet ardentis falerni
Pocula prætereunte lympha?

Et ces champisses contenances de nos laquais y estoyẽt aussi,

O Iane à tergo quem nulla ciconia pinsit,
Nec manus auriculas imitata est mobilis albas,
Nec linguæ quantum sitiet canis Apula tantum.

Les Dames Argienes & Romaines, portoyent le deuil blanc, comme les nostres auoiẽt accoustumé, & deuoyẽt continuer de faire, si i'en estois creu. Mais il y à des liures entiers faits sur cet argument.

De Democritus & Heraclitus.

CHAP. L.

LE iugement est vn vtil à tous subiects, & se mesle par tout. A cette cause aux essais, q̃ i'ẽ fay icy, i'y employe toute sorte d'occasion. Si c'est vn subiect que ie n'entende point, à cela mesme ie l'essaye, sondant le gué de bien loing, & puis le trouuant trop profond pour ma taille, ie me tiens à la riue; & cette recõnoissance de ne pouuoir passer outre, c'est vn traict de son effect, voire de ceux, dequoy il se vãte le plus. Tantost à vn subiect vain & de neant, i'essaye voir s'il trouuera dequoy luy donner corps, & dequoy l'appuyer & estançonner. Tantost ie le promene à vn subiect noble & tracassé, auquel il n'a rien à trouuer de soy-mesme, le chemin en estant si frayé & si batu, qu'il ne peut marcher que sur la piste d'autruy. Là il fait son ieu à eslire la route quy luy semble la meilleure; & de mille sentiers, il dict que cettuy-cy, ou celuy là, à esté le mieux choisi. Au demeurant ie laisse la fortune me fournir les subiects; d'autant qu'ils me sont également bons: & n'entreprens pas de les traicter en-

Plate 1. The Bordeaux copy of the 1588 *Essais*, plate 253, recording Montaigne's revisions.

its compositional and early editorial history. It is, as David Maskell said in 1978, a pleasing irony that the posterity of the *Essais* has turned out in this way: as a continuous exercise in essaying.

Essaying in Book I

We are now ready to return to 'Of Democritus and Heraclitus' and to the problems that the chapter's opening poses editors and readers. The passage is different in each of the four most important states of the text. The differences between 1580–2 and 1588 are minimal – a word is removed here and there – but the changes made after 1588 are significant. The most significant of these is the overhaul and expansion of the second half of the passage. That overhaul adds, in particular, the strongly physical description of Montaigne's treatment of his subjects and the long penultimate sentence that describes his attitude towards his samples and speaks of ignorance as his ruling quality. This is a sentence that resonates with other late additions to the *Essais*, those made to a nearby chapter in Book I, 'Of vain subtleties' (I.54: 'Des vaines subtilitez'), and to 'Of physiognomy' (III.12), in particular.

The Bordeaux copy and the 1595 edition agree on most, but not all, of the post-1588 changes made to 'Of Democritus and Heraclitus'. Both texts provide indispensable help in the hazardous business of construing what Montaigne is most likely to have wanted us to read. The first eleven words of the C-text are no more than a conjecture, derived from the 1595 edition, replacing a chunk of text at the top of a page in the Bordeaux copy that went under the binder's knife. Various minor differences of lexis and phrasing in 1595 are so inconsequential that they are most easily explained as a whim on the part of the author: they fit the hypothesis that such instances are most likely the result of Montaigne's own interventions. Two differences in 1595, however, are consequential: the first is the punctuation of the word 'essais' at the beginning of the passage; the second is the punctuation of the penultimate sentence. Both go beyond the merely technical in that they raise fundamental interpretative questions about the passage.

Let us deal with the second difference first. The penultimate sentence varies in its punctuation to such an extent between the Bordeaux copy and the 1595 edition that it may not even be appropriate to call it a 'sentence'.

Here is my transcription of the Bordeaux copy at this point in the text (see Plate 2, left margin), followed by Frame's translation, but with his punctuation altered accordingly:

> Semant icy un mot icy un autre: Eschantillons depris de leur piece: escartez. Sans dessein & sans promesse, ie ne suis pas tenu d'en faire bon. Ny de m'y tenir moi mesme sans varier quand il me plaist. Et me rendre au doubte et incertitude & à ma maistresse forme, qui est l'ignorance.

> Scattering a word here there another: Samples separated from their context: dispersed. Without a plan and without a promise, I am not bound to make something of them. Or to adhere to them myself without varying when I please. And giving myself up to doubt and uncertainty and my ruling quality, which is ignorance.

The Bordeaux copy offers here not one sentence, as per Villey's 'modernized' punctuation, but four clauses marked by full stops. The first two clauses, further segmented by commas and colons, reflect in their form the dispersal of which they speak. Each segment corresponds to a separate thought – its sudden appearance disrupting the onward flow of which it is a part – the flow to which the act of reading must eventually return it. The word 'Eschantillons' ('Samples') is lent emphasis by being capitalized. The final two clauses run on with the greater freedom of movement that they claim for themselves, but even there a full stop intervenes to emphasize the wilful choice of variation in the treatment of the samples. The punctuation of this passage, though difficult to follow in some places, nonetheless offers a classic case of the new 'clipped style' ('langage coupé') of the Bordeaux copy, rehabilitated by Tournon, and it is clearly no accident: in the draft instructions to the printer included in the copy, Montaigne tells him not to spare the full stops and capital letters of this style, stressing that commas should not be substituted where full stops are required. This clipped style is the one that seems truly modern – innovative and unsettling – and not Villey's taming of it.

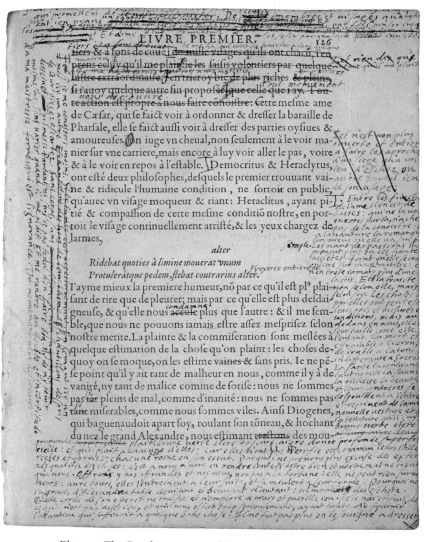

Plate 2. The Bordeaux copy of the 1588 *Essais*, plate 254,
recording Montaigne's revisions.

Here is the 1595 version, as found in the new Pléiade edition, with Frame again repunctuated accordingly:

> Semant icy un mot, icy un autre, eschantillons dépris de leur piece, escartez, sans dessein, sans promesse: je ne suis pas tenu d'en faire bon, ny de m'y tenir moy-mesme, sans varier, quand il me plaist, et me rendre au doubte et incertitude, et à ma maistresse forme, qui est l'ignorance.

> Scattering a word here, there another, samples separated from their context, dispersed, without a plan, without a promise: I am not bound to make something of them or to adhere to them myself, without varying when I please, and giving myself up to doubt and uncertainty, and my ruling quality, which is ignorance.

After the disruptive segmentations of the Bordeaux copy, the 1595 edition offers one long meander of a sentence, its various clauses stitched together by commas and a colon, an altogether softer thread of punctuation whose effect is accumulative rather than emphatic. While softer, the punctuation nonetheless changes the meaning of the sentence decisively in various ways: for example, the placing of a colon after the phrase 'sans dessein, sans promesse' ('without a plan, without a promise') means that the phrase now qualifies the dispersal of the samples and not the 'je' who thereby frees himself from the obligation to make sense of them.

The wording of this so-called sentence from 'Of Democritus and Heraclitus', to sum up, is identical in the Bordeaux copy and the 1595 edition, give or take an ampersand, and one might be tempted to think that too much could be made of the commas, colons, and full stops that differ. But these marks alter the fabric and in some cases the sense of the writing; and, if the deletions and redraftings it undergoes in the margin of a page in the Bordeaux copy are anything to go by, getting it right mattered to Montaigne; so it should matter to us.

The second of the consequential differences between the Bordeaux copy and the 1595 edition concerns whether or not the word 'essais' should be capitalized in the second sentence of our passage from 'Of Democritus and Heraclitus'. The 1595 edition gives 'Essais', whereas all of the editions published during Montaigne's lifetime read 'essais', and there is not a trace of an alteration to the word in the Bordeaux copy. So which is it to be? To follow 1595 would mean seeing this passage as a marked first step in the invention of the essay as a literary genre and accepting that Montaigne, at the last, transforms his use of the word here so that it no longer refers in a general sense to the testing of his judgement, as before, but instead to the specific production of the text. There is little evidence to support this view. It is untypical of Montaigne to alter an existing occurrence of the word 'essai' in this way. The alteration would have the unhappy consequence, too, of weakening the force of the adverb 'here' ('ici') in the same phrase and rendering it all but superfluous. Is this one example of a change made not by Montaigne, but by his 1595 editors, in a lapse of fidelity? That is certainly what the new Pléiade editors suggest. Remaining consistent with their decision to use the 1595 edition as the basis for their own, they give 'Essais', but they point out the change – and dissociate themselves from it – in an endnote: 'Mlle de Gournay here significantly alters the sense of this term by capitalizing it [...]: its initial sense was without a doubt vaguer and more general' ('Mlle de Gournay infléchit ici notablement le sens de ce terme en lui attribuant une majuscule [...]: le sens initial était sans aucun doute plus vague et plus vaste'). The Pléiade editors' fidelity to the 1595 edition prevents them from following the logic of their own endnote by removing the capital E in the main text. There is, of course, no certain means of knowing who made the alteration. It is possible that Montaigne, developing further in the so-called second copy the clipped style of the Bordeaux copy, capitalized the word 'Essais' to pair it with 'Eschantillons' ('Samples') in the same passage, thereby emphasizing the connotations of his title, and that the 1595 editors removed the capital from 'Eschantillons' but left it on 'Essais' – losing the echo. It is possible too, though I admit the conjecture is fanciful, that Montaigne deliberately capitalized 'Essais' in the second copy while leaving it unchanged in the Bordeaux copy so as to set his unborn editors, translators, and readers a puzzle – and a chance to essay their judgement in the company of his text. The puzzle, in any case, remains.

Book I puts into practice all the varieties of essaying that Montaigne describes in 'Of Democritus and Heraclitus'. That chapter is itself a case in point. Having said at its outset that he likes most often to take subjects from some unaccustomed point of view, Montaigne goes on to treat the stock comparison of laughing Democritus and weeping Heraclitus in precisely this paradoxical way, preferring the former's humour not because it is more pleasant to laugh at life than to weep at it but because it is more scathing: 'it seems to me that we can never be despised as much as we deserve' ('il me semble que nous ne pouvons jamais estre assez mesprisez selon nostre merite'; F 268, VS 303). Similarly paradoxical treatments of other subjects are close to hand. 'Of the education of children' (I.26), as we saw in chapter 2 above, is one example. 'Of cannibals' (I.31) is another. Proceeding through successive redefinitions of the term 'barbarous', Montaigne launches his attack on common European attitudes towards the peoples of the New World, and particularly towards the so-called barbarities of the Brazilian Tupinambá. He judges their practice of cannibalism to be indeed cruel, but less so than the atrocities of the Europeans who condemn them, blind to their own faults. The argument is not relativistic, then, but contrarian in its reversal of perspectives: the chapter offers ethnographic information in the place of ethnocentric prejudices, and ends by reporting the observations of three Tupinambá on French society, aiming a parting ironic jibe at the insularity of an imagined European interlocutor. And – last but not least – 'Of age' (I.57: 'De l'aage'), at the end of Book I, counters the common idea that there is a natural span (of three-score years and ten) to a life. In reviewing the activities that occupy different phases of a life, Montaigne notes not only the thousand shocks that flesh is heir to but also the gradual processes of physical and mental decline, thus ending Book I in a vision of human frailty from which the author is not spared.

The various other forms of essaying of which Montaigne speaks in 'Of Democritus and Heraclitus' are also to be found scattered across Book I. Montaigne may be seen seeking the best chosen paths through well-worn subjects such as death, in the chapter 'That to philosophize is to learn to die' (I.20: 'Que philosopher c'est apprendre à mourir'), fortune, in the chapter 'Fortune is often met in the path of reason' (I.34: 'La fortune se rencontre souvent au train de la raison'), and the desire for literary glory, in 'Of solitude' (I.39) and the two chapters that follow it. He may be seen attempting to lend substance to vain and nonexistent subjects, in 'Of vain subtleties' (I.54) and 'Of smells' (I.55: 'Des senteurs'), a chapter that grows progressively more whimsical in and after 1588 to include autobiographical notes and scientific and cultural reflections on smells and their senses – ending with the stench of Venice and Paris in its nostrils; and he may be seen acknowledging his inability fully to comprehend perplexing subjects such as the cause of perfect friendship, in 'Of friendship' (I.28), and the force of poetry, in 'Of Cato the Younger' (I.37: 'Du jeune Caton').

This is not to say that essaying is the only approach that Montaigne takes to the writing of Book I. He tries out other methods and styles, too, already encountered in the course of this book: these include the letter form and the dialogue, discussed in chapter 1 above, as well as argumentation 'on both sides of a question' (*in utramque partem*), mentioned in the previous chapter, a rhetorical exercise to which he adds a characteristic twist of epistemological uncertainty in 'Of the uncertainty of our judgement' (I.47: 'De l'incertitude de notre jugement').

Above all, Book I contains various exercises in his earliest style, in which he sews together examples and quotations culled from his reading in the manner of the miscellaneous compilations popular in his day. 'One man's profit is another man's harm' (I.22: 'Le profit de l'un est dommage de l'autre') is a case in point. Another is 'Of the parsimony of the ancients' (I.52: 'De la parsimonie des anciens'). A compilation detailing the thriftiness of various ancients in spite of their prestige, this is the shortest chapter of the *Essais*, as if emulating the quality of which it speaks. While the two chapters just mentioned show Montaigne's early style at its simplest and purest, it may also be seen at work in longer chapters such as 'Of war horses' (I.48: 'Des destriers'), whose listing of the uses of horses – particularly in war – shows its author at his most Quixotic: as a gentleman and a soldier who is happiest in the saddle.

Book I is a miscellany. But it is a miscellany in which clusters form and patterns emerge. The most consistent of these patterns is the one that Montaigne comes to call the essaying of his judgement. Time after time, chapters examine those very forces and constraints that tend to obscure the judgement or to hinder its liberty of movement, while also – in Montaigne's view – providing, on occasions, a necessary curb on innovation and change. External forces that work in this two-edged fashion include customs and laws: these are put under scrutiny in 'Of custom, and not easily changing an accepted law' (I.23: 'De la coustume et de ne changer aisément une loy receuë'), 'Of the custom of wearing clothes' (I.36: 'De l'usage de se vestir'), 'Of sumptuary laws' (I.43: 'Des loix sumptuaires'), and 'Of ancient customs' (I.49: 'Des coustumes anciennes'). Some of these forces, however, operate from within the mind. Examples of such internal forces, also intensely studied in Book I, include the passions: these are examined in all their power and inconstancy in chapters including 'Of sadness' (I.2: 'De la tristesse'), 'How the soul discharges its passions on false objects when the true are wanting' (I.4: 'Comme l'âme descharge ses passions sur des objects faux, quand les vrays luy defaillent'), and 'Of fear' (I.18: 'De la peur'). The chapter 'Of a saying of Caesar's' (I.53: 'D'un mot de César') prolongs this sequence by offering a brief moral reflection on humankind's constitutive restlessness and a call to self-study that resonates throughout the *Essais*.

Judgement is never better essayed, as Montaigne says in the sentences that open 'Of Democritus and Heraclitus', than when it is forced to encounter subjects that reveal to it its own limits. Offering as it does a way of understanding what surrounds it, that chapter acts like a belated preface to Book I and a mirror-image of an earlier prefatory exercise, 'Of idleness' (I.8). But where, as was said earlier, 'Of idleness' describes a writer in hot pursuit of his runaway mind, 'Of Democritus and Heraclitus' presents essaying as the best way for him to give his mind free rein – while remaining in the saddle.

4

Two Cheers for Free-Thinking

Our mind is an erratic, dangerous, and heedless tool; it is hard to impose order and moderation upon it. And in my time those who have some rare excellence beyond the others, and some extraordinary quickness, are nearly all, we see, incontinent in the licence of their opinions and conduct. It is a miracle if you find a sedate and sociable one. People are right to give the tightest possible barriers to the human mind. In study, as in everything else, its steps must be counted and regulated for it; the limits of the chase must be artificially determined for it. They bridle and bind it with religions, laws, customs, science, precepts, mortal and immortal punishments and rewards; and still we see that by its whirling and its incohesiveness it escapes all these bonds. It is an empty body, with nothing by which it can be seized and directed; a varying and formless body, which can be neither tied nor grasped. [B] Indeed there are few souls so orderly, so strong and wellborn, that they can be trusted with their own guidance, and that can sail with moderation and without temerity, in the freedom of their judgements, beyond the common opinions. It is more expedient to place them in tutelage. The mind is a dangerous blade, [C] even to its possessor, [A] for anyone who does not know how to wield it with order and discretion. [C] And there is no animal that must more rightly be given blinkers to hold its gaze, in subjection and constraint, in front of its feet, and to keep it from straying here or there outside the ruts that custom and the laws trace for it. [A] Wherefore it will become you better to confine yourself to the accustomed routine, whatever it is, than to fly headlong into this unbridled licence. But if one of these new doctors tries to show off his ingenuity in your presence, at the risk of his salvation and yours; to rid yourself of this dangerous pestilence that spreads day by day in your courts, this preservative, in case of extreme necessity, will keep the contagion of that poison from harming either you or the others present.

Nostre esprit est un util vagabond, dangereux et temeraire; il est malaisé d'y joindre l'ordre et la mesure. Et, de mon temps, ceux qui ont quelque rare excellence au dessus des autres et quelque vivacité extraordinaire, nous les voyons quasi tous desbordez en licence d'opinions et de meurs. C'est miracle s'il en rencontre un rassis et sociable. On a raison de donner à l'esprit humain les barrieres les plus contraintes qu'on peut. En l'estude, comme au reste, il luy faut compter et regler ses marches, il luy faut tailler par art les limites de sa chasse. On le bride et garrote de religions, de loix, de coustumes, de science, de preceptes, de peines et recompenses mortelles et immortelles; encores voit-on que, par sa volubilité et dissolution, il eschappe à toutes ces liaisons. C'est un corps vain, qui n'a par où estre saisi et assené; un corps divers et difforme, auquel on ne peut asseoir neud ny prise. [B] Certes il est peu d'ames si reiglées, si fortes et bien nées, à qui on se puisse fier de leur propre conduicte, et qui puissent, avec moderation et sans temerité, voguer en la liberté de leurs jugements au delà des opinions communes. Il est plus expedient de les mettre en tutelle. C'est un outrageux glaive [C] que l'esprit à son possesseur mesme, [A] pour qui ne sçait s'en armer ordonnéement et discrettement. [C] Et n'y a point de beste à qui plus justement il faille donner des orbières pour tenir sa veuë subjecte et contrainte devant ses pas, et la garder d'extravaguer ny çà ny là, hors les ornieres que l'usage et les loix luy tracent. [A] Parquoy il vous sera mieux de vous resserrer dans le train accoustumé, quel qu'il soit, que de jetter vostre vol à cette licence effrenée. Mais si quelqu'un de ces nouveaux docteurs entreprend de faire l'ingénieux en vostre presence, aux despens de son salut et du vostre; pour vous deffaire de cette dangereuse peste qui se respand tous les jours en vos cours, ce preservatif, à l'extrême necessité, empeschera que la contagion de ce venin n'offencera ny vous ny vostre assistance.   (F 509–10, VS 559)

Free-thinking, as I said in chapter 2 above, is a form of intellectual engagement that Montaigne reflects upon and practises with characteristic complexity. Nowhere in the *Essais* is that complexity more apparent than in the enigmatic and emblematic chapter entitled 'Apology for Raymond Sebond' (II.12: 'Apologie de Raimond Sebond'). The passage from the chapter, quoted above, powerfully illustrates the point. In its perspective and tone it may come as something of a surprise, to put it mildly, after the texts analysed in the earlier chapters of this book. Its authoritarian imposition – upon its reader and itself – of closure and constraint, of bridles and bonds, sits uneasily with the passages scattered across the three Books in which Montaigne opens up his writing and its processes to the reader and seeks to be treated with the same openness in return. It sits even more than uneasily, one might say, with his advocacy of free-thinking as an anti-authoritarian principle of intellectual engagement and his invention of essaying as the method whereby he puts free-thinking into practice: it appears, in fact, as nothing less than a flat contradiction of the principle and the method alike. How could the author of chapters like 'Of the education of children' and 'Of Democritus and Heraclitus' also write the text quoted above? The free-thinking Montaigne seems to have found his own inverse. Perhaps what he says in the 'Apology for Raymond Sebond' is not to be taken at face value. Or has he perhaps changed his mind?

What Montaigne does in the 'Apology', I shall argue in what follows, is neither conceal his free-thinking and his essaying nor abandon them but bring them together in ways that produce disconcerting shifts of perspective and tone. For not only does he animate the process of essaying with the spirit of free-thinking, but he also reverses the charge, putting the principle of intellectual freedom to a searching examination, a thought-trial, of its own. One way of describing the result might to be to say that he puts his thinking about free-thinking into a swerve.

By far the longest chapter of the *Essais*, the largest and most prominent island in the middle of the textual archipelago, the 'Apology for Raymond Sebond' also applies most systematically its author's essaying method. It pursues, page after page, a single line of argument about the weakness and uncertainty of human reason. Along the way, it surveys a vast range of philosophical doctrines and schools of thought, putting ideas to the test, discarding those that do not pass, and appropriating to its own purposes and idiom those that do. It judges the most congenial of these philosophies to be the ancient tradition of radical scepticism and offers a detailed presentation of its modes of thinking and ways of talking. In this radical tradition, the freedom to think is the freedom to doubt, and the 'Apology' not only presents the exercise of this freedom with evident sympathy but also incorporates it within its own method. When the method is in turn applied to the principle, as in the passage quoted above, intellectual freedom is put under searching scrutiny and a number of critical questions are raised about its conditions of possibility and the uses to which it may be put. These may be phrased as a series of responses to the free-thinking adage 'Plato is my friend but a greater friend is truth'. What kind of freedom makes it possible to call truth a greater friend than Plato? Is it a good thing or a bad thing? What kind of person is able to consider Plato – let alone truth – with such familiarity? What is the truth that Plato missed, and which other authorities are likely to be pushed to one side in the search for it? Is there an end to the subversions of which free-thinking is capable? The shifts of perspective in the 'Apology' leave it delicately poised between support for the principle of intellectual freedom and anxiety about its conditions of possibility and its uses.

A Strange Defence

The 'Apology', as its title suggests, is framed as a defence of the Catalan theologian Ramon Sibiuda (Raimundus Sabundus) (*d.* 1436), whose *Natural Theology, or, The Book of Creatures* (*Theologia naturalis sive Liber creaturarum*) Montaigne translated from Latin into French, and first published at the request of his father in 1569 (a second edition followed in 1581). Screech's edition of Montaigne contains English versions of the two short texts that preface Montaigne's French version of the *Natural Theology*: a letter dedicating the translation to his father and his translation (and adaptation) of Sebond's prologue to the work. These two texts, published over a decade before the first edition of the *Essais*, give a flavour of Montaigne's earliest prose style and of his attitude to Sebond's work. The work is a 'natural theology' in that it reads the natural world as a book, written by the hand of God, in which the creatures serve as letters and combine to spell out the science of human salvation. Sebond's work turns articles of Christian faith into objects that are susceptible to human enquiry and knowledge. Its dogmatic confidence in the power of human reason was held to be excessive and detrimental to the theology of relevation and grace. The indications are that these objections came from both sides of the confessional divide in the sixteenth century. The Roman Index prohibited Sebond's *Natural Theology* in 1559, limiting its prohibition to the work's prologue in 1564. Montaigne seems to have been unaware of this until 1581, a year after his 'Apology' was first published, when papal censors in Rome apprised him of the prohibition. He makes no reference in the 'Apology' to Catholic censure of Sebond's work. He seems instead to allude to its Protestant detractors, as we shall see, and he sets out in the 'Apology' to defend the *Natural Theology* – and to justify his decision to translate it into French – in the face of their objections.

What he offers, through detailed replies to two particular criticisms of Sebond's work, is a strangely sinuous defence. The first of those two criticisms says that a rationalist natural theology is fundamentally misguided since Christian belief is based only on faith and the inspiration of divine grace. Montaigne effectively defers to this criticism before redefining the value of Sebond's arguments: they are not in themselves capable of securing faith, but they can and do prepare the way to faith for apprentice believers or waverers, leaving the revelation of grace to add the finishing touch (F 389–97, VS 440–8). The second criticism says that the arguments Sebond offers in support of his thesis are weak (F 397, VS 448). Montaigne's reply to this takes up almost the entire chapter, and it sweeps away Sebond and his detractors alike, for it throws into doubt the idea that certainty of any kind is possible, given the weakness of human reason when left to its own devices. In its earliest formulation, offered as an afterthought in Montaigne's reply to the first of the two criticisms, this argument maintains the apologetic value of Sebond's propositions: taken even as merely human fancies, these propositions will serve to combat the enemies of the faith, since they are as solid as any that could be used to oppose them (F 396–7, VS 448). But the exuberance, not to mention the sheer length, of the attack that the 'Apology' then mounts on human reason unaided by faith – an attack that draws particular sustenance, as we shall see, from a radical version of philosophical scepticism – produces an unstable balance between the chapter's framing as an orthodox contribution to apologetic discourse, which is reasserted in the closing pages of the chapter, and its encounter with an extreme and corrosive form of doubt that not only unseats the work that it set out to defend but shakes the foundations of knowledge itself.

The text that I quoted at the outset of this chapter is taken from the end of the section in which Montaigne interrupts the flow of his argument to address the princess for whom, he says, he has, against his custom, written at such length in this chapter (F 508–10, VS 557–9). This is the first of two instances in Book II, remember, in which a lady is apostrophized without warning in the middle of a chapter: I examined the other, in 'Of the resemblance of children to their fathers' (II.37), in chapter 1

above. One major difference between the two instances is that in the
'Apology' the identity of the apostrophized princess remains concealed.
She is nonetheless widely thought to be Marguerite de Valois (1553–1615),
whose colourful life Alexandre Dumas *père* (1802–70) fictionalized in *La
Reine Margot* (1845), a novel that became the subject of a 1994 film adaptation, of the same name, directed by Patrice Chéreau. Marguerite, the
daughter of a Catholic King of France, Henri II (1519–59), and his Italian
queen consort Catherine de Médicis (1519–89), was married in August
1572 to the Protestant King of Navarre, the future Henri IV of France, in
an attempt to seal the peace between the two sides in the middle of the
Wars of Religion. Within days the massacre of Protestants had begun,
but Henri survived, and so did his marriage to Marguerite. This means
that when, in the late 1570s, Montaigne wrote the 'Apology', his addressee
was a Catholic princess at the Protestant court of Navarre. An allusion to
her situation may be seen in the last sentence of our text: by 'new doctors'
('nouveaux docteurs') Montaigne seems to mean Protestant theologians
at the court of Navarre – he refers at the beginning of the chapter in
similar terms to 'the innovations of Luther' ('les nouvelletez de Luther';
F 388, VS 439) – who might try to talk Marguerite out of her admiration
for Sebond's work of Catholic devotion. Montaigne keeps the identity of
the princess concealed – to avoid, doubtless, taking a position that could
appear hostile to Henri de Navarre – but this does not prevent him from
alluding, in the final sentence of our text, to her situation and the com-
mission which she seems to have given him: to provide her with arguments to answer anyone at court who wishes to spread the 'pestilence'
of reformist theology by using a discussion about Sebond as a means of
attempting to make her waver in her Catholic faith.

That final sentence witnesses a change of perspective from what had
gone before. On this and other occasions the chapter heads in a particular direction before abruptly changing course and even, sometimes,
turning back on itself. Terence Cave describes this boomeranging of the
argument by applying to it the notion of 'antiperistasis', which was used
in sixteenth-century science to explain similar processes of contrariness
observed in nature, as for example the burning sensation caused by touch-
ing ice. The logic of antiperistasis characterizes other sixteenth-century
presentations of radical scepticism in apologetic texts, as Cave shows,
but it works in particularly complex ways in the 'Apology'. Cave's analysis offers a way out of the impasse in which critics find themselves when

they try to resolve the chapter's apparently contradictory arguments by choosing to fix Montaigne to the position either of an orthodox defender of Christian faith over reason or of a discreet proponent of irreligious philosophical scepticism. Cave portrays instead a Montaigne who moves between radically different attitudes. The antiperistatic movements of Montaigne's thought, I suggest, can be seen with particular clarity in the reversals of perspective that free-thinking undergoes inside the apostrophe to the princess and within the chapter as whole. The chapter first takes the liberty of thinking freely with the sceptical doubters about the infirmities of human reason. It then reverses its perspective on that liberty, condemning it as a dangerous licence, before qualifying that reversal in turn and allowing itself the possibility to proceed, with caution, in the free-thinking direction it had earlier adopted. These two antiperistatic reversals of perspective produce an S-shaped curve in the argument of the chapter at this, its mid-point, in the apostrophe to the princess.

The chapter describes more curves than that, however, in its sinuous progress. By the time the apostrophe makes its abrupt appearance, the chapter has already changed direction once in escaping the confines of its apologetic frame and adopting the freer, experimental mode of the essay. Montaigne announces this shift when he presents his reply to the second criticism levelled at Sebond as an initial and provisional investigation of the certainty to which human reason, considered for now on its own terms alone, can ever reasonably aspire (F 398–9, VS 449). He starts by comparing his method with that of St Augustine and comes, after a preliminary sounding, to narrow his field of investigation to that of secular philosophy on the grounds that it represents the finest achievements of the unaided human mind (F 450–1, VS 501–2). One hundred or so pages after starting his reply, he is still going strong, with no end in sight. This is essaying on an unprecedented scale, and as we have seen, Montaigne comments on the unusual length of the chapter at the beginning of his apostrophe to the princess.

Its absorbing encounter with the ancient tradition of radical anti-dogmatic scepticism – called 'Pyrrhonism' after its first proponent, Pyrrho of Elis (*fl.* 340 BCE) – best explains the exorbitant length to which the chapter goes. That encounter also gives the essaying of the 'Apology' a new philosophical focus. Montaigne judges Pyrrhonism to offer the approach most congenial to his own, and a detailed presentation of the school follows (F 451–6, VS 502–6). That presentation draws on the accounts of Cicero and the late Greek historian of philosophy Diogenes Laertius but above all on the compilation of Sextus Empiricus (*fl. c.* 200 CE), the *Outlines of Pyrrhonism* (*Pyrrhoniarum hypotyposeon*), which was translated for the first time from Greek into Latin by the French humanist Henri Estienne (1531–98), in 1562, and which Montaigne is thought to have discovered in the mid-1570s. Montaigne, paraphrasing Sextus, divides philosopers into those who think they have discovered the truth (the dogmatists), those who assert that the truth cannot be discovered (the academics), and those who call the matter into doubt and are still investigating (the Pyrrhonians). Unable to accept or deny any truth proposition, the Pyrrhonians practise suspension of judgement (*epoche*) on all matters of opinion, a practice that brings them peace of mind (*ataraxia*). Montaigne lists the phrases they systematically use to express doubt, the so-called 'sceptical phrases' (*phonai skeptikai*), such as their keyword, επεχω (*epecho*), which he gives in Greek before translating it as 'I hold back, I do not budge' ('je soutiens, je ne bouge'), and similar phrases like 'I establish nothing' ('je n'establis rien') and 'appearances are equal on either side' ('les apparences sont égales par tout') (F 454, VS 505). He ends his first presentation of the school and its philosophy with a ringing endorsement: 'There is nothing in man's invention that has so much verisimilitude and usefulness' ('Il n'est rien en l'humaine invention où il y ait tant de verisimilitude et d'utilité'; F 455, VS 506). A little later, he considers the linguistic problems raised by the art of perpetual doubt and offers a motto, 'Que sçay-je?' ('What do I know?'), as the first element of a new language, since its form as a question allows one to avoid asserting even that one knows one is in doubt (F 477, VS 527). In the same sentence, he pairs this motto with the visual emblem of a level pair of scales, representing the perpetually balanced judgement of the Pyrrhonians.

The chapter grows and grows as Montaigne, inspired by the Pyrrhonians, warms to his theme. We know, too, that in 1576 he had a medal struck bearing the same emblem and the keyword mentioned above, *epecho* ('I hold back'), and that about the same time he had that and others of the sceptical phrases inscribed on the rafters of his study (though not his motto 'Que sçay-je?', which does not figure on Montaigne's medal either, despite what is often said: in both cases it is the Greek keyword of the Pyrrhonians that appears). These various signs inside the text of the 'Apology' – as well as in the object world surrounding its composition – suggest that there is to be found, in someone so eclectic and independent in his thinking as Montaigne, an uncharacteristic degree of personal commitment to Pyrrhonism.

This commitment takes the form of support for the Pyrrhonians' understanding of – and appeal to – free-thinking. Montaigne voices support during his initial presentation of their school in a passage that was added in, and expanded after, 1588 (F 452–3, VS 504–5). Having described their extreme practice of doubt, he points out how far apart this sets them from other philosophers, for whom truth is, say, either green or yellow – whereas they maintain that they cannot be sure. Free-thinking, for the Pyrrhonians, is nothing other than the free exercise of doubt: they radically alter the thrust of the adage 'Plato is my friend but a greater friend is truth', not by discarding the idea of truth, but by doubting that it could ever be found and initiating a perpetual quest for it. We saw in chapter 2 above that, in 'Of the education of children', doubt is one of the two possible outcomes that Montaigne imagines for free-thinking. Here it is the only one left standing.

Having emphasized just how disquieting this outcome is to everyone but the Pyrrhonians themselves, Montaigne then reports their appeal to intellectual freedom as follows:

[B] Why, they say, since among the dogmatists one is allowed to say green, the other yellow, are they not also allowed to doubt? [...] And where others are swept – either by the custom of their country, or by their parental upbringing, or by chance – as by a tempest, without judgement or choice, indeed most often before the age of discretion, to such or such an opinion, to the Stoic or Epicurean sect, to which they find themselves pledged, enslaved, and fastened as to a prey they have bitten into and cannot shake loose – [C] *to whatever doctrine they have been driven, as by a storm, to it they cling as to a rock* [Cicero, *Academic Philosophy (Academica)*, II.3] – why shall it not be granted similarly to these men to maintain their liberty, and to consider things without obligation and without servitude? [C] *The more free and independent because their power to judge is intact* [Cicero, *Academic Philosophy*, II.3]. Is it not an advantage to be freed from the necessity that curbs others?

[B] Pourquoy ne leur sera il permis, disent ils, comme il est entre les dogmatistes à l'un dire vert, à l'autre jaune, à eux aussi de doubter? [...] Et, où les autres sont portez, ou par la coustume de leur païs, ou par l'institution des

parens, ou par rencontre, comme par une tempeste, sans jugement et sans
chois, voire le plus souvant avant l'aage de discretion, à telle out telle opinion,
à la secte ou Stoïque ou Epicurienne, à laquelle ils se treuvent hippothequez,
asserviz et collez comme à une prise qu'ils ne peuvent desmordre: – [C] *ad
quamcunque disciplinam velut tempestate delati, ad eam tanquam ad saxum
adhaerescunt* – [B] pourquoy à ceux cy ne sera il pareillement concedé de
maintenir leur liberté, et considerer les choses sans obligation et servitude?
[C] *Hoc liberiores et solutiores quod integra illis est judicandi potestas.* N'est
ce pas quelque avantage de se trouver desengagé de la necessite qui bride
les autres?   (F 452–3, VS 503–4)

Montaigne reports the Pyrrhonians' appeal with evident sympathy and
persuasive power: the passage continues, beyond the extract just quoted, in
the same vein for a further five rhetorical questions in a crescendo of support for the freedom to remain forever freed by – suspended in – doubt.

Note that this entire passage was added in and after 1588, as if
Montaigne felt able by then to strengthen the case for freedom of thought
in the 'Apology', thus counterbalancing the note of caution sounded in
the apostrophe to the princess in the middle of the chapter. The B-text
echoes the anti-authoritarian arguments put forward in 'Of the education of children' (I.26), and the highly physical metaphors in which these
arguments are couched, when Montaigne refers to the loss of intellectual
freedom that the young suffer when they find themselves walled in by
the opinions to which their education forces them to cling. It broadens
the focus of the earlier chapter, however, in seeing not only the education and upbringing of the young, but also the customs of the country
in which they grow up, and even chance, as so many bricks in the wall.
Notice that the hindrances to the free exercise of judgement mentioned
here – education, custom, and chance – are, as I suggested at the end of
the previous chapter, the three that Book I most consistently probes. It is
as if Montaigne were looking back here, in and after 1588, to the 1580 text
of Books I and II and detecting in its loose weave a recurring pattern of
preoccupations with the limits of and obstacles to free-thinking.

The C-text uses a quotation from Cicero and a further rhetorical question to press home the superlative claim that the Pyrrhonians, liberated
as they are from the need to rein in and confine their judgement to one
choice, are not just free in their thinking but the freest of them all: they
alone may freely range, in the zodiac of their own doubt, to places that other

philosophers, those bound and shackled by dogma, simply cannot reach. Montaigne goes on immediately after this passage to spell out the unassailable force this gives Pyrrhonist arguments; these are the same arguments, of course, he had used in his reply to Sebond's detractors. In presenting the Pyrrhonians' appeal to intellectual freedom with a considerable degree of personal support in this passage, then, he is also provisionally incorporating their exercise of free-doubting within his own method.

The impression given in these pages is that Montaigne has found in the ever-provisional and free-wheeling enquiry of Pyrrhonism a philosophy to match the informal mode of essaying as he has so far practised it. This has led many of his readers to see the 'Apology' as its author's philosophical manifesto. Many studies continue to talk of 'Montaigne's scepticism' as if this were a position, in some cases the defining intellectual position, to which he adhered: the distillation of his wisdom. The most influential of these studies remains Richard Popkin's ground-breaking history of scepticism, which was published first in 1960, then revised and expanded in 1979 and again in 2003. Popkin describes Montaigne as animated by a single intention in the 'Apology', namely, to unify the sceptical tendencies already present in sixteenth-century theology, philosophy, and science within what Popkin calls a total Pyrrhonist crisis. He claims that the 'Apology' brought the pre-modern intellectual world to an end, in a seismic epistemological shift, and proved to be 'the womb of modern thought, in that it led to the attempt either to refute the new Pyrrhonism, or to find a way of living with it.' He offers the reception of Montaigne as evidence to support his narrative: he declares that throughout the seventeenth and eighteenth centuries, Montaigne was seen not as 'a man off the main roads of thought, but as the founder of an important intellectual movement.' Montaigne claims his place in the pantheon of early modern thinkers, according to this account, as the father of modern scepticism. It is indisputable that Montaigne shows an unusual degree of interest in and support for Pyrrhonism in much of the 'Apology', and that the success of his book and its translations into other vernacular languages made available for educated readers of a middling sort across early modern Europe a set of sceptical arguments and phrases that had, up until that point, been the preserve of the learned. This is not the place for me to join the list of those who have in recent years contested or revised Popkin's thesis at length. I will simply observe that, in decisively reducing the essaying of a vast range of philosophical schools and doctrines in the 'Apology' to the expression of a single adherence, Popkin drains the chapter – and Montaigne's encounter with Pyrrhonism – of its adventure, straightens out the twists and turns it takes, subdues its antiperistatic volatility.

The most visible sign of that volatility is the unease that the chapter shows at its heart about the hold that Pyrrhonism itself appears to have taken over it. First introduced as a means to an end, that school's practice of extreme doubt seems to have outgrown its stated purpose and to have become the text's end in itself, subordinating Montaigne's independence of mind and distorting his chapter's apologetic framework along the way. Of what precisely, one is left wondering, is this chapter a defence?

A Fine Balance

Montaigne redresses the balance in two ways. First, he asserts his control over the Pyrrhonist material he has introduced. In a late addition inserted a few pages before the apostrophe to the princess, he pauses to claim that his caprices and attitudes are untutored, in other words that they are merely his own; it was only when he started looking for ways to make them appear more decent in public that he discovered, by accident, how closely they coincided with philosophical examples and ideas. He is, he exclaims with a flourish, a new figure: 'an unpremeditated and accidental philosopher' ('un philosophe impremedité et fortuite'; F 497, VS 546). There is a considerable irony to this remark given its setting – Montaigne's most sustained engagement with the Western philosophical tradition – but it is an irony that serves his purpose. It allows him to take his distance from the tradition of formal or (as Ann Hartle calls it) 'deliberate' philosophy, which he dislikes, and to dislodge Pyrrhonist arguments from the central position they were threatening to assume in the chapter by reimposing on them an instrumental role. It allows him, furthermore, to restate the idea that his purpose in writing his book is to record his way of seeing the world, to track a mind on the move, through the open-ended essaying method that is his own.

The method is not overrun by Pyrrhonist ideas but, on the contrary, is applied to them. Montaigne discards those he finds wanting and claims a share in those that pass the test by making them his own.

The interrogatively phrased 'Que sçay-je?' is only the most visible of the nearby instances in which he absorbs and recasts elements of Pyrrhonism in this way. It is for all the world as though Montaigne had foreseen what Popkin and many of his other readers would make of his encounter with Pyrrhonism and had decided to smuggle in an early reply to them: it is no more according to Pyrrho than according to me, as he might have put it here, since – as it turns out – he and I understand and see it in the same way.

The second way in which he redresses the balance is by inserting an apostrophe to the princess warning her of the risks that Pyrrhonist arguments carry. This is the first of the two about-turns in the S-curve that the chapter performs at its mid-point. Having earlier escaped the confines of an apologetic frame and adopted a freer mode, it now condemns that mode and reimposes the apologetic frame.

That about-turn moves the terrain on which the discussion is conducted from the provisional speculations of secular philosophy to the politics of security and constraint. It is not that Montaigne reverses his assessment of the force that Pyrrhonist arguments carry but that, precisely because of the unassailable force he recognizes in them, he places a restraining order upon their use. These are weapons of last resort, he says, because they destroy both sides of any argument – your own as well as your opponent's. We might think here of the weapons of mass destruction produced by the nuclear age in which we live. The metaphors Montaigne uses in this passage are similarly pregnant with violence: he adds in and after 1588 examples from military history of actual suicide missions involving swords and gunpowder. These examples underscore the moral fear and loathing that now surround the thrilling force of Pyrrhonist arguments. One short sentence in the middle of the apostrophe captures this uneasy mixture: 'Here we are shaking the barriers and last fences of knowledge, in which extremity is a vice, as in virtue' ('Nous secouons icy les limites et dernieres clotures des sciences, ausquelles l'extremité est vicieuse, comme en la vertu'; F 509, VS 558). The thrill felt in the first half of the sentence gives way to a shudder of disapproval as the extreme force of Pyrrhonist arguments is identified as a vice. These arguments are also associated with innovation, a term last used at the beginning of the chapter to condemn the theology of Luther and the erosion of religious belief it has brought about (F 388, VS 439), so that some of the moral opprobrium first attached to that theology seems now to besmirch the practice of Pyrrhonist doubt. Montaigne probably has both Reformation theology and Pyrrhonist doubt in mind when he declares to the princess his own irritation at all forms of innovation that stray beyond the bounds of custom: 'All deviant ways irritate me' ('Toutes les voyes extravagantes me faschent'; F 509 (translation modified), VS 558). The Pyrrhonians might justifiably reply that they peacefully observe the existing laws and customs, since they doubt that there is sufficient evidence to adhere to (let alone establish) any alternative, a point that Montaigne made in his initial presentation of the school (F 455, VS 506). The advice he now offers the princess is, for all that, unequivocal: use the customary arguments, presented with moderation and temperance, to defend your Sebond and your Catholic faith; you tamper with the innovations of the Pyrrhonians at your peril.

Montaigne's advice to the princess does not, however, end there. The final sentence of our chosen passage ends the apostrophe by performing the second of the two turns in its S-curve. It lifts the restraining order it had placed on Pyrrhonist arguments and awards its author and a select band of others a licence to think with those arguments. Previously associated by their dangerous novelty with Reformation theology, they are now seen as a potential remedy to that greater ill, since they are powerful enough to neutralize the arguments of the Reformist doctors of divinity at court. This second turn in the argument establishes its course for most of the rest of the chapter: Montaigne returns to his earlier critique of human reason and continues appropriating Pyrrhonist strategies to that end for a further forty pages (VS 559–601, F 510–53). He does so, of course, with the apostrophe's moral alarm at the risks of those strategies fresh in the mind of the reader. For this reason it does indeed seem, as Terence Cave suggests, that the apostrophe to the princess looks two ways in the chapter and serves both as a kind of postface to the encounter with Pyrrhonism that precedes it and as a preface to the encounter that follows. Montaigne reimposes the apologetic framework at the very end of the chapter by placing there a 'most religious conclusion' in praise of an unchanging God who knows no beginning or end (F 553–6, VS 601–4). There is nothing to suggest that Montaigne's attitude towards this conclusion is any less sincere than his presentation of radical Pyrrhonist thinking. But the fact that he mischievously borrows his devout conclusion from one of his favourite pagan writers, Plutarch, can only remind us of the intrinsically dynamic character of the 'Apology', of its disconcerting ability to swerve from the straight and narrow when least expected.

The S-curve of the text that I quoted at the outset of this chapter is particularly visible in its treatment of free-thinking. The first half of the passage reverses the chapter's earlier support for the Pyrrhonians in their appeal to the liberty of unfettered thinking: it redescribes that liberty as a dangerous licence of the mind that must be constantly held within firm limits. At first, it seems that this is merely a local reversal of values, since Montaigne is complaining that this licence of thought and conduct afflicts nearly all of the best minds of his age. But the first sentence of the passage already made the observation one of general application, and this generality is preserved and even strengthened in the A-text that follows, making as it does a series of normative assertions about the free-wheeling fickleness of the mind and the steps that human societies rightly take to control and regulate its extravagances. Liberty reappears in the guise of unbridled licence. Also making a reappearance here are laws and customs (including, this time, religion), educational precepts, and the other means listed earlier of keeping the mind in confinement. The difference from what went before is that this confinement is now met with warm assent in the sphere of study and learning as in all other things: 'People are right to give the tightest possible barriers to the human mind' ('On a raison de donner à l'esprit humain les barrieres les plus contraintes qu'on peut'). This assent is reinforced in the single sentence added to the passage after 1588:

> And there is no animal that must more rightly be given blinkers to hold its gaze, in subjection and constraint, in front of its feet, and to keep it from straying here or there outside the ruts that custom and the laws trace for it.

> Et n'y a point de beste à qui plus justement il faille donner des orbières pour tenir sa veuë subjecte et contrainte devant ses pas, et la garder d'extravaguer ny çà ny là, hors les ornieres que l'usage et les loix luy tracent.

The rhyme 'orbières' ('blinkers') / 'ornieres' ('ruts') imitates, at a phonetic level, the constraints under which the runaway horse of the mind described in 'Of idleness' (I.8) is now placed. Curbs and blinkers are seen not only as expedient but as the right response to the tendency of this erstwhile galloping Rosinante, when given the reins, to deviate from the norm. Free-thinking is seen here as an error of 'unbridled licence' that requires correction.

However, once the second turn of the S-curve has been performed and an exception made for the strategic use of Pyrrhonist arguments in extreme circumstances, the language of free-thinking reappears in a positive guise. The sentence that follows the end of our passage starts: 'Thus the liberty and wantonness of these ancient minds …' ('La liberté donq et gaillardise de ces esprits anciens …'; F 510, VS 559). That 'thus' ('donq') signals a return to the perspective on free-thinking first adopted when the chapter surveyed the various ancient traditions of secular philosophy and came to express support for that of Pyrrho (F 452–3, VS 503–4). The unbridled licence identified in the apostrophe has reverted to being a salutary liberty that the ancients enjoyed but that the present age, with its schools and the certainties of its common opinions, has stifled: the anti-authoritarian arguments put forward in 'Of the education of children' (I.26), repeated in the first half of the 'Apology' and appreciably strengthened there (as we saw earlier) by the 1588 and post-1588 additions, come back to the fore. These arguments are now directly addressed to the princess: Montaigne briefly calls on her to bear witness to the credit commonly given to palm-reading as one example of the alacrity with which their age will swallow any argument enjoying common currency (F 510–11, VS 559–60). His support for the Pyrrhonians soon returns, too, as he declares their infinite irresolution to be the most plausible position to take in relation to the truth (F 512, VS 561). The ability to call truth a better friend than Plato, while remaining in doubt about what that truth might be, is reinstated here as a thoroughly good thing. Free-thinking – the free-wheeling doubt of the Pyrrhonians in particular – once more requires personal cultivation and appropriation instead of public correction.

The reversal of perspective may seem as abrupt as it is radical. It has already been prepared, however, by a sentence added in 1588 to the middle of our text:

> Indeed there are few souls so orderly, so strong and wellborn, that they can be trusted with their own guidance, and that can sail with moderation and without temerity, in the freedom of their judgements, beyond the common opinions.

Certes il est peu d'ames si reiglées, si fortes et bien nées, à qui on se puisse fier de leur propre conduicte, et qui puissent, avec moderation et sans temerité, voguer en la liberté de leurs jugements au delà des opinions communes.

That opening 'Indeed' ('Certes') suggests that the sentence is going to confirm and amplify Montaigne's recent negative assertion, in the A-text at the beginning of our chosen passage, that licence of thought and conduct afflicts nearly all of the best minds of his age. In fact the sentence produces a more positive variation on the same theme. The conclusion to which it leads in the B-text, about the policing of minds, is still repressive: 'It is more expedient to place them in tutelage' ('Il est plus expedient de les mettre en tutelle'). But the policing of thought is seen merely as the expedient course of action, rather than the right one, and the reader's attention is now directed not to the unbridled licence of nearly all the best minds of the age but to the well-tempered liberty with which a few chart their sober and self-restrained course through the dangerous waters that lie beyond the common opinions. The emphasis has shifted. The text goes on after 1588, as was mentioned earlier, to strengthen its language of repression in applauding the attachment of blinkers to the runaway horse of the mind. Coming as it does in the middle of a remarkably authoritarian sequence, the 1588 sentence about the high-minded few shows that the apostrophe is even more complex in its argumentation and perspective than the image of an S-shaped curve suggests and that it is marked by momentary reversals of thought and tone, often – as here – belonging to separate chronological strata of composition. The reversal introduced in 1588, by achieving a fine if momentary balance between unbridled licence and absolute constraint, creates the conditions in which, for some at least, an art of free-thinking is glimpsed as a possibility.

The Happy Few

But who are the happy few capable of such an art? What kind of mind is able to treat Plato, let alone the truth, with such freedom?

Montaigne uses three adjectives here to describe such minds – 'orderly' ('reiglées'), 'strong' ('fortes'), and 'wellborn' ('bien nées') – and links them by means of the intensifying adverb 'so' ('si') to form a formidable trio of criteria: these are people 'so orderly, so strong and wellborn, that they can be trusted with their own guidance'. What distinguishes them from nearly all the best minds of the age is not, it appears, freedom of thought: the latter, too, have that 'rare excellence' and 'extraordinary quickness'. It is, rather, the ability to exercise control over their freedom of thought in the moral sphere and to proceed with moderation. This is an ability lacking in those who are incontinent in the licence of their opinions and conduct alike – and such people, Montaigne says in the second sentence of our text, account for nearly all of those who are capable of thinking for themselves. Moral self-restraint, then, is the bridle that the rider needs to place on the runaway horse. It is the quality that distinguishes liberty of thought from licence, liberty's secret sharer, its very own Mr Hyde. It is what shapes free-thinking into a well-tempered art.

That quality of self-restraint is certainly captured by the first two adjectives that Montaigne applies to the best free-thinking souls, 'orderly' ('reiglées') and 'strong' ('fortes'), but what about 'wellborn' ('bien nées')? Why should circumstances of birth matter? The two current senses of 'wellborn' in English (as of 'bien né' in French), in the words of the *Oxford English Dictionary*, are as follows: first, 'of good birth or lineage, of gentle blood', distinguished from the illborn and the ungentle; second, 'having the personal qualities naturally associated with good birth', 'noble in nature or character'. Those two senses, one social and the other moral, are available to Montaigne, and he may well not distinguish between them, thinking that self-restraint is 'naturally associated with good birth', as the *OED* seems to, or at least choosing to imply so on this occasion. He is, after all, talking to a princess! In the context, however, it seems most likely that he is predominantly using the term in its second, moral, sense to refer to souls equipped at birth with good qualities. It may be, indeed, that orderly, strong, and wellborn are not items in a list of three require-ments, but that the pair 'so strong and wellborn' ('si fortes et bien nées') is intended to qualify 'so orderly' ('si reiglées'), meaning that the orderliness of the well-tempered free-thinking few is the result of a moral strength that comes, at least in part, from inherited predispositions.

A further context for understanding why Montaigne calls these happy few 'wellborn' is suggested by their strong association with the rarefied world of classical antiquity. 'Wellborn' in this sense would mean something like 'born after the pattern of a better age than this'. The licentious and incontinent free-thinkers of the second sentence are explicitly marked as being of Montaigne's time. But no such temporal marker is attached to the wellborn few. The positive phrase referring to 'the freedom of their judgements' ('la liberté de leurs jugements') finds a strong echo a few sentences later when Montaigne, as has already been said, repeats the word 'liberté': 'Thus the liberty and wantonness of these ancient minds...' ('La liberté donq et gaillardise de ces esprits anciens...'). The lexical link is strong enough to suggest that Montaigne may be attributing to the happy few of his age the well-tempered liberty that flourished in ancient Greece and Rome.

The term 'wellborn' ('bien né'), when used in this context, belongs within an entirely different set of oppositions: it distinguishes, not the aristocrats of pre-Revolutionary France from the commoners, but the citizens or 'free-men' of an ancient democracy from the rest. Athens in the time of Plato and Aristotle offers the canonical example of such a democracy. All resident adult male Athenians were citizens of the *polis* – so the simplest baker and the smartest banker each had one vote – but by no means all residents were citizens: slaves, women, free foreigners ('metics'), and children were all excluded. A metic or a child suffered no more than a temporary exclusion: they might enjoy citizenship in another place or at another time. But slaves (considered to be inhuman objects of property) and women (considered to be defective, unreasoning versions of men) were unquestioningly and universally excluded from citizenship and the freedoms that accompanied it – free-thinking among them – on the grounds that they were incapable not only of independent judgement, but equally of friendship, which, as we will see in chapter 6 below, was held to be not a private matter for individuals of all kinds but rather, and exclusively, a bond between citizens of the *polis*. On both counts, then, the slaves and women of ancient Athens could never hope to become universal subjects or to call truth a greater friend than Plato. The republican theory of liberty, which became fundamental to Roman law and was later associated with Venice and the other city-states of Renaissance Italy, derives from the same view of citizenship. According to that theory, as Quentin Skinner puts it, 'the paramount distinction in civil associations is between those who enjoy the status of *liberi homines* or "free-men" and those who live in servitude.' That theory has clear implications for free-thinking, since what follows from it is that only the *liberi homines* could possibly claim *libertas philosophandi*. Being a free-man, while not a sufficient condition of free-thinking, is certainly a necessary one. Others need not apply.

Montaigne often shows, in the 'Apology' as elsewhere, a Renaissance humanist's nostalgia for the classical past and its great minds, noble deeds, and alpha males. The exclusion of slaves, women, and the rest in that past from citizenship's freedoms and responsibilities does not strike him in the same way that it does modern eyes. But his are not modern eyes, of course, and we would be doing him an injustice if we judged his attitudes and reactions according to the ethical and political standards of our age. He belongs to an age in which slavery was a common practice and women were treated as second-class citizens, in the sphere of learning as well as in society at large, and his way of seeing things is to a certain degree conditioned by those attitudes. He writes from the privileged position of being 'wellborn' in the first sense of that word – of gentle blood – and a man. In 'Of the inequality that is between us' (I.42: 'De l'inequalité qui est entre nous') he observes the quasi-republican liberty enjoyed in his age by wellborn men in France:

> In truth, our laws are free enough, and the weight of sovereignty scarcely touches a French nobleman twice in his life […] Anyone who wants to esconce himself by his hearth, and who can manage his house without quarrels and lawsuits, is as free as the Doge of Venice.

> A la verité, nos loix sont libres assez, et le pois de la souveraineté ne touche un gentil-homme François à peine deux fois en sa vie […] Qui se veut tapir en son foyer, et sçait conduire sa maison sans querelle et sans procès, il est aussi libre que le Duc de Venise.   (F 236, VS 266)

He is perfectly capable of expressing the prevalent attitudes of others in the same position. But he is equally capable of testing the foundations and limits of that position and of the attitudes that go with it – of subjecting these to a thought-trial – and of opposing certain opinions commonly held by others in his position: those, for example, concerning the inhabitants of the New World, in 'Of cannibals' (I.31) and 'Of coaches' (III.6: 'Des coches'), and, in 'On some verses of Virgil' (III.5: 'Sur des vers de Virgile'), those conditioning male attitudes towards women. We saw, at the end of chapter 1 above, a tension in Montaigne's sense of his entire literary project between the conservation of a stable position and a radical testing of that position. That tension also characterizes his ethical and political thought, I would suggest, and nowhere more strikingly than in the S-curves of the 'Apology'.

The chapter's account of who is capable of the art of free-thinking offers a case in point. Montaigne, as we have seen, says that this art was the invention of ancient minds: citizens of the *polis* to a man. He says, too, that practitioners of the art in his own age are vanishingly rare. His nostalgia for the classical past is keenly felt. It does not prevent him, however, from reworking ancient ways of thinking about free-thinking. His decision to attach no temporal marker to the sentence about the well-tempered few leaves ajar the possibility that their art may continue to exist in modern times. He appropriates and adapts to his own purposes the Pyrrhonians' freedom to doubt while also advocating that it needs to be surrounded by the strictest controls. In so doing, he offers no more than two cheers for free-thinking in the 'Apology', and thereby suggests that he himself is capable of sailing with the requisite moderation through its treacherous waters: that he is, in other words, capable of mastering the art. He makes the same suggestion, in the final sentence of our text, about its addressee, the anonymous princess, when he invites her in the last resort to use Pyrrhonist arguments against the Protestants at court. In social terms, a princess could of course hardly be in a more privileged position, but she is nonetheless a woman – so Montaigne has at least opened up to that extent the circle of free-thinkers as fixed by the great minds of ancient Athens and Rome.

He goes on to make room in the circle for others besides the princess and himself. These 'others' include his readers. This becomes clear in the following page of the chapter when Montaigne, returning to the language of essaying, states: 'I do not leave off sounding and testing what my powers cannot discover; and by handling again and kneading this new material, [...] I open up to whoever follows me some facility to enjoy it more at his ease' ('Ce que ma force ne peut descouvrir, je ne laisse pas de le sonder et essayer; et, en retastant et pétrissant cette nouvelle matiere, [...] j'ouvre à celuy qui me suit quelque facilité pour en jouir plus à son ayse'; F 511, VS 560). Free-thinking is seen here, in the middle of Book II, as an art to be continued by those who accompany his text in its afterlife.

5

Two Freedoms

Not long after the 'Apology for Raymond Sebond' (II.12), in which he presents the free-wheeling doubt of the Pyrrhonians as permitting an orthodox Catholic response to the heterodox innovations of Protestant theology, Montaigne places a short chapter devoted to an issue of freedom fundamental to religious conflict in general. 'Of freedom of conscience' (II.19: 'De la liberté de conscience') concerns the freedom to adhere to a faith other than the established or dominant one. The alternative faith in question is that of the Protestant Reform movement within Western European Christianity. The freedom of belief that might be available to such a movement is not to be confused with freedom of thought in the sphere of religion, whereby one claims independence of any church or creed, with, that is, freedom *from* belief. Nowhere in 'Of freedom of conscience' does Montaigne consider that possibility: his headline theme is not freedom from belief but the freedom to believe otherwise. Related as it is to movements of Reformation and Counter-Reformation across Europe during this period, freedom of conscience is one of the cardinal early modern freedoms, perhaps the most fragile and contested of them all. Why support this kind of freedom? What are its likely effects? Is it a principle to which a society should aspire in the first place?

In examining Montaigne's approach to these questions, I suggest in what follows that for him, freedom is more than just a policy towards alternative creeds: it is also the cast of mind that we see at work in the chapter 'Of freedom of conscience' itself, an anti-authoritarian and anti-partisan way of thinking that he brings to his headline theme, and which he attempts to cultivate in his readers. We saw, at the end of the previous chapter, how in his 'Apology for Raymond Sebond' Montaigne imagines free-thinking as an art he hopes will be continued by those who follow him in the afterlife of his text. In 'Of freedom of conscience', I want to argue, he puts his readers through what might be called a warm-up exercise in that art. He does so by subjecting them to a thought-trial of their own in order to see whether they are capable of upholding freedom of conscience in their reading of the chapter. The only chapter of the *Essais* to include the word 'freedom' ('liberté') in its title contains, in other words, not one but two freedoms. Their interplay raises the dizzying possibility that the chapter might be an essaying of freedom: an attempt to think with freedom about freedom of conscience. I think that the chapter is just such an attempt, but that it also upsets the excessive neatness of that formulation, revealing in various ways how difficult a thing freedom is to live and think by: its fragility and peril as a policy and a cast of mind alike.

Contemporary Troubles

The chapter opens with a series of reflections on the distortions that thoughts and deeds suffer when they fall prey to the partisan dictates, the passionate intensity, of religious zeal. These reflections are initially made in the most general terms. The first sentence reads: 'It is usual to see good intentions, if they are carried out without moderation, push men to very vicious acts' ('Il est ordinaire de voir les bonnes intentions, si elles sont conduites sans moderation, pousser les hommes à des effects très-vitieux'; F 615, VS 668). The mention of 'moderation' and its lack puts us in mind of the apostrophe to the princess, examined in the previous chapter, in which Montaigne describes the few capable of sailing with 'moderation' and without temerity in the freedom of their judgements. 'Of freedom of conscience' confronts us, at its outset, with the opposite of these happy few: the many who act with a lack of moderation and on the promptings of a judgement distorted by zeal. It is immediately clear that the point of view adopted in the chapter will be contrarian, given over to criticism of those with whom one might be otherwise inclined to agree, but the field of reference remains at this stage general. Montaigne goes on, in the sentences that follow, to specify the two main points of temporal reference for his reflections throughout the chapter: present-day civil-war-torn France, in which he criticizes the zeal of certain of his fellow Catholics, and the period of early Christianity in the Roman Empire, particularly during the reign of the so-called 'apostate' emperor Julian (331–63 CE), in which he criticizes many early Christians and their supporters for the same partisan lack of moderation in their thoughts and deeds.

It is no surprise that he should start with the long-running and, for him at the time of writing, ongoing wars between Catholics and Protestants in France: they are at the heart of the politics of the age in which he lived.

Montaigne was nearly 30 when the first major battle between the two sides took place, at Dreux on 19 December 1562, an episode on which he reflects in 'Of the battle of Dreux' (I.45: 'De la bataille de Dreux'). The spirit of moderate evangelical reform that had characterized the initial mainstream reaction in France to the growth of Lutheran Protestantism in Germany was, by then, a distant memory. The French humanists who, inspired by the example of the Dutch humanist Erasmus, had promoted non-schismatic reform in the 1520s under the patronage of Marguerite de Navarre (1492–1549), sister to King François I (1494–1547), were dead. French Protestantism had changed under the radical influence of the schismatic French exile in Geneva, Jean Calvin (1509–64), and the infusion of Calvinism in France (or Huguenotism, as it was often called) was particularly strong in the towns of the South, including Bordeaux, where Montaigne held the office of magistrate in the *Parlement* from 1557 to 1570 and of Mayor from 1581 to 1585. The attitude of the French crown towards the ever-strengthening Huguenot minority vacillated between repression and reconciliation throughout the second half of the century. The death of François I's son Henri II (1519–59) after a freak jousting accident triggered a power struggle between the noble families of Guise, Bourbon, and Montmorency for influence at the heart of government. Since those families represented different tendencies in the struggle between Catholics and Huguenots, the conflict in France was fuelled by an explosive mixture of religious conflict and political rivalry, as is often the case in such situations. Henri II's queen consort Catherine de Médicis, who ruled France as regent from 1560 to 1574, first sought reconciliation with the Huguenots: under the guidance of her moderate chancellor Michel de l'Hospital (1505?–70), she issued in 1562 the Edict of January, which permitted Huguenots freedom of conscience and a limited freedom to practise their cult in the privacy of their own homes. The reaction of hardline Catholics, led by the house of Guise, was swift and deadly: in March 1562, a Huguenot congregation was massacred at

Vassy, and the civil wars began with the battle of Dreux in December of the same year.

The civil wars continued on and off until the last years of the sixteenth century. They touched Montaigne closely: Montaigne the place – since southwest France, with its strong Huguenot sympathies, was a theatre of the conflict – as well as Montaigne the man. He makes his basic allegiance clear throughout the *Essais*: in the second sentence of his chapter 'Of freedom of conscience', for example, he declares the best side to be that which maintains the established religion and government of the country, in other words, the Catholic majority. But he lived alongside Huguenots, in his region and even in his family, and remained on good terms with them.

What, then, was Montaigne's political position? This question has long divided commentators, with some pronouncing him a conservative and others a liberal, their aim being more often than not to press the great man into the service of their own cause. Montaigne's desire to protect and sustain the established order of things can make him look like a strict conservative; his corrosive analysis of that order as being based on mere convention – and often damaging to the individual – can make him look like a radical liberal. Neither tag makes much historical sense when applied to Montaigne, in truth, as Peter Burke has shown. The apparently contradictory so-called 'conservative' and 'liberal' elements in his thinking, meanwhile, coexist in the ancient philosophical traditions that interested him: stoics tend to emphasize the duty of submission while also laying bare the illusions of public life, for example, and Pyrrhonists systematically call all matters of opinion into doubt while following the laws and customs of the place in which they live. Montaigne knew all this. His politics are pragmatic and moderate, in keeping with his desire to shore up the established order against the prospect of something worse, and he appears to have attempted to steer a middle course through the civil wars. Allied with the *Politiques* – a loose confederacy of moderate Catholics and Protestants united by no identifiable political agenda other than their desire to preserve the state against the partisan conflicts of the Bourbon-led Huguenots and the Guise-led Catholic hardliners – Montaigne acted at various times as a mediator between the two opposing sides. He served as an unofficial adviser to Henri de Navarre in various capacities and, after the assassination of Henri III (1551–89), supported the Protestant Bourbon king's claim to the throne of France even before his conversion to Catholicism. He lived to see Henri de Navarre become Henri IV of France in 1589. But it was only in the years following Montaigne's death in 1592 that the civil wars came to an end. In 1593, Henri IV finally converted to Catholicism, seizing the initiative and reunifying France in the process; in 1595, the Pope absolved Henri IV; and in 1598, Spain relinquished its claim on the French throne in favour of Henri IV, who in April of the same year imposed the Edict of Nantes, which instituted on a lasting basis freedom of conscience, full civil rights, and a wide degree of freedom of cult for Huguenots.

The civil wars are an indispensable contemporary context for understanding 'Of freedom of conscience'. It is generally thought, although Montaigne does not explicitly refer to it, that the immediate context for the chapter, composed around 1578 and first published in 1580, is the 1576 Edict of Beaulieu, and that, when he refers to 'our kings' ('nos Roys') in that chapter, he has in mind the Edict's architects, Henri III of France, Henri de Navarre, and Henri III's younger brother François d'Alençon (1554–84), otherwise known as 'Monsieur', a leader of the *Politiques*. The Edict of Beaulieu was an attempt to repair the damage done to national unity by the massacres of Huguenots in 1572, most notoriously on 24 August of that year, St Bartholomew's Day. It condemned the massacres and went further than the Edict of January 1562 in recognizing freedom of conscience and also of cult (outside Paris) for the Huguenots. It was more liberal in its provisions than the 1598 Edict of Nantes that eventually replaced it. It had beneficial effects for the Huguenots: the Peace of Bergerac in 1578 and the Peace of Fleix in 1580, in the signing of which Montaigne directly participated, repeated its guarantees. It strengthened, for a short while, the position of the *Politiques*. But it provoked bitter resentment among hardline Catholics who, under Henri de Guise (1550–88), promptly formed a national League to combat the Huguenots. The Edict was an attempt at reconciliation, in other words, that proved to be deeply divisive. Montaigne reflects on it in the passage that ends 'Of freedom of conscience', which I will later examine in some detail, when he refers to a recent provision of 'our kings'. The reference to a recent past makes it more likely that he is talking of the Edict of Beaulieu than of, as has sometimes been suggested, the Edict of January 1562. It is striking that, in later years, Montaigne refrains from altering or adding to the account that he gives of the Edict in 'Of freedom of conscience', as he might have well done, when he could have considered its effects with hindsight. It is as though he wished to preserve the advent of freedom of conscience – and the response it elicited – in all its contextual freshness and ambiguity.

The Truth about Julian

Sandwiched between the opening reference to France's contemporary troubles and the final part of the chapter, in which Montaigne treats directly the theme of freedom of conscience, is a substantial account of Julian the Apostate and his place in history. Nephew of the first Roman emperor to espouse Christianity, Constantine the Great (272?–337 CE), Julian was Roman emperor from 361 to 363. On the death of Constantine in 337, his son Constantius II (317–61) had all of the other pretenders to the empire assassinated, including Julian's father and eight of his relatives. Julian was spared and, in keeping with the new orthodoxy of the imperial elite, raised as a Christian. Constantius II eventually sent him to Gaul on a military campaign. Its success proved the making of Julian. He was proclaimed emperor by his troops in Gaul in 360 and, on the death of Constantius II the following year, he took sole charge of the Roman Empire. He announced, shortly thereafter, his reversion to the traditional polytheistic beliefs and practices that had obtained in the empire for some eight centuries until Constantine had replaced them, a few decades earlier, with his Christian innovations. Or, to put the matter according to a Christian perspective, Julian had no sooner come to power than he announced his conversion to paganism. Taking precisely this view of events, his early Christian detractors, St Cyril of Alexandria (375?–444), author of a virulent tract *Against Julian* (*Contra Julianum*), and Theodoret of Cyrrhus (393?–458?) chief among them, lent Julian his epithet, 'the Apostate'. Among Christians, at least, it stuck.

The pagan Roman emperor who introduced freedom of conscience across his empire was a figure of considerable historical interest in sixteenth-century France. Other contributions to the debate about the policy of freedom of conscience, from the time of the Edict of January 1562 onwards, cite Julian, either – in the case of the *Politiques* – as a ruler admirable for having tolerated religious difference in the interests of peace in his empire, or – in the case of Huguenot writers such as Theodore

Beza (Théodore de Bèze) (1519–1605) and Innocent Gentillet (1535–95?) – as an atheist and tyrant who introduced of freedom of conscience as a Machiavellian policy designed to divide and rule. There was a different Julian for each faction in the French civil wars, in short, each reflecting its attitude towards the policy of the French crown. Historians of the same period argued about which was the true Julian. In chapter four of his work on approaches to the writing of history, *The Method of History* (*Methodus ad facilem historiarum cognitionem*) of 1566, Jean Bodin (1530–96), a humanist scholar allied with the *Politiques*, offers Julian as an example of a figure ill-served by those Christian historians who are blinded to the emperor's qualities by his faults. Montaigne, who seems to have read Bodin's *Method* shortly before composing 'Of freedom of conscience', shares with him an interest in the challenges that Julian poses as an object of historiography. It is clear, then, that in choosing to think about recent developments in French politics by means of history, in particular the case of Julian, Montaigne is deliberately intervening in a contemporary debate. I suggest that he treats Julian distinctively in that he makes the controversial Roman emperor the point of intersection between the chapter's two freedoms: freedom of conscience and freedom as a cast of mind; for only after he has presented Julian as the object of judgements vitiated by zeal and therefore lacking freedom – as a victim of partisan thought – does he turn to the emperor's policy of freedom of conscience.

The case of Julian is first introduced as an illustration of, and corrective to, the chapter's opening observation about the distortions that truth suffers at the hands of the zealous and the partisan. Having taxed some of his fellow Catholics with passion-fuelled temerity, Montaigne widens his criticism to include Christians of the past, in particular those over-zealous early Christians who destroyed pagan books of all kinds. He clinches the point boldly: 'I consider that this excess did more harm to letters than all the bonfires of the barbarians' ('J'estime que ce desordre ait plus porté de nuysance aux lettres que tous les feux des barbares'; F 615, VS 668). The zealots of 'our' religion, as Montaigne calls it, are responsible for having caused unjustifiable and irreparable material damage to learning and letters. Montaigne might have argued, as many Christian commentators did, that, in destroying the fabrications of the pagans in this way, these zealots were in fact protecting the truth divinely revealed to them. He chooses, instead, to argue that they were responsible for a serious distortion of historical truth in lending false praise to the Roman emperors who helped their cause while universally condemning those who were hostile to it. Distortion of the truth, whether through excessive praise or blame, belongs among those very vicious acts to which good intentions, under the sway of immoderate passion, ordinarily lead. Montaigne's provocative assertion here is that the many over-zealous early Christians, rather than their pagan and barbarian contemporaries, were guilty of just such a distortion.

Julian is introduced at this point in the argument as an example of a Roman emperor excessively blamed by Christian historians. Montaigne, from the outset, places his portrait of Julian under the sign of a search for a truth about him that runs counter to the deepest convictions of Julian's opponents: 'He was, in truth, a very great and rare man' ('C'estoit, à la verité, un très-grand homme et rare'; F 616, VS 669). Much of the portrait is given to a list of Julian's many qualities and the anecdotes that bear them out: his virtue, the fruit of a philosophical soul, shown in his chastity and sobriety; the impartiality of his justice and his lack of cruelty towards Christians despite his opposition to their faith; and his preeminence in letters as well as arms. As the list turns towards his military virtues, it appears to take on the shape of a life of Julian, ending with his death, which he met (like all the best military leaders) on the field of battle, in the flower of his age, at thirty-one, and which has about it, says Montaigne, something of the demise with which the Theban Epaminondas (*d.* 362 BCE) met. This comparison is high praise indeed from Montaigne, as his chapter 'Of the most outstanding men' (II.36: 'Des plus excellents hommes') confirms, containing as it does a panegyric to Epaminondas as a military leader of exceptional virtue and the ideal statesman. The writer visibly leans against the excessive blame heaped on Julian by his Christian detractors.

There is more to Montaigne's portrait of Julian, however, than praise alone. Universal praise, as a response to the universal condemnation offered by Julian's opponents, would after all risk being *merely* contrarian – a revisionist exercise that was subject to an equal and opposite distortion of the truth – and that greater friend would have been lost. Julian certainly had vices, most notably in the realm of religion, where Montaigne's judgement is unequivocal: 'In the matter of religion he was bad throughout' ('En matiere de religion, il estoit vicieux par tout'; F 618, VS 670). He supports this judgement with examples of the superstitious beliefs and the infatuation with divination that stayed with Julian until the moment – and that reconciled him to the manner – of his death. There is a note of admiration to Montaigne's account of Julian's acceptance of death, but it is an admiration tinged with reserve, since it is clear that Montaigne considers that acceptance to have been the product of Julian's religious vices as much as of his philosophical virtues.

The impression given, then, is of a search on Montaigne's part for a truth about Julian that sits somewhere between immoderate praise and blame. Montaigne reveals in the interstices of his portrait something of how his search for that truth is conducted. When describing the emperor's dispensation of justice, he introduces the two main historians from which his portrait is drawn, Eutropius (*b.* 320 CE?) and Ammianus Marcellinus (330–95). In 369 Eutropius dedicated his brief introduction to eleven centuries of Roman history, the *Abbreviated History of Rome from its Beginning* (*Breviarium ab urbe condita*), to the eastern Roman emperor Valens, who ruled from 364 to 378. His history ends with events, including the reign of Julian (X.14–16), which he had witnessed. Ammianus Marcellinus' thirty-one books of *Chronicles of Events* (*Rerum gestarum libri*), published in the early 390s, were intended to serve as a continuation of the earlier history of Tacitus (56–120? CE) by covering Roman history of the period 96 to 378 CE. Only the last eighteen books, covering the years 353–78, survive. Ammianus draws on Eutropius and other historians as well as on his own experience in his account of Julian's life and reign (XV.8–XXV.4). His account, to which Montaigne is referring in the opening sentences of our chosen passage, is much longer than that of Eutropius, and even more favourable to Julian, although it also finds fault with him: Ammianus, though no more of a Christian than Julian, in particular criticizes the emperor's harsh treatment of them on more than one occasion (see, for example, XXII.9, 12 and XXII.10, 7).

How does Montaigne treat his two main sources? He stresses the proximity of Eutropius and Ammianus Marcellinus to the events that they describe: 'We have two good historians who were eyewitnesses of his actions' ('Nous avons deux bons historiens tesmoings oculaires de ses actions'; F 616, VS 669). Reliable personal testimony is important to Montaigne in his search for truth across a range of topics. In 'Of cannibals' (I.31), he requires from travellers' accounts of the New World the same qualities, commenting: 'We ought to have topographers who would give us an exact account of the places where they have been' ('Il nous faudroit des topographes qui nous fissent narration particuliere des endroits où

ils ont esté'; F 184, VS 205). The man from whom he claims to derive his
information about the New World has the same advantage as Eutropius
and Ammianus: he has seen that of which he speaks. Montaigne stresses
that his eyewitness source in 'Of cannibals' is all the more reliable in that
he is simple enough to be wedded to no theory or conviction. But he does
not say the same of the two historians on whom he draws in 'Of freedom
of conscience'. While Ammianus' remarks about Christians attracted
conflicting interpretations in the early modern period, Montaigne was
by no means alone in considering them to be the words of someone
genuinely sympathetic to the plight of the Christians in Julian's empire,
and he immediately spells out what he sees as Ammianus' pro-Christian
perspective: the Roman historian was, Montaigne says, 'well affected
to our side' ('bien affectionné à nostre party'; F 616, VS 669). He uses
his two historical sources to correct what he considers to be distortions
about Julian propagated by his enemies: he dismisses the idea that Julian
behaved with cruelty towards Christians, for example, by pointing out
that no such episode appears in Ammianus who, given his perspective,
would have hardly neglected to mention it; he gives the same reason,
later, for rejecting as apocryphal – a move that, as we will see in chapter 7
below, attracted censure from a 1581 Vatican report – the idea that Julian,
on receiving his death-wound, acknowledged that Christ had defeated
him (VS 671, F 618). Montaigne turns among the various sources at his
disposal to those that he can most trust. But he never awards them an
absolute trust.

He chooses, instead, to think with them, comparing them against
one another and other sources, seeking to build up a picture that is
consistent and probable. He appeals directly on two occasions to a particular notion of probable truth, that which is 'vray-semblable' because
founded on the authority of a witness, in order to moderate the stories
told about Julian: it is probable, he says, that Ammianus would not
have neglected to mention Julian's cruelty, had such cruelty been in
evidence, and it is more probable that Julian merely feigned Christian
belief until he became emperor than that he was guilty of true apos-
tasy. In that last instance, Montaigne makes no appeal to his sources,
presenting the probable thought as his own: 'This theory seems to
me more likely' ('Cette opinion me semble plus vraysemblable'; F 618,
VS 670). The use of a first-person perspective adds here to the image
of Montaigne thinking with history, searching for a truth about Julian

that he knows can only ever be probable, but passionately committed to that search nonetheless.

A Puzzle and a Question

Montaigne continues to think with history in the final part of the chapter, but the direction of his thinking alters as he comes, finally, 'to the purpose of his theme', freedom of conscience. 'Of freedom of conscience' ends thus:

> And to come to the subject of my discussion, he [Emperor Julian] had incubated paganism, says Marcellinus, for a long time in his heart; but because all his army was composed of Christians, he dared not reveal it. Finally, when he saw himself strong enough to dare to proclaim his will, he had the temples of the gods opened and tried in every way to set up idolatry. To attain his effect, having found the people in Constantinople at odds and the prelates of the Christian Church divided, he had them come to him at the palace and earnestly admonished them to lull these civic dissensions and urged that each man should serve his own religion without hindrance and without fear. This solicitation he made very urgently, in the hope that this complete freedom would augment the schisms and factions that divided them and would keep the people from uniting and consequently strengthening themselves against him by their concord and unanimous understanding; for he had learned by experience, from the cruelty of some Christians, that there is no beast in the world so much to be feared by man as man. Those are very nearly his words. Wherein this is worthy of consideration, that Emperor Julian uses, to kindle the trouble of civil dissension, that same recipe of freedom of conscience that our kings have just been employing to extinguish it. It may be said, on the one hand, that to give factions a loose rein to entertain their own opinions is to scatter and sow division; it is almost lending a hand to augment it, there being no barrier or coercion of the laws to check or hinder its course. But on the other hand, one could also say that to give factions a loose rein to entertain their own opinions is to soften and relax them through facility and ease, and to dull the point, which is sharpened by rarity, novelty, and difficulty. And yet I prefer to think, for the reputation of our kings' piety,

that having been unable to do what they would, they have pretended to will what they could.

> Et pour venir au propos de mon theme, il [l'Empereur Julien] couvoit, dit Marcellinus, de long temps en son cœur le paganisme; mais, par ce que toute son armée estoit de Chrestiens, il ne l'osoit descouvrir. En fin, quand il se vit assez fort pour oser publier sa volonté, il fit ouvrir les temples des dieux, et s'essaya par tous moyens de mettre sus l'idolatrie. Pour parvenir à son effect, ayant rencontré en Constantinople le peuple descousu avec les prelats de l'Eglise Chrestienne divisez, les ayant faict venir à luy au palais, les amonnesta instamment d'assoupir ces dissentions civiles, et que chacun sans empeschement et sans crainte servist à sa religion. Ce qu'il sollicitoit avec grand soing, pour l'esperance que cette licence augmenteroit les parts et les brigues de la division, et empescheroit le peuple de se réunir et de for- tifier par consequent contre luy par leur concorde et unanime intelligence; ayant essayé par la cruauté d'aucuns Chrestiens qu'il n'y a point de beste au monde tant à craindre à l'homme que l'homme. Voylà ses mots à peu près: en quoy cela est digne de consideration, que l'Empereur Julien se sert, pour attiser le trouble de la dissention civile, de cette mesme recepte de liberté de conscience que nos Roys viennent d'employer pour l'estaindre. On peut dire, d'un costé, que de lácher la bride aux pars d'entretenir leur opinion, c'est espandre et semer la division; c'est prêter quasi la main à l'augmenter, n'y ayant aucune barriere ny coerction des loix qui bride et empesche sa course. Mais, d'autre costé, on diroit aussi que de lascher la bride aux pars d'entre- tenir leur opinion, c'est les amolir et relácher par la facilité et par l'aisance, et que c'est émousser l'éguillon qui s'affine par la rareté, la nouvelleté et la difficulté. Et si croy mieux, pour l'honneur de la devotion de nos rois, c'est que, n'ayans peu ce qu'ils vouloient, ils ont fait semblant de vouloir ce qu'ils pouvoient.   (F 618–19, VS 671–2)

Montaigne approaches the issue of freedom of conscience here by jux- taposing two examples, the one from the Roman past, the other from the present of French politics. That juxtaposition contains an interpre- tative puzzle about the past and raises a political question about the present. The puzzle has to do with Julian's motivation: to what end did he instigate freedom of conscience as a policy? The question has to do with the recent introduction of the same policy in France: is it to be welcomed?

While the puzzle and the question emerge from Montaigne's thinking with history, he chooses to resolve neither, putting them instead to the reader. We saw in chapter 2 above that two steps are required if one is to call truth a greater friend than Plato and the other authorities on a given topic: the first is to understand what those authorities mean by what they say about the topic, on their own terms, whereas the second involves trying out what they say against one's own sense of where the truth lies. We saw, too, that in 'Of the education of children' (I.26) Montaigne imagines and prepares for the situation in which, for his reader, the privileged inter-locutor – and the friend to be discarded as and when the truth demands it – will be not Plato but Montaigne himself. If 'Of freedom of conscience' can be read as a warm-up exercise in the art of readerly free-thinking, it is because the chapter takes the reader through both stages, requiring us first to consider what its author might mean by what he says – which is the puzzle – and then to think for ourselves about the question he raises.

The puzzle is posed by the last anecdote about Julian that Montaigne takes from Ammianus Marcellinus and that he relates in our passage. It takes, as André Tournon says, the form of a discordant utterance. Ammianus' account of Julian's policy of freedom of conscience as Machiavellian, which Montaigne appears to accept here, flatly contra-dicts his earlier characterization of a great and just ruler in the chap-ter. Ammianus says that Julian implemented his policy of freedom of conscience not to calm the conflicts between Christians in his empire but to exacerbate those conflicts in order to divide and rule. He offers a detailed account of Julian's public words and deeds but also of his secret, unvoiced, motivations as emperor: his single-minded determination to see paganism restored, his hope that the licence of complete religious liberty would achieve this restoration, and his abiding fear of Christian cruelty. Purposive clauses – such as 'to attain his effect' ('pour parvenir à son effect') and 'in the hope that' ('pour l'espérance que') – underscore the connection between Julian's secret intentions and his public deeds. This account is marked out in the first sentence as being the direct speech of Ammianus, but it continues for a further three sentences without the repetition of any such marker, and sixteenth-century French has of course no system of direct quotation marks. The effect created is akin to that of Flaubertian free indirect style whereby, in this case, it is temporarily unclear whether the character or narrator – Ammianus or Montaigne – is speaking. This is a common feature of the practice of citation in the *Essais*. On this occasion, however, the fusion of voice is only temporary: Montaigne, in using a formula of authentication – 'Those are very nearly his words' ('Voylà ses mots à peu près') – to signal that the passage of more-or-less direct speech is over, retrospectively insists upon the distinctness of Ammianus' speech from his own. This insistence, as André Tournon points out, is unusual in the *Essais* as a whole, and marks a departure from Montaigne's practice elsewhere in this chapter, where he silently reproduces Ammianus' testimony of Julian in his portrait of the emperor. Why the insistence? One might assume that Montaigne is seeking to distance himself from Ammianus' account of Julian's motivations in order to take issue with it. In the sentence of commentary that follows the passage of direct speech, however, he appears to do the opposite and to accept that account. We are left with a puzzling discordance.

What is to be done with it? Does Montaigne really accept Ammianus' portrayal of Julian as a Machiavellian liberator of conscience in a pagan cause? The choice is ours. One option would be to acknowledge the authority of Ammianus and to see the discordance as internal to Julian: the expression of a pagan emperor's hostility towards the faith he rejected, a religious hostility – paranoia, even – that vitiated his political rule, despite his qualities as emperor celebrated by Eutropius and Ammianus. Another option would be to dispute in this respect the testimony of Ammianus, citing the reason given earlier by Montaigne himself that the Roman historian was 'well affected to our side', and to see the discordance as internal to Ammianus: the expression of a pro-Christian commentator's hostility towards the apostate emperor, a partisan hostility that vitiated his writing of history, despite his other qualities as a historian celebrated by Bodin. A third option would be to see the discordance as internal to Montaigne: a reversal of perspective in which the earlier excessive praise of Julian veers towards an equally excessive blame. We saw in the previous chapter how abruptly the argument changes direction and turns back on itself in the 'Apology for Raymond Sebond' (II.12). In 'Of vanity' (III.9), Montaigne alludes to this feature of his own thinking and writing, saying that its purpose is not simply to meander at greater length and adding: 'Besides, perhaps I have some personal obligation to speak only by halves, to speak confusedly, to speak discordantly' ('Joint qu'à l'adventure ay-je quelque obligation particuliere à ne dire qu'à demy, à dire confusément, à dire discordamment'; F 927, VS 995–6). He does not spell out or make it clear what that obligation might be – the sentence is, in this sense, self-confirming – but it might be explained as an act of self-restraint in a dangerous age, a philosophical and literary response to the confusion and discordance of the political world, or the antiperistatic volatility of a mind – and a pen – on the move. It might be a mixture of those things that varies according to the context. Montaigne does not say. He emphasizes, instead, the extra work it imposes on a reader who wishes to understand what he means, that is, the kind of reader he is looking for.

Seen in this way, the discordance becomes a matter for the reader, an essaying of their judgement. Tournon says that 'Of freedom of conscience' stages a 'virtual trial' of Julian, in which Ammianus plays the role of star witness, and that we – playing at judges – would have good reasons for ruling this part of his testimony out of court on several grounds: it makes an uncorroborated claim about Julian's secret intentions, one that goes against everything otherwise known about the accused, and which cannot be materially proven. It is worth pointing out that there is one other uncorroborated claim about secret intentions to be found in this passage: the one made in the final sentence by Montaigne in relation to 'our kings'. That claim, which is charitable about the intentions of the kings while explicit about the limits of their power, he phrases as nothing more than a subjective belief. It stands, therefore, as a silent reproach to the uncharitable claim that Ammianus presents as fact. Behind the virtual trial of Julian, then, lies a thought-trial to which Montaigne puts his reader: the judicial and the experimental senses of the word 'trial' here meet. What that thought-trial will reveal is whether the reader shows signs of the distortion that, as the first part of the chapter demonstrated, thoughts suffer when they fall under the sway of religious zeal; or whether the reader is capable of upholding freedom of conscience in finding an apostate innocent of the charge against him.

The discordance, whatever its cause, allows Montaigne to pose a question about freedom of conscience that reaches beyond the particular historical situation of Julian:

> Those are very nearly his words. Wherein this is worthy of consideration, that Emperor Julian uses, to kindle the trouble of civil dissension, that same recipe of freedom of conscience that our kings have just been employing to extinguish it.

Voylà ses mots à peu près: en quoy cela est digne de consideration, que
l'Empereur Julien se sert, pour attiser le trouble de la dissention civile, de
cette mesme recepte de liberté de conscience, que nos Roys viennent d'em-
ployer pour l'estaindre.

Notice that – in an odd shift of temporal sequence – Montaigne here
chooses to apply the verb 'se servir de' ('to use') to Julian in the present
tense whereas his earlier portrait of the emperor was a narration entirely
made up of verbs in the various past tenses. This choice does not by
itself resolve the discordance of Montaigne's sentence. But it suggests an
alternative reading: that he is wishing to move swiftly from his concrete
historical example about Julian to the more general statements that follow
about the effects that freedom of conscience may have in other cases, and
so extracts from Ammianus' account what is 'worthy of consideration',
suspending for this purpose the puzzle of its truth status. That puzzle
ceases to be of primary importance.

The next two sentences present the reader with a new question. It
appears, says Montaigne as he compares the past of early Christianity
with the recent past of Christian conflict, that the policy of freedom of
conscience may either spread division between different religious factions or, on the contrary, soothe it. In the one case, the argument is that
freedom of conscience removes the ability of the law to control religious
divisions, that liberty stokes the fires of conflict. In the other case, the
argument is that freedom of conscience transforms religious divisions
into legitimate differences, that liberty tempers the conflict. Which is it
to be? The symmetrical formulation of the two possibilities – in particular through the repetition of the phrase 'to give factions a loose rein to
entertain their own opinions' ('lascher la bride aux pars d'entretenir leur
opinion') – underscores their status as strict alternatives. Montaigne, in
presenting the choice between those alternatives to the reader, reaches
the second stage in his initiation of that reader in the art of free-thinking.
He does so not because he hovers, unable to choose, between the alternatives. There is no Pyrrhonist suspension of judgement here or elsewhere
in 'Of freedom of conscience': the appeal to the notion of the probable
earlier in the chapter and in its final sentence, for example, is distinctly
foreign to Pyrrhonist modes of doubt. Montaigne knows on this occasion where his beliefs and engagements tend. But he knows equally well
that his readers have beliefs and engagements of their own and that those

of his contemporary readers in France will help to determine the reception given to the French crown's policy of freedom of conscience. If the thoughts and deeds of his compatriots are vitiated by religious zeal, whichever side of the conflict they are on, their new liberty will fan the flames; if they are able to think and live with freedom of conscience, the conflict will lose its intemperate heat, and the crown will have brought peace to the kingdom. The outcome of the policy – and therefore its meaning – is not in the hands of the rulers, let alone Montaigne's, but in the hands of his compatriots. All he can do is confront those compatriots – and his readers – with the question.

Montaigne's decision to present freedom of conscience in the form of a question open to debate, as we will see in chapter 7 below, attracted criticism from the 1581 Vatican report on the *Essais* prepared for the censors of the Roman Index. The report appears to take the view that the Roman Catholic Church had effectively answered the question once and for all by rejecting the policy of toleration. Montaigne, meanwhile, does not simply raise the question: he goes so far as discreetly to voice his support for the policy as instigated by France's rulers in recent times. He chooses to offer a direct view about the effects of the Edict of Beaulieu neither at the initial time of writing (around 1578) nor when revising his text over the next decade and more. Instead, in the final sentence of the chapter, he chooses to offer a view about what motivated the authors of the Edict to promote freedom of conscience: 'And yet I prefer to think, for the reputation of our kings' piety, that having been unable to do what they would, they have pretended to will what they could' ('Et si croy mieux, pour l'honneur de la devotion de nos rois, c'est que, n'ayans peu ce qu'ils vouloient, ils ont fait semblant de vouloir ce qu'ils pouvoient'). Unable to achieve what they wanted, namely to bring about the victory of the Catholic faith in France, they pretended to want what they were able to achieve – freedom of conscience for both sides – in order to secure peace in the kingdom.

Anyone wishing to see in Montaigne an early modern champion of the larger principle of tolerance or freedom of conscience – a kind of Voltaire *avant la lettre* – is in for a disappointment here. It was possible to advocate the principle in the period, and a few sixteenth-century humanists did, using either the ecumenical argument that the world's major religions are united by common tenets, despite their superficial differences, or the sceptical argument that all religious beliefs are characterized by such insurmountable uncertainty and diversity that to impose one religion would be quite wrong. Guillaume Postel (1510–81) puts forward the ecumenical argument in his work of 1544. Two French writers repeat that argument and advance its sceptical counterpart in the second half of the sixteenth century: these are the liberal Reformer Sebastian Castellio, in his published response of 1554 to the case of Miguel Serveto which I mentioned in chapter 2 above, and Jean Bodin, in a treatise composed in the late 1580s and unpublished before 1857, entitled *The Colloquium of the Seven about the Secrets of the Sublime* (*Colloquium heptaplomeres de rerum sublimium arcanis abditis*). These are important but rare sixteenth-century interventions in favour of freedom of conscience as a principle.

Other interventions are altogether more ambiguous, and none more so than that of Thomas More (1478–1535) in Book 2 of *Utopia* (1516), where his narrator includes, in his description of the ways and customs of a far-flung island from which he has just returned to Europe, an account of the religions in Utopia. The account starts with the assertion that, ever since the island's conqueror, King Utopus, first decreed it thus, it has been lawful on Utopia for everyone to follow the religion of their choosing and unlawful for anyone to proselytize with violence or zeal. Utopus's reasons for introducing and protecting freedom of conscience are portrayed as having been both pragmatic and principled: he wished not only to preserve peace, but also to further the cause of true religion, which he felt would best come to the fore in a society that admitted freedom of conscience and peaceful debate in the search for truth. The text's description of religious tolerance on Utopia is surrounded by the sharp ambient irony that the island is, as its name suggests in Greek, a 'no-place' as much as a 'good-place'. And the description conforms to the general pattern in *Utopia* described by Stephen Greenblatt, whereby 'freedoms are heralded, only to shrink in the course of the description'. We come to learn that those who believe the soul dies with the body are not considered human, for example, and that irreligious people are excluded from all honours and offices. Freedom *from* belief is not tolerated in Utopia, then, and even the principle of freedom of belief, having been announced with a flourish, is all but qualified out of meaningful existence.

There is no sign in his chapter on the topic that Montaigne even considers it possible to view freedom of conscience as a principle in which one might believe for its own sake. The absence of this possibility marks a limit to the horizon of Montaigne's thought, imposed, no doubt, by his response to the situation of civil war in which he writes. He treats freedom of conscience in a much more restricted way: not as a principle but as a policy, and a second-best policy at that, whose effects depend on how it is received by the warring factions. It is, for all that, a policy to which he lends his support. That support is cautiously phrased, offered by implication alongside his charitable interpretation of what motivated 'our kings' to institute the policy, but it is unmistakable.

Two verbal reminiscences of earlier chapters lend discreet emphasis to this support. The first is the suggestion made in the penultimate sentence about the purpose of allowing freedom of conscience: '[It] is to dull the point, which is sharpened by rarity, novelty, and difficulty' ('C'est émousser l'eguillon qui s'affine par la rareté, la nouvelleté, et la difficulté'). This suggestion links 'Of freedom of conscience' back four chapters to 'That our desire is increased by difficulty' (II.15: 'Que notre desir s'accroist par la malaisance'). Launched by a Pyrrhonist sentence, this chapter explores its headline proposition in threading its way through different realms of human experience, from erotic relations to religious and political conflict. In a long concluding passage added after 1588, Montaigne personalizes the discussion by explaining how he has protected his house from the ravages of the civil wars not by making a fortress of the place, but by allowing free and open access to it. Freedom dulls the desire that is sharpened by difficulty. The reminiscence between the two chapters suggests a parallel between Montaigne's domestic policy and the national policy of 'our kings'.

The second verbal reminiscence comes in the chiasmus that ends the chapter on a note of quiet irony about the limited power of those kings who, finding they could not do what they wanted, pretended instead to want what they could do. That very formula, taken from a play by the Roman comic dramatist Terence (195–159? BCE), *Andria* (II.1.305), appears in other sixteenth-century texts relating to the policies of the French crown, including the Edict of Beaulieu. It appears on one other occasion in the *Essais*: in the closing sentences of the chapter 'Of custom' (I.23). There Montaigne uses it in order to suggest, in cases of extreme necessity, an exception to his general rule that the commonly received laws of a country should be obeyed: 'For in truth, in these ultimate necessities where there is nothing more to hold on to, [...] it would be better to make the laws will what they can do, since they cannot do what they will' ('Car, à la verité, en ces dernieres necessitez où il n'y a plus que tenir, [...]

vaudroit mieux faire vouloir aux loix ce qu'elles peuvent, puisqu'elles ne peuvent ce qu'elles veulent'; F 108, VS 122). The formula, when repeated in the sentence that ends 'Of freedom of conscience', focuses attention on the dilemma in which kings, those who make the laws, find themselves at such moments: bound to act for the good of the country and yet powerless to do so without the consent and goodwill of their subjects. The politics of freedom appears here as the dark art of a near-impossible.

Montaigne expresses his view of what motivated 'our kings' in deliberately subjective as well as limited terms: 'And yet I prefer to think' ('Et si croy mieux'), he says, no more and no less. The reader is given the freedom to agree or disagree with his view of the Edict of Beaulieu and, beyond that restricted instance, to choose between the alternative effects, set out in the preceding sentences, that freedom of conscience may have in other times and other places. It is in the sentence that brings 'Of freedom of conscience' to an end that the chapter's two freedoms finally meet.

Two Middles

We have now explored two chapters in the middle of Book II – the 'Apology for Raymond Sebond' (II.12) and 'Of freedom of conscience' (II.19) – in which Montaigne reflects on and practises the art of free-thinking. I hope it has become clear just how perilous an undertaking that is in the dangerous and restricted age, marked by religious and political division and the shedding of blood, during which Montaigne lived out his days and wrote his book. That age, as he makes clear, forms an indispensable context for understanding both chapters and, in particular, the volatility and indirection with which they treat the notion of free-thinking. In them, Montaigne reaches out beyond the confines of his own historical moment, attempting to imagine what it was like to be alive and thinking in the past – particularly the ancient Greek and Roman past – and using the fragments that survive from that past as materials for a thought-experiment, an essay of his judgement, in the present. In both chapters, he expects his readers to do the same in turn, and provides the means for them to think with history in trying out the independence of their judgement on the questions he raises. We will see in the Epilogue to this book how some of his readers have made use of this invitation. For now, though, I want simply to point out the extra weight of meaning that the two chapters appear to take on by being in the middle of Book II and – once, from 1588 onwards, a third Book has appeared – of the *Essais* as a whole.

The two chapters have different claims for being in the middle. The sheer length of the 'Apology' – on which, as we have seen, Montaigne comments – means that it expands to fill the physical centre of Book II. It has been pointed out that, in the editions of 1580 and 1595 alike, the middle page of the Book is the one in which Montaigne, reviewing his presentation of Pyrrhonist arguments to the princess, declares: 'All deviant ways irritate me' ('Toutes les voyes extravagantes me faschent'; F 509 (translation modified), VS 558). The middle, on this showing, is occupied by the austere first turn in the S-curve of the apostrophe and the move Montaigne makes there against freedom of thought.

'Of freedom of conscience', meanwhile, is the median point of Book II's thirty-seven chapters. Various readers have observed that there is, arranged with exact numerical symmetry around this centrepiece, a pair of chapters in which Montaigne condemns cruelty in general and torture in particular – 'Of cruelty' (II.11: 'De la cruauté') and 'Cowardice, mother of cruelty' (II.27: 'Couardise mere de la cruauté') – and that this pair brings into sharp relief his praise of Julian in 'Of freedom of conscience' for the lack of cruelty he showed his Christian enemies (F 616, VS 669). The middle, on this showing, is reserved for Montaigne's advocacy of the need to preserve freedom of thought and deed in the midst of cruelty and zeal. An extension of the same argument says that 'Of freedom of conscience' corresponds to the centrepiece of the first Book, 'Of friendship' (I.28), in making a place at the heart of the second Book for a work of the lost friend Etienne de La Boétie, in this case, the *Memorandum* (*Mémoire*) of 1562 on Catherine de Médicis and Michel de l'Hospital's Edict of January 1562, a text that Montaigne refers to in 'Of friendship' (F 165, VS 184) and to which, Géralde Nakam suggests, he indirectly replies in 'Of freedom of conscience'. The middle of each of the two Books first published in 1580, on this reading, is occupied by Montaigne's reflections, in the company of La Boétie, on the politics of freedom.

Notice how, when such claims are made, the 'Apology for Raymond Sebond' (II.12) and 'Of freedom of conscience' (II.19) are thought to occupy not just the middle but also the symbolic centre of the text and its preoccupations. Those who place the 'Apology' in the middle also see that chapter's presentation of Pyrrhonism as a philosophical blueprint for its author's thinking. At the heart of the *Essais*, for such readers, is Montaigne the sceptic. Those who place 'Of freedom of conscience' in the middle, by contrast, see that chapter's treatment of cruelty and clemency as a major contribution to its author's central exploration of political and ethical themes. At the heart of the *Essais*, for these readers, is Montaigne the *moraliste*. The alternative middles could be – have already been – described in terms of free-thinking, with the 'Apology' offering two cheers for its art, and 'Of freedom of conscience' entangling its practice and that of its readers in the politics of religious difference. Readers are right to see both chapters as central to themes and modes of thinking that recur in the *Essais*, I would suggest, but something has gone wrong when they start arguing about which of the two chapters constitutes the middle of Book II. Neither chapter can claim a monopoly on this position, as should now be clear, and nor is the importance of being in the middle to be exaggerated in the first place. Book II does not contain, as Book I does, a place set aside for a centrepiece. The ordering of its chapters reveals, in some places, an architectural organization; in other places, however, the underlying principle is the serial recording of thought-experiments on a miscellany of topics. Chapter 1 above explored the closing pages of Book II's final chapter, 'Of the resemblance of children to their fathers' (II.37), which capture this unstable tension between a sense of textual symmetry and the recognition that the text and its author are caught in the onward flow of time. Book II is marked, as a whole, by a similar instability. If anything, it has two middles, and what this suggests is that the centre has ceased to hold.

6

Of Free-Thinking and Friendship

In true friendship, in which I am expert, I give myself to my friend more than I draw him to me. I not only like doing him good better than having him do me good, but also would rather have him do good to himself than to me; he does me most good when he does himself good. And if absence is pleasant or useful to him, it is much sweeter to me than his presence; and it is not really absence when we have means of communication. In other days I made use and advantage of our separation. We filled and extended our possession of life better by separating; he lived, he enjoyed, he saw for me, and I for him, as fully as if he had been there. One part of us remained idle when we were together; we were fused into one. Separation in space made the conjunction of our wills richer. This insatiable hunger for bodily presence betrays a certain weakness in the enjoyment of souls.

En la vraye amitié, de laquelle je suis expert, je me donne à mon amy plus que je ne le tire à moy. Je n'ayme pas seulement mieux luy faire bien que s'il m'en faisoit, mais encore qu'il s'en face, qu'à moy; il m'en faict lors le plus, quand il s'en faict. Et si l'absence luy est ou plaisante ou utile, elle m'est bien plus douce que sa présence; et ce n'est pas proprement absence, quand il y a moyen de s'entr'advertir. J'ay tiré autrefois usage de notre esloingement et commodité. Nous remplissions mieux et estandions la possession de la vie en nous separant: il vivoit, il jouissoit, il voyoit pour moy, et moy pour luy, autant plainement que s'il y eust esté. L'une partie demeuroit oisive quand nous estions ensemble: nous nous confondions. Cette faim insatiable de la presence corporelle accuse un peu la foiblesse en la jouyssance des ames.

(F 907–8, VS 977)

Montaigne's claim to be an expert in the art of true friendship, in the opening sentence of the passage from 'Of vanity' (III.9: 'De la vanité') quoted above, is striking in an author who consistently belittles his gifts and powers. It reasserts, as central to his character, the capacity for friendship already established in the much earlier chapter 'Of friendship' (I.28). Posterity has confirmed this claim of expertise: friendship is one of the themes with which he is most closely associated in the Western philosophical and literary tradition. What, though, is the 'true' friendship of which he speaks? On what grounds does he claim to be expert in it? What role does this claim play in a chapter whose headline theme is vanity? What bearing, if any, does his account of friendship in 'Of vanity' have on his relationship with the reader? Answering those questions will mean not only exploring that chapter but also setting it in the context provided by 'Of friendship'. What such a comparison shows is that the reflections on friendship in 'Of vanity' both return to 'Of friendship' and lead away from it in new directions. This, we will see, is true of other reflections on the same topic in the *Essais*. It means that a new question needs to be added to our list. How are we to understand the shifting of the author's position on friendship between his first and third Books?

'Of vanity' is emblematic of Book III in that it constitutes a criss-crossing extension of Montaigne's earlier thoughts on several topics. Its opening sentence establishes vanity as a property that defines the chapter's manner as well as its matter. This sets the tone for one of the most self-reflexive and freewheeling chapters of Book III – and indeed of the *Essais* as a whole – in which Montaigne presents his love of travelling and his writing as examples of a vanity that he acknowledges as his own. He then goes further than simple acknowledgement on his own account by claiming that this vanity is an intrinsic feature of what it is to be human. He presents this claim as a fruit of the labour of introspection that he enjoins others to undertake by quoting at the end of the chapter the famous and paradoxical – because shocking to common usage – motif of the Delphic oracle: 'Know thyself.' Along the way, he reflects on the rotten state of civil-war-torn France, the imminence of death, and the obligations of public service: all obstacles that might prevent him from climbing back in the saddle and setting off on another journey, were he not determined to maintain his freedom of movement.

Three Licences, in a Digression or Two

The various licences that he takes in the course of the chapter reflect that determination – to be free – in the domain of his own writing and thinking. I shall pause for a moment to single out three. The first is the licence that he takes in Book III to extend his discussion of topics already broached in Books I and II; the second is the licence he takes to continue thinking freely about those topics; the third is the licence he takes to roam from topic to topic. These three licences are variously interconnected and, when taken together, they characterize the mode of a text for which freedom of movement is as much a literary matter as a literal one. While present throughout, these licences rise to the surface of the text in 'Of vanity', where they become in turn an object of the chapter's reflection on its own processes.

Montaigne claims the licence to extend his earlier thoughts in the course of his third Book early in 'Of vanity' when he directly addresses the reader for the first time. Digressing from his description of the civil wars in France, he reflects on the development of his own writing, commenting in an aside: 'Reader, let this essay of myself run on, and this third extension of the other parts of my painting. I add, but I do not correct' ('Laisse, lecteur, courir ce coup d'essay et ce troisiesme allongeail du reste des pieces de ma peinture. J'adjouste, mais je ne corrige pas'; F 894, VS 963). Here is yet another example from Book III of the belated prefatory discourse – in which the writer disarms a potential objection by rehearsing it and appealing to the reader's goodwill – that reappears throughout the *Essais*.

We encountered earlier the idiomatic phrase 'coup d'essai', meaning a first attempt or specimen sample, during our discussion of the lexicon of essaying. Montaigne uses the phrase in the sentence just quoted to refer specifically to the thought-experiment he undertakes in 'Of vanity'. He immediately, thereafter, widens the same sentence's field of reference to include the 'third extension' of his 'painting', namely, Book III as a whole. When he declares in the following sentence that he is in the habit of adding new material to this portrait, we might well be reminded of the numerous interpolations and additions that he makes to the existing chapters of Books I and II. What he clearly has in mind here, however, is the writing of Book III. He declares that, when adding to his portrait, he does so without correcting what already exists. This is a partial truth – Montaigne does correct his text as well as adding to it, particularly after 1588, as the pages of the Bordeaux copy testify – but it is nonetheless an important one: it captures the open-ended extension of the *Essais* forwards into a new, third, Book.

Montaigne reflects on the third of his licences – to meander – towards the end of 'Of vanity'. After pointing out that he has digressed yet again from the subject he has in hand, he pauses to consider the manner of his digressions themselves, commenting in an aside to the reader: 'I go out of my way, but rather by licence than carelessness. My ideas follow one another, but sometimes it is from a distance, and look at each other, but with a sidelong glance' ('Je m'esgare, mais plutost par licence que par mesgarde. Mes fantasies se suyvent, mais par fois c'est de loing, et se regardent, mais d'une veuë oblique'; F 925, VS 994). His licence to meander is related to the other two he takes – to rehearse and revisit earlier topics, and to do so freely – since it also describes a particular movement of the mind and the text. But it is distinct from them, and more local, in that it governs the relationship between the sentences within a given chapter rather than his treatment of a particular topic or question across the three Books. He goes on to point out various features of his text associated with this licence to meander: the oblique relation between his chapter titles and their subject-matter; the leaps and gambols of his vagabond style and mind; and the greater length, compared with those of Books I and II, of the chapters in Book III (F 925–7, VS 994–6). He underlines the fact that the longer chapters, in offering him greater room to roam, require greater attention from the diligent reader wishing to follow him. He adds here the enigmatic sentence, mentioned in chapter 5 above, in which he suggests that he also writes longer chapters out of some unexplained personal obligation to speak elliptically, confusedly, and discordantly. His licence to meander is presented, finally, as a stroke against reason, which he brands 'kill-joy' ('trouble-feste'), and as a pleasurable use of the 'vanity' – his headline topic in the chapter – that underlies his thirst for freedom (F 927, VS 996).

It is in the middle of the chapter, framed by the earlier discussion of his licence to extend and the later discussion of his licence to meander, that Montaigne claims the second of his licences: namely, to think again, and to do so in all freedom. He does so particularly in relation to the topic of friendship. The adage 'Plato is my friend but a greater friend is truth', whose fortunes we have traced throughout this book, comes into its own here because it not only encapsulates the way in which Montaigne thinks and writes about friendship but also reveals, in its very formulation, that free-thinking is itself enmeshed in the thematics of true friendship. Everyone in the world can see things their way, but only a friend can also see things your way, and it is your difficult and precious task to do the same in return. Not only is that capacity for understanding shared in a true friendship, it is no less than what makes the friendship true, and it helps the friends undertake together the still harder task of making a greater friend of truth.

Montaigne undertakes this formidable challenge in his writings on the topic. These writings place him, from 'Of friendship' (I.28) onwards, in a free-thinking dialogue with Plato, Aristotle, Cicero, and other authorities on friendship in the Western classical tradition of ethical philosophy. They increasingly place him in the same dialogue with himself, or at least with the Montaigne that first wrote about friendship all those years ago, and whose search for the truth, it now appears, fell short on that occasion. When it comes to friendship, in other words, Montaigne takes in 'Of vanity' not only a licence to extend what he has already said but also, and all importantly, a licence to think again in the search for truth.

He extends to his readers the same licence. Every Don Quixote, after all, needs a Sancho Panza, and every Sancho Panza aspires to govern an isle, that utopia in which the governor's greatest duty is not to his friends but to the truth. From 'To the Reader' onwards, as I have suggested throughout this book, Montaigne maintains a direct relationship with his reader. That relationship, initially characterized in 'To the Reader' by an ideal of mutual openness, comes, in 'Of the education of children' (I.26) and 'Apology for Raymond Sebond' (II.12), to be shaped by the notion of free-thinking. As the writer of those two chapters exercises the freedom to think with or against Plato and other friends in the search for truth, he recognizes that the same freedom ought perhaps to be open to his readers, and that for them he may become one of the friends over whom the truth is to be preferred. The art of free-thinking as Montaigne practises it, in other words, implies befriending not just the thinkers of the past but also those of the present and future.

Befriending any stranger can be hard enough, involving the risk of misunderstanding on both sides, but how do you set about it when the stranger comes from that undiscovered country called the future? That question represents one major addition to Montaigne's treatment of friendship as it appears in 'Of vanity'. Friendship, in that chapter, is not simply a topic involving reflection on personal experience and the legacy of times past: it becomes a means of imagining the ideal relationship between author and reader. That friendship, as Montaigne sees it, is to be characterized on both sides by freedom of thought. One consequence of the friendship and free-thinking he attempts to cultivate in his readers is that they may end up disagreeing with him in their search for the truth. Montaigne accepts this possibility on condition that they read him, without prejudice, like a friend: like the kind of friend he is to Plato. If they choose to do otherwise, as we shall see, they risk a visit from his ghost.

The Friendship Archipelago

The passage from 'Of vanity' that I took as my point of departure is one instance in a prominent cluster of references to friendship in the chapter. And if one widens the focus, that cluster appears as one 'island' in an archipelago, scattered across the *Essais*, devoted to the question of true friendship.

Friendship, on its first appearance in 'Of vanity', is presented as a potential obstacle to free movement: it is a reason for staying at home rather than an incitement to travel. The topic surfaces when Montaigne reports how he justifies his love of travel to foreign parts. His justification is immediately political: he would rather leave a bad state for an unknown one than remain in a France torn apart by civil strife; and he likes making new friends abroad (F 903, VS 972–3). One accusation he commonly has to face as a result, he says, is that he neglects his relationships with his household and, particularly, with his wife. These relationships are seen as forms of friendship. He talks first of '[les] devoirs de l'amitié maritale', which Frame renders as 'the duties of marital love', thus losing the lexical connection between this and the other forms of 'amitié' ('friendship') of which Montaigne goes on to speak in relation to his family and other members of his household (F 905–6, VS 975). The gist of his response to the charge of neglect is contained in our passage (F 907–8, VS 977). Montaigne moves on in the following paragraphs to consider, as further potential objections to his travels, his old age and the imminence of death (F 908–19, VS 977–88). One might expect the theme of friendship to disappear from view at this point. No sooner has he set out his attitude towards dying, however, than he undertakes two important digressions on the subject of his writing (F 911–12 and 913–14, VS 981 and 982–3) – as though the prospect of his demise irresistibly brought to mind the question of his literary achievements and posterity – and friendship resurfaces on both occasions as something Montaigne imagines enjoying with his reader. The island of friendship is, therefore, one place in which the chapter's key topics of travel and writing – the free movement of the author and his text – meet.

How does Montaigne respond in our passage to the charge that his travelling amounts to a neglect of his friendships? By arguing, first in principle and then from experience, that the physical separation of true friends serves not to enfeeble their union but to enrich it. His point of departure in the passage is an ethical principle of friendship, namely, that it means espousing what is good for one's friend as being best for oneself. The example he chooses of this principle in action is a hypothetical one in which his friend chooses to go away from him: if doing so is useful or pleasing to the friend, Montaigne says, then his absence will be sweeter, will make the heart grow fonder, than his proximity could. The implication is that he expects the same treatment in return. He confirms his espousal of separation in negative terms some five sentences later, at the end of the passage, when he criticizes as 'insatiable' the hunger for physical presence that characterizes common friendships. Before he does so, he offers a positive example of bodily separation in true friendship, drawn from his own experience. The example begins abruptly: 'In other days I made use and advantage of our separation' ('J'ay tiré autrefois usage de nostre esloignement et commodité'). The change of tenses at this point in the passage, from present to past, shifts the writing from a discussion of principles to a remembrance of things past. There is no need for Montaigne to name the friend to whom he is referring. His claim to be 'expert' in true friendship has already unmistakably referred the reader back to 'Of friendship' (I.28), the centrepiece of Book I. There Montaigne had considered classical accounts of the topic in the light of his intense intimacy with a legal colleague and fellow humanist, Etienne de La Boétie, who had died some seventeen years before the chapter was first published in 1580. Montaigne returns in our chosen passage to the memory of this intimacy and extends the account he gives of it in 'Of friendship' by defending his love of travelling against the charge that it is a dereliction of friendship.

Exactly what kind of extension of the earlier chapter on friendship does 'Of vanity' represent? Montaigne presents his intimacy with La Boétie in 'Of vanity' as one part of a spectrum of affectionate relationships, including those within his own household, which he calls by the name of friendship; and he offers his experience of that true friendship as an exemplary instance of an ethical principle that holds good in other cases. Does this square with the account of friendship to be found in 'Of friendship'? The answer is, in brief, not entirely! 'Of vanity' prolongs 'Of friendship' but also takes it in new directions. The extension in Book III reveals a complex interplay of continuity with – and divergence from – what went before. It shows Montaigne looking back and thinking again.

A fundamental continuity between the two chapters is provided by the fact that, in both cases, Montaigne is thinking about friendship with the same classical authorities on the topic in mind: Aristotle and Cicero, in particular, but also Lucian and Plutarch. 'Of vanity' reflects on how true friends ought to conduct themselves in order to lead a good and happy life together. Its preoccupations, for that reason, may be called 'ethical' in character. Montaigne uses the adjective in this sense in a C-addition to 'Of experience' (III.13): 'Ethical laws [...] concern the individual duty of each man in himself' ('Les loix éthiques [...] regardent le devoir particulier de chacun en soy'; F 998, VS 1070). His treatment of ethical themes in the *Essais* has been the subject of much recent scholarship. Ullrich Langer, among others, has shown that the underlying context for Montaigne's thinking in this area is the Aristotelian-Ciceronian ethical tradition, in other words, the body of thought that takes as its main point of reference the account of the good life found in Aristotle and Cicero and which remained largely dominant in the sixteenth century: 'a practice-centered, contingent ethics, one that passes through the virtues, and relies on example as a mode of argumentation.' One distinguishing feature of that tradition is its commitment to the idea that the virtuous behaviour in individuals of which it speaks contributes not only to their well-being but, more importantly, to that of the state, the *polis*, as a whole. Aristotle demonstrates this commitment at the beginning of the *Nicomachean*

Ethics when he defines the entire work as a study in politics: 'For even if the end is the same for a single man and for a state, that of the state seems at all events something greater and more complete whether to attain or to preserve' (I. 2). The search for the good life leads, even as it subordinates, ethics to politics; and the bridge between the two discursive realms is none other than friendship. Aristotle announces this idea, at the beginning of the two books (VIII and IX) devoted to the topic in the *Nicomachean Ethics*, when he says that friendship is not only an ethical virtue but also a political one: it 'seems too to hold states together' (VIII. 1). Cicero extends the same line of thought in his treatises on friendship (*Laelius de amicitia*) and on duties (*De officiis*). Generalized friendship is seen as the end to which the *polis* should aspire. The Aristotelian-Ciceronian ethical tradition formulates, to echo the title of Jacques Derrida's study of the same subject, a 'politics of friendship'.

'Of friendship' and 'Of vanity' fit squarely within this tradition in so far as both might be said to advocate a particular view of friendship by portraying its virtues in the setting of an exemplary case. How far, though, does Montaigne go along with the tradition in its account of true friendship? Does friendship, for instance, constitute an ethical and political ideal in the *Essais* as it does for Aristotle and Cicero?

The argument has ebbed and flowed since Hugo Friedrich offered an influential 'no' to this question in his classic study, *Montaigne*, first published in 1949. Friedrich portrays a Montaigne who views perfect friendship as an irreducibly private event and, in this respect, departs from the classical tradition. Timothy J. Reiss, writing in 1986, is one of the many critics to have followed the line taken by Friedrich: 'For [Montaigne], in a rather untypical anti-Ciceronian move, friendship is a private affair.' Various critics sketched counter-moves in the argument in the following decade. Eric MacPhail concludes his 1989 article with a direct refutation of Reiss's claim: 'For Montaigne, friendship is not strictly a private affair, as some critics have contended, but rather a public, political engagement.' David Quint suggests, in his 1998 study of ethical and political themes in the *Essais*, that the text presents conversation between friends as a 'model' for 'larger social relations' and for a 'national discussion in [...] strife-torn France'.

The shift towards ethical and political readings of friendship in Montaigne has not convinced all his readers. But it does seem to have helped elicit more careful formulations from those who take a different view. In his 1994 study, for example, Ullrich Langer agrees with Friedrich's assertion that perfect friendship, for Montaigne, is irreducibly private. But he qualifies that assertion: it does not mean that Montaigne entirely deprives friendship of its social dimension, he says, but that 'the articulation of the inner "sentiment" of friendship with the life of social activity is unclear'. In his analysis of the role of friendship in the history – and future – of political philosophy, Jacques Derrida places Montaigne in the middle, characterizing his thought as caught in a tension between an inherited classical commitment to friendship as a political structure and a strong inner impulse to the contrary. Rather than assign their author to a clear position, as interventions on either side of the critical debate have done, Langer and Derrida describe in Montaigne altogether less clear and more complex attitudes towards the ethical and political dimensions of friendship.

You may well be wondering how this issue can have caused so much disagreement – most but not all of it friendly – among Montaigne's readers. An obvious point to make is that they tend to be reading different parts of the text. Those who see friendship in Montaigne as irreducibly private tend to be extrapolating from 'Of friendship', and those who portray it as ethical and political, from other areas of the *Essais*. This division of interpretative labour may help to explain why the critical debate has at times, perhaps, been more polarized than it need be. Once one asks how, if at all, the various important islands on friendship might be connected in the archipelago of the *Essais*, the picture changes, and becomes more puzzling.

The chapter from which all such explorations must start, 'Of friendship' (I.28) proves to be a puzzle in its own right, an altogether less stable mixture of elements than first meets the eye. Weighing existing treatments of the topic against his intense experience of friendship with La Boétie, whose loss he mourns, Montaigne insists that perfect friendship is compatible with good citizenship while also stressing its mysterious nature and fusional power. The result is a tension in the chapter between different views of friendship: as an ethical and political virtue rooted in the classical tradition, on the one hand, and, on the other, as something so powerful and so difficult to assimilate that coming to terms with it requires a break-out from the classical tradition as well as from common notions of friendship.

That tension may be seen as a product of the free-thinking approach that Montaigne takes towards the Aristotelian-Ciceronian tradition in

'Of friendship'. He starts the chapter by paraphrasing Aristotle's view that friendship is the ultimate perfection of human society. He repeats the fundamental distinction made in the *Nicomachean Ethics* (VIII. 3) between three kinds of friendship on the basis of what motivates them: pleasure, profit, and – in the perfect kind – the good (VS 184, F 165). He goes on to list the four species into which friendship is commonly divided: that which exists between kith and kin, neighbours, host and guest, and finally lovers. His review of these various classifications, however, obeys an underlying syntax of negation that says: 'Perfect friendship is not that, or that, or that again.' What, in that case, is perfect friendship? It is in his treatment of this question that Montaigne thinks against the classical tradition, as well as with it, and that his chapter reveals its unstable mixture of elements.

Montaigne's initial and closing response is classical in its inspiration: what makes friendship perfect is the fact that it is freely chosen. The greater the part obligation plays in a relationship, he says, the less that relationship deserves the name of friendship. Friendship is an expression of freedom, and not just one expression among others, but the greatest of them all: 'Our free will has no product more properly its own than affection and friendship' ('Nostre liberté volontaire n'a point de production qui soit plus proprement sienne que celle de l'affection et amitié'; F 166, VS 185). It follows from this that only the free are capable of friendship. We are back here in the classical past of Aristotle's Athens and Cicero's Rome, last explored in chapter 4 above, in which the possibility of friendship, like that of free-thinking, is the preserve of free-men in the *polis*. Just as it is for free-thinking, freedom is a necessary condition for the cultivation of friendship, but not a sufficient one: while all friends are by definition free-men, in other words, not all free-men are capable of being friends. Friendship, then, is a political virtue as well as an ethical one – Aristotle says, as we have seen, that it holds states together – and those who attain it do the state some service: they are better citizens for being good friends. Montaigne, at various moments in 'Of friendship', makes this ancient model of friendship his. He refers to the consensus among the ancient philosophical schools that women have no place in the circle of perfect friendship, for example, and assents to their exclusion on the grounds that their sex has in no instance yet succeeded in attaining it (F 167–8, VS 186–7). Friendship is for men only, and free-men, at that. He and La Boétie were not only perfect friends, but good citizens too, jealous of the preservation of the state in these agitated times. He discreetly illustrates the political virtue of their friendship with reference to his own decision, discussed in chapter 1 above, to remove from the middle of Book I his friend's political defence of liberty after it was published by French Protestants to their partisan ends. His last word about La Boétie in 'Of friendship' is a eulogy in a pure classicizing vein: 'His mind was moulded in the pattern of other ages than this' ('Il avoit son esprit moulé au patron d'autres siècles que ceux-cy'; F 176, VS 194). Along with disgust at the present age, here is a keen nostalgia for the classical past, its stabilities, and its perfect friendships.

Montaigne sounds a powerful new note in the middle of the same chapter when he presents himself and La Boétie as free-men in whom the classical model of friendship was not just reborn but surpassed. Their experience of friendship was so intense as to seem to him suddenly unassimilable: hard to put into words, and harder still to fit within the classical paradigm, let alone the pattern of common friendships. Montaigne sums up this shift of the chapter's argument and sensibility in explaining why he expects to find no good judge of his account among his readers: 'For the very discourses that antiquity has left us on this subject seem to me weak compared with the feeling I have' ('Car les discours mesmes que l'antiquité nous a laissés sur ce subject, me semblent lâches au pris du sentiment que j'en ay'; F 174, VS 192). Even the classical model, in the face of his lived experience, starts to come undone.

Montaigne first sounds this new note when he considers why it was that he felt such friendship for La Boétie. He produces a sequence of sentences as famous as they are difficult to understand:

> If you press me to tell why I loved him, I feel that this cannot be expressed, [C] except by answering: Because it was he, because it was I. [A] Beyond all my understanding, beyond what I can say about this in particular, there was I know not what inexplicable and fateful force that was the mediator of this union.

> Si on me presse de dire pourquoy je l'aymois, je sens que cela ne se peut exprimer, [C] qu'en respondant: Par ce que c'estoit luy; par ce que c'estoit moy. [A] Il y a, au delà de tout mon discours, et de ce que j'en puis dire particulierement, ne sçay quelle force inexplicable et fatale, mediatrice de cette union.   (F 169, VS 188)

The first sentence dramatizes the search for explanation by imagining an impersonal interlocutor pressing Montaigne to explain what caused the friendship. In reply, he offers only a sublime tautology: 'Because it was he, because it was I' ('Par ce que c'estoit luy; par ce que c'estoit moy'). Montaigne added the second half of this phrase in the margins of the Bordeaux copy some time after he had written the first half. It is, in its completed state, a perfect example of the twelve-syllable alexandrine metre that acquires canonic status in French poetry thanks to his near-contemporaries Joachim Du Bellay (1525–60) and Pierre de Ronsard (1524–85). Montaigne's alexandrine, by keeping the line's twinned half-lines or hemistichs on either side of a marked caesura, effectively puts one soul in two bodies and so weaves his idea of friendship into the fabric of the writing: two they were and the heart was one.

In the next sentence, Montaigne names what brought the friends together. He starts by announcing that there was indeed something but then uses the long prepositional clause to delay the revelation of what that mysterious something may be. The revelation, when it comes, only deepens the mystery: it was 'I know not what inexplicable and fateful force' that brought them into friendship. 'Inexplicable' here reinforces the semantic power of the preceding adjectival phrase 'I know not what' ('[je] ne sçay quelle'). That adjectival phrase is related to the emergence of the *je-ne-sais-quoi* in early modern French as a key literary strategy for putting into words a 'certain something' that proves as difficult to explain as its effects are transformative. As Montaigne describes it here, perfect friendship is a *je-ne-sais-quoi* that resists explanations, ancient and modern. It is his free-thinking approach to the topic that allows him to say so.

Montaigne, exceptionally, repeats the same adjectival form of the phrase a few sentences later in his continuing attempt to make sense of the friendship with La Boétie:

> It is not one special consideration, nor two, nor three, nor four, nor a thousand: it is I know not what quintessence of all this mixture, which, having seized my whole will, led it to plunge and lose itself in his; [C] which, having seized his whole will, led it to plunge and lose itself in mine, with equal hunger, equal rivalry.

> Ce n'est pas une speciale consideration, ny deux, ny trois, ny quatre, ny mille: c'est je ne sçay quelle quinte essence de tout ce meslange, qui, ayant saisi toute ma volonté, l'amena se plonger et se perdre dans la sienne; [C] qui, ayant saisi toute sa volonté, l'amena se plonger et se perdre en la mienne, d'une faim, d'une concurrence pareille.   (F 169–70, VS 189)

Montaigne here describes the friendship, not as the expression of free will, but as its loss. His free-thinking approach seems to have dislodged freedom itself from its earlier supremacy over friendship. Or perhaps this particular friendship was different. Where the 1580 text describes Montaigne's will plunging and disappearing into that of his friend, the post-1588 addition repeats the same description with reference to La Boétie's will, repeating the 1580 clause while inverting the relative positions of the pair to produce a chiasmus of mutual loss. But 'loss' is hardly the right word, Montaigne says in the following sentence, since the loss of individual free will is simply the most visible effect of the inexplicable quintessence at the heart of that absolute fusion which is perfect friendship.

Perfect friendship has by now taken us a long way from the ethical and political ideal of the classical tradition celebrated elsewhere in 'Of friendship'. The absolute fusion of souls, says Montaigne, frees them from the ethical obligations with which friendship is commonly associated (F 171, VS 190). There is no need for one friend to recognize or respect the other's difference for the simple reason that between such friends no difference exists. He reflects, in a post-1588 addition, that constructing a politics on the basis of such a friendship seems inconceivable, for it is hard to imagine how the friendship might admit a third person, let alone extend to an entire polity:

> And he who supposes that of two men I love one just as much as the other, and that they love each other and me just as much as I love them, multiplies into a fraternity the most singular and unified of all things, of which even a single one is the rarest thing in the world to find.

> Et qui presupposera que de deux j'en aime autant l'un que l'autre, et qu'ils-s'entr'aiment et m'aiment autant que je les aime, il multiplie en confrairie la chose la plus une et unie, et dequoy une seule est encore la plus rare à trouver au monde.   (F 172, VS 191)

Montaigne strains here, using a cluster of terms around the number one, to capture perfect friendship in its singularity, that rarest of qualities which frees it from the ethical and political obligations that spring up as soon as one friend becomes two or three or more.

The passage from 'Of vanity' that I took as my point of departure contains strong verbal echoes of the manner in which 'Of friendship' describes the bond Montaigne shared with La Boétie. These echoes are to be found in the sentences that offer a supporting example, drawn from past experience, of a true friendship. The first of these sentences places the first and third person singular, 'him' and 'me', in a chiasmus to stress the reciprocal character of friendship even in separation: 'he saw for me, and I for him' ('il voyoit pour moy, et moy pour luy'); this recalls the more complex chiasmus that Montaigne uses in 'Of friendship' in an attempt to describe the quintessence that bound them together. The second sentence describes friendship as a kind of fusion: 'we were fused into one' ('nous nous confondions'). The first person plural, 'we', here marks the seamless intermingling of 'him' and 'me' in perfect friendship. The same verb, 'se confondre', is used in a similar context in 'Of friendship': 'In the friendship I speak of, our souls mingle and blend with each other so completely that they efface the seam that joined them, and cannot find it again' ('En l'amitié dequoy je parle, elles [nos ames] se meslent et confondent l'une en l'autre, d'un meslange si universel, qu'elles effacent et ne retrouvent plus la couture qui les a jointes'; F 168, VS 188). Perfect friendship, in the exemplary case of Montaigne and La Boétie, fuses two in one. In 'Of vanity' Montaigne extends this thought in a new direction by insisting that, since true friends can never be apart, they hardly need to be together. What was in 'Of friendship' a remembrance of absolute confusion becomes in 'Of vanity' a defence of the virtues of distance.

In 'Of vanity' Montaigne applies to the topic of friendship his licence to think again. But this licence could be seen as little more than an extension of the free-thinking approach taken in 'Of friendship'. There, as we have seen, Montaigne thinks with and against classical accounts, particularly those of the Aristotelian-Ciceronian tradition, in the light of his own experience. In 'Of vanity', one of the thinkers to whom Montaigne responds besides Aristotle and Cicero is none other than the Montaigne of the earlier chapter, at least in his incarnation as the high priest of a friendship that was as remote from the world of ethical and political interactions as it was singular. What connects the two chapters is not a shared vision of friendship so much as a determination to think freely, and to think again, about this most transformative of experiences.

'Of friendship', in its anti-classical vein, refuted the traditional idea in ethics that friendship exists between husbands and wives and within households. 'Of vanity' returns to the idea, as we have already seen, and blurs the distinctions between perfect friendship and other kinds that 'Of friendship' drew so clearly. It sees friendship as having a place in the part of philosophy the early moderns called 'economics' and which, dealing with the interactions between members of the same household, provides a bridge between the realms of ethics and politics. 'Of friendship' dismissed the virtues of generosity, gratitude, and the like as foreign to perfect friendship because revealing of a residual difference between the friends. 'Of vanity', by contrast, reintroduces the importance to true friendship of a kind of generosity for which Montaigne offers his own practice as the example. We are suddenly a long way from the sublime fusion that 'Of friendship' describes and closer to the magnanimity of the 'great-souled man' portrayed in Book IV of Aristotle's *Nicomachean Ethics*. Such a man prizes his honour with such jealousy that he is often regarded as haughty. To maintain his honour, he shrinks from benefits and favours that would put him in a position of obligation towards their authors, and he is always the harshest judge of his own actions. Early in 'Of vanity', Montaigne lays claim to the selfsame character traits, saying that he avoids putting himself under any kind of obligation and that he subjects everything he does to what he calls, in a strikingly physical metaphor of self-restraint, 'the grip of my conscience' ('l'estreinte de ma conscience'; F 897, VS 967). He ascribes these traits, however, not to a keen sense of honour but rather to his intrinsic thirst for freedom. He drives home his point in a post-1588 addition to this passage by apostrophizing 'liberty' ('franchise') itself: 'Blessed liberty, which has guided me so far! May it continue to the end!' ('Bienheureuse franchise, qui m'a conduit si loing. Qu'elle acheve'; F 899, VS 968). That freedom needs to be tempered, of course, and the grip of his conscience provides for this by imposing an internal constraint upon his freewheeling adventures. Freedom tempered by conscience: this defines the great-souled man that Montaigne embodies in 'Of vanity', and it makes him an expert in the virtues of true friendship, a master in the art of giving himself to his friend more than he draws the friend to him.

The shift of perspective from 'Of friendship' is not as clear and distinct, however, as first appears. There are continuities between the two chapters. 'Of friendship', for example, contains the idea that the great-souled man of the classical tradition exercises civic virtue in his choice of friends and his behaviour towards them. As Jacques Derrida points out, this thought occurs to Montaigne in that chapter when he considers the example of Caius Blossius, condemned by Cicero for saying that he would do anything his friend asked of him. Montaigne's discussion of this case is one example of his attempt in 'Of friendship' to temper that chapter's unstable mixture of elements by showing that friendship, despite having the power to fuse and confuse the free will of citizens, poses no threat to the state and its laws. In a post-1588 addition, he further defends Blossius' remark as entirely proper, arguing that the yoke of unconditional friendship that made of these friends a team must have been guided by reason and commenting of reason in a parenthesis: 'indeed it is quite impossible to harness it without that' ('aussi est-il du tout impossible de l'atteler sans cela'; F 170, VS 189). Like generosity in 'Of vanity', reason is viewed here as a necessary condition of friendship, a virtue of the free-man without which his friendships cannot be sustained. 'Of friendship' thus indicates, within the space of a parenthesis, a line of thought about the virtues of friendship that runs through 'Of vanity'. This marked convergence should not surprise us: Montaigne added the parenthesis to 'Of friendship' after he had first published 'Of vanity', after all, and his habit of making additions to the existing chapters of his book means that he is just as capable of thinking again in 'Of friendship' about 'Of vanity' as he is in 'Of vanity' about 'Of friendship'. Note, meanwhile, that the dialogue between the two chapters is characterized by convergences as well as divergences. This is because what relates them is not a common 'position' on friendship, but a readiness to change position, to think again in pursuit of the truth about friendship: in other words, a shared freedom of thought.

Montaigne brings the same freedom of thought to the other islands on friendship in Books II and III. Friendship, once broached in the middle of Book I, becomes a major preoccupation of the *Essais*. I shall briefly single out two islands in Book II and two more in Book III from among this archipelago of instances.

The two islands in Book II show Montaigne, in different ways, putting ideas advanced in 'Of friendship' to the test. 'Of the affection of fathers for their children' (II.8) reopens a question that 'Of friendship' answers in the negative: is the relationship between parents and children, as is commonly thought, a kind of friendship? The term 'amitié' has already appeared more than once in the opening pages of the chapter to characterize that relationship when Montaigne, again after 1588, shifts the perspective of the chapter by repeating and even emphasizing the firm line taken in 'Of friendship': 'Will it ever be said enough how precious is a friend, and how different a thing from these civil bonds?' ('Aura l'on jamais assez dict de quel pris est un amy, et de combien autre chose que ces liaisons civiles?'; F 347–8, VS 395).

My second example from Book II is to be found in the closing section of 'Of presumption' (II.17: 'De la présomption'). The writer eulogizes various people he has known and admired, ending after 1588 with a warm appreciation of his adoptive daughter and future editor, Marie de Gournay. This appreciation leads Montaigne to question the exclusion of women from the sphere of perfect friendship in the classical tradition:

> If youthful promise means anything, her soul will some day be capable of the finest things, among others of perfection in that most sacred kind of friendship which, so we read, her sex has not yet been able to attain.

> Si l'adolescence peut donner presage, cette ame sera quelque jour capable des plus belles choses, et entre autres de la perfection de cette tres-saincte amitié où nous ne lisons point que son sexe ait pu monter encores. (F 610, VS 661)

One of the several places in which 'we read' that women are constitutionally incapable of perfect friendship is, as we saw earlier, 'Of friendship' (F 167–8, VS 186–7). In 'Of presumption', Montaigne distances himself from this claim and thinks again. He describes Marie de Gournay's reading of the early *Essais* and her desire for his friendship in terms reminiscent of the *je-ne-sais-quoi* that characterized his intimacy with La Boétie: as a strange phenomenon for which no ready-made explanation, classical or otherwise, exists (F 610, VS 662). This is one further occasion, it seems, in which not only Aristotle and Cicero but even Montaigne himself, in another place, will need to be put to one side in the search for the truth about friendship. The added spice to this passage is that it does not appear in the Bordeaux copy, but only in the 1595 edition, which Marie de Gournay herself supervised. Montaigne's twentieth-century editors, who followed the text of the Bordeaux copy, doubted the passage's authenticity: Pierre Villey, in his edition, suggests Gournay might have written it. Its authenticity is generally accepted today on the grounds of its stylistic coherence, its consistency with other records of Montaigne's affection and esteem for his literary executor, and its greater plausibility than the hypothesis of an otherwise scrupulous editor not only daring but even, in the first place, wishing to fabricate so prominent a eulogy of herself and to smuggle it into the text. What can be added to those arguments is that, in returning to 'Of friendship' and putting its claim about the capacity of women for friendship to the test, the passage is typical of Montaigne's wider free-thinking approach to the topic.

The two instances in Book III show Montaigne looking forwards to friendships new and considering how they might be kindled and sustained. In 'Of three kinds of association' (III.3: 'De trois commerces'), he portrays his three favourite occupations, in turn, as conversation with friends, love, and reading. He starts the first section by recalling a single perfect friendship that he experienced in his youth and which has given him a lasting distaste for what he calls 'these numerous and imperfect friendships' ('ces amitiés nombreuses et imparfaictes'; F 755, VS 821). He goes on to describe the kind of friends, few and far between in truth, he seeks: 'I know my men even by their silence and their smiles' ('Je connois mes gens au silence mesme et à leur soubsrire'; F 759, VS 824).

My second example from Book III is to be found in 'Of husbanding your will' (III.10: 'De mesnager sa volonté'), the chapter directly following 'Of vanity' and to which we shall turn next. Montaigne returns to the idea that friendship with others starts in legitimate self-love or what he called, in 'Of friendship', 'the friendship I feel for myself' ('l'amitié que je me porte'; F 171, VS 190). This idea, which Aristotle examines in the *Nicomachean Ethics* (IX. 4), helps Montaigne in 'Of husbanding your will' to imagine how to strike the right balance when, as so often happens, one's social and political commitments threaten one's independence of will. Friendship offers him a conceptual instrument with which to articulate and pursue the ethical principle around which the chapter turns: 'We must lend ourselves to others and give ourselves only to ourselves' ('Il se faut prester à autruy et ne se donner qu'à soy-mesme'; F 932, VS 1003). In this chapter, as in 'Of vanity' and the other islands scattered throughout the *Essais*, Montaigne returns to a thought about friendship he has already articulated and takes it in a new direction. In a reformulation of a free-thinking expression, one might say that he considers himself a friend, but a lesser friend than truth.

Befriending the Reader

For Montaigne, still mourning the perfect friend and living in a dangerous age, the best hope of rediscovering true friendship may lie in his book. He ends the island devoted to the topic in 'Of vanity' by imagining friendship with the reader. By 1588, when he first published Book III, Montaigne knew that earlier editions of his book had proved a success. The knowledge that his book is reaching a wide circle of readers serves only to nourish Montaigne's hope that he will be read in intimacy.

He says as much of his female readers in 'On some verses of Virgil' (III.5: 'Sur des vers de Virgile'): 'I am annoyed that my essays serve the ladies only as a public article of furniture, an article for the parlour. This chapter will put me in the boudoir' ('Je m'ennuie que mes essais servent les dames de meuble commun seulement, et de meuble de sale. Ce chapitre me fera du cabinet'; F 781, VS 847). There is an erotic charge to this imagined intimacy: the imagined scene of female reading is not the parlour but the boudoir. Montaigne's chapter on sex and marital relations, proceeds, as its title suggests, by means of a commentary on the poets and a confession in their company: this is free-thinking and free-speaking in action. The writer comes to his theme by extending the principle of diversion, set out in the previous chapter, into this particular area of experience: talking about sex is his way of turning his mind away from the woes of old age, while he still can, and a form of public confession whose licence he justifies. The first question he examines – why so few talk about the coital act in a serious manner – sends him to the Latin poets who do, starting with Virgil (70–19 BCE), first among equals. He quotes the description that Virgil gives of the coupling of Venus with her husband, in Book 8 of the *Aeneid*, before subjecting it to a commentary that provides the impetus for much of the chapter: its distinction between marriage (in its ideal form, a lasting friendship, though much satirical space is devoted here to its less-than-ideal instantiations) and love (subject to the fiery evanescence of desire); its analysis of the inequalities that men visit on women in marriage; and its condemnation of jealousy. The introduction of a second passage about Venus, this time by Virgil's contemporary Lucretius, brings from Montaigne an appreciation of the vigour with which the two poets write and think, a reconsideration of his own project, and praise for the art of suggestion that the poets deploy. He then offers his own thoughts on – and advice to – men and women caught up, as he has been, in the game of desire, stressing the moderation with which they should play that game, and emphasizing the virtues of sincerity and reciprocity. He digresses, after 1588, to justify the frankness with which he has just revealed his own sexual inadequacies by stressing the need for freedom in speech as well as in thought on this topic as on every other. He ends the chapter by first imagining the good that it would do him to fall in love again and then preferring the pleasures that the imagination, fed and fired by the poets, affords an old man. He uses the final passage of poetry that he quotes, from Catullus (84–54 BCE), to suggest an erotic analogy for the 'flux' of commentary and of prose that has escaped from him in the course of the chapter. But he reserves the last word, its serious intent lightened by the old saying concerning pots and kettles in which it is couched, for the equality of the sexes.

In 'Of vanity', after advertising his expertise in true friendship, he sends out an open invitation to the men in his growing readership: 'I hope [...] that if my humours happen to please and suit some worthy man before I die, he will try to meet me' ('J'espere [...] que, s'il advient que mes humeurs plaisent et accordent à quelque honneste homme avant que je meure, il recerchera de nous joindre'; F 911, VS 981). If such a man does exist, then the *Essais* will have given him an intimate knowledge of its author, which would have otherwise taken several years to acquire. Montaigne is prepared to go very far to find such a man, he says, for nothing is sweeter than friendship: 'Oh, a friend!' ('O un amy!'; F 912, VS 981). The perspective on friendship has shifted once again: it no longer appears as a topic on which Montaigne essays his judgement but also, simultaneously, as a means of imagining the ideal bond between author and reader.

What kind of friend, then, does he imagine the reader to be? He has in mind a companion in the search for truth capable of listening to him and pursuing the questions he raises with the openness of mind that characterizes his writing. A reader, therefore, who brings to questions an independent, experimental, anti-dogmatic, and non-partisan cast of mind, qualities that he not only advocates but practises in the *Essais*, as we have seen. A reader, equally, who does not allow liberty of judgement to slide into licence of conduct, as so often happens in his age, but who exercises that liberty with sufficient self-restraint to be trustworthy: a well-tempered free-thinker, then, of the kind that the 'Apology for Raymond Sebond' (II.12) allows might just be out there among the nameless many. When in a post-1588 addition to 'Of presumption' (II.17), Montaigne directly asks himself for whom it is that he writes, he characterizes his implicit readers in the same fashion once again – as neither professional pedants nor untutored peasants but a third group of readers who think for themselves – while stressing how hard they are to find:

> The third class into whose hands you come, that of minds regulated and strong in themselves, is so rare that for this very reason it has neither name nor rank among us; it is time half wasted to aspire and strive to please this group.

> La tierce, à qui vous tombez en partage, des ames reglées et fortes d'elles-mesmes, est si rare que justement elle n'a ny nom, ny rang entre nous: c'est à demy temps perdu, d'aspirer et de s'efforcer à luy plaire.   (F 605–6, VS 657)

Notice that, for Montaigne, the time is only *half* wasted: the class of well-tempered free-thinking readers for whom he writes may be vanishingly small, it is true, but it is out there somewhere all the same. 'Are you that kind of reader?' That is the unvoiced question to his actual readers that Montaigne whispers in the corners of his sentences on the topic. Anyone wishing to play Sancho Panza to his Don Quixote has their work cut out. The free-thinking friendship he offers his readers is every bit as demanding as it is liberating.

Montaigne extends his thinking on this topic in 'Of vanity' by spelling out an indispensable condition of the friendship that such free-thinking involves, namely, the need for dispassionate understanding. It is no act of friendship to rush to the judgement that what Plato or one's other friends have to say on a question is simply to be discarded in the search for truth; that search is and must remain a collective undertaking and a dialogue among friends; so the first task is to listen to what one's friends have to say and to try to understand it on their terms. Montaigne challenges his own readers to treat him in this way. That challenge takes the form of a ghostly threat. He wants to be spoken of truly and justly after his death, and if the opposite happens, he reserves the right to return:

> I would willingly come back from the other world to give the lie to any man who portrayed me other than I was, even if it were to honour me. Even the living, I perceive, are spoken of otherwise than they really are. And if I had not supported with all my strength a friend that I lost, they would have torn him into a thousand contrasting appearances.

> Je reviendrois volontiers de l'autre monde pour démentir celuy qui me formeroit autre que je n'estois, fut ce pour m'honorer. Des vivans mesme, je sens qu'on parle toujours autrement qu'ils ne sont. Et si à toute force je n'eusse maintenu un amy que j'ay perdu, on me l'eust deschiré en mille contraires visages. (F 914, VS 983)

Montaigne looks for a well-tempered free-thinking reader who will approach his book as one needing to be understood – read freely and without prejudice – rather than distorted by praise or blame. That he sees this work of understanding to be a defining feature of friendship as well as of free-thinking is confirmed by the fact that, having looked forward to his own posterity in the sentences just quoted, he immediately refers to the conflict-ridden one that awaited La Boétie – the friend he lost – and to his defence of his friend's work and reputation in 'Of friendship' and elsewhere.

Does Montaigne leave behind a reader anywhere near as affectionate and understanding towards him as he was towards his friend? The answer that he gives in the 1588 edition is an unequivocal 'no', penetrated with the memory of La Boétie, who he says alone enjoyed his true image and took it with him:

> I know well that I leave behind no sponsor anywhere near as affectionate and understanding about me as I was about him. There is no one to whom I would be willing to entrust myself fully for a portrait; he alone enjoyed my true image, and carried it away. That is why I decipher myself so painstakingly.

> Je sçay bien que je ne lairray apres moi aucun respondant si affectionné bien loing et entendu en mon faict comme j'ay esté au sien. Il n'y a personne à qui je vousisse pleinement compromettre de ma peinture: luy seul jouissoit de

ma vraye image, et l'emporta. C'est pourquoy je me deschiffre moy-mesme,
si curieusement.   (F 914, n. 14; VS 983, n. 4)

After 1588, Montaigne deletes that melancholy passage, perhaps – we
might conjecture – because he felt he had found such a friend in Marie
de Gournay or, at least, because he wanted to encourage her sponsorship
of his work after his death. In any case, while that passage is removed in
the Bordeaux copy and does not figure in the 1595 edition, in both texts
the earlier call to dispassionate understanding, issued to readers of the
future, remains in place. As does Montaigne's ghostly threat.

7

Of Keeping Your Freedom Alive

Earlier chapters of the *Essais* have already established free-thinking as an art that the writer wishes to see continued by those who follow him in the afterlife of his text. Where, in 'Of freedom of conscience', Montaigne puts his readers through a warm-up exercise in that art, in 'Of vanity' he steps back from the exercise and reflects upon it. He makes the notion of dispassionate understanding central to the twinned arts of free-thinking and friendship, and he suggests that those twinned arts bear on the very act of reading the *Essais*, for he uses them to imagine the relationship between the ideal reader and himself.

In 'Of husbanding your will' (III.10: 'De mesnager sa volonté'), the chapter that directly follows 'Of vanity', he goes a step further. He presents himself as someone who not only espouses the principles of free-thinking, but does so even in a rotten age, and who brings these principles to bear on his thoughts and deeds in the sphere of political action: as someone, that is, able freely to comment on the virtues of his enemies and the vices of his allies. In declaring his opposition to excessive zeal and his espousal of free-thinking, he attempts to win the reader over to the same point of view, presenting examples in a way that he hopes will speak volumes.

Of these, the examples drawn from his experience are of particular interest, for two reasons: they reveal the role that free-thinking plays in his public life and in his writing; and they bear witness to the degree of official censorship that his writing has already undergone when, in 1588, he publishes 'Of husbanding your will' for the first time. He looks backwards, in the chapter, to that censorship and describes his response to it. In so doing, he looks not only backwards but also forwards to future receptions of the text, challenging others to accompany him on a journey without end in search of truth: to be the kind of free-thinking friend that he has been to Plato and Co. The rich and contested afterlife of the *Essais* has seen – and continues to see – Montaigne's readers responding to that challenge, galvanized, as well as haunted, by the company of his ghost.

'Of husbanding your will' takes its place alongside the other chapters of Book III – especially 'Of the useful and the honourable' (III.1: 'De l'utile et de l'honneste'), 'Of vanity' (III.9), and 'Of physiognomy' (III.12: 'De la phisionomie') – in which Montaigne reflects on contemporary events, particularly the civil wars in France, and on the role he has played in them. The two terms that he served as Mayor of Bordeaux (in the years 1581–5) fall under his particular scrutiny in 'Of husbanding your will'. That chapter is one of his most sustained reflections on the ethical and political dimensions of his abiding thirst for individual freedom. He describes this thirst as intrinsic to his character in 'Of vanity', as we have seen, and he does so again in 'Of husbanding your will': 'If anyone wants to use me according to my nature, let him give me tasks in which vigour and freedom are needed' ('Qui se voudra servir de moy selon moy, qu'il me donne des affaires où il face besoing de la vigueur et de la liberté'; F 950–1, VS 1021). The situation imagined in that sentence poses the question around which the entire chapter turns: that of how much individual will you should properly invest in the service of the collective good. It offers, in response to the question, the thought that, whatever else you do, you should certainly keep alive the freedom that made you fit for service in the first place.

How might 'husbanding your will' ('ménager sa volonté'), as the chapter's title has it, help you to keep this freedom alive? The chapter starts from the fundamental precept that you should offer your dispassionate concern in the service of the public good but never invest your passion: you should merely lend yourself to others and give yourself to no one but yourself. Montaigne, in exploring this precept, espouses it as a paradox: it distinguishes him, he suggests, from most people, including his father, whom he remembers worn down by the same public office – that of Mayor of Bordeaux – to which he, the son, was himself later elected. He makes a strong link in the chapter between 'freedom' ('liberté') and 'will' ('volonté'). Having first made 'will' the object of exploration, in the chapter title, he substitutes it for 'freedom' in the following formulation: 'We must husband the freedom of our soul and mortgage it only on the right occasions' ('Il faut mesnager la liberté de nostre ame et ne l'hypothequer qu'aux occasions justes'; F 933, VS 1004). This confirms the semantic link between 'freedom' and 'will'. Are the two terms therefore synonymous? Not quite. The will is the part of the soul that is directed to choice and action: it acts in concrete instances, and its actions are not only made possible by the freedom of the soul, but also help to preserve that freedom. Montaigne prefers 'will' to 'freedom' in the title of his chapter, no doubt, because the chapter is chiefly concerned with concrete instances in which public obligation may be reconciled with individual freedom only if – as he did – you act in such a way as to husband your will. The aim of such careful husbandry is to keep alive the freedom that Montaigne claims is intrinsic to his nature.

The middle part of the chapter sketches out the approach required of anyone wishing to preserve freedom of mind in the midst of political engagement. Taking this approach means cultivating your ability to recognize truth, wherever it is found, and so to discriminate between appearance and reality, between public causes and private interests, and between things as they are and things as you would wish them to be. As Montaigne sketches what this free-thinking approach entails and advocates it to his readers, he also examines why so few of his contemporaries adopt it, so that this part of the chapter is as much an analysis of the forces that prevent or vitiate freedom of thought as it is a description of its constituent features and virtues. Those baleful forces, as we have already seen in previous chapters, exert themselves from without as well as from within. In 'Of husbanding your will' the emphasis is on internal forces, such as our passions and interests, which have the potential – if not properly managed – to rob the will of its freedom.

What is striking about the middle part of the chapter is that it delivers its advocacy of free-thinking in a portrait of the author. Montaigne starts by asserting the independence of his thought from his private allegiances and interests. The example he offers is embedded in the context of the civil wars: 'In the present broils of this state, my own interest has not made me blind to either the laudable qualities in our adversaries or those that are reprochable in the men I have followed' ('Aus presens brouillis de cet estat, mon interest ne m'a faict mesconnoistre ny les qualitez louables en nos adversaires, ny celles qui sont reprochables en ceux que j'ay suivy'; F 941, VS 1012). The civil wars remain in the foreground throughout this part of the chapter. So does the author:

I want the advantage to be for us, but I do not fly into a frenzy if it is not. [C] I adhere firmly to the healthiest of the parties, but I do not seek to be noted as especially hostile to the others and beyond the bounds of the general reason. I condemn extraordinarily this bad form of arguing: 'He is of the League, for he admires the grace of Monsieur de Guise.' 'The activity of the king of Navarre amazes him: he is a Huguenot.' 'He finds this to criticize in the king's morals: he is seditious in his heart.' And I did not concede even to the magistrate that he was right to condemn a book for having placed a heretic among the best poets of this century. Should we not dare say of a thief that he has a fine leg? And if she is a whore, must she also necessarily have bad breath? In wiser ages, did they revoke the proud title of Capitolinus, which they had previously given to Marcus Manlius as the preserver of public religion and liberty? Did they smother the memory of his liberality and his feats of arms and the military rewards accorded to his valour, because he afterwards aspired to kingship, to the prejudice of his country's laws? If they have formed a hatred for an advocate, the next day in their view he becomes ineloquent. I have elsewhere touched on the zeal that impels good men into similar faults. For my part, I can perfectly well say: 'He does this wickedly and that virtuously.' Likewise in predictions or in the unfavourable outcome of affairs, they want everyone to be blind and stupid in his own cause, and our conviction and judgement to serve, not the truth, but the aim of our desire. I should rather err toward the other extreme, so much do I fear being suborned by my desire. Besides, I am somewhat tenderly distrustful of the things I wish for.

Je veux que l'avantage soit pour nous, mais je ne forcene point s'il ne l'est. [C] Je me prens fermement au plus sain des partis, mais je n'affecte pas qu'on me remarque specialement ennemy des autres, et outre la raison generalle. J'accuse merveilleusement cette vitieuse forme d'opiner: Il est de la Ligue, car il admire la grace de Monsieur de Guise. L'activeté du Roy de Navarre l'estonne: il est Huguenot. Il treuve cecy à dire aux mœurs du Roy: il est seditieux en son cœur. Et ne conceday pas au magistrat mesme qu'il eust raison de condamner un livre pour avoir logé entre les meilleurs poëtes de ce siècle un heretique. N'oserions nous dire d'un voleur qu'il a belle greve? Et faut-il, si elle est putain, qu'elle soit aussi punaise? Aux siecles plus sages, revoqua-on le superbe tiltre de Capitolinus, qu'on avait auparavant donné à Marcus Manlius comme conservateur de la religion et liberté publique? Estouffa-on la memoire de sa liberalité et de ses faicts d'armes et recompenses

militaires ottroyées à sa vertu, par ce qu'il affecta depuis la Royauté, au prejudice des loix de son pays? S'ils ont pris en haine un avocat, l'endemain il leur
devient ineloquent. J'ay touché ailleurs le zele qui poussa des gens de bien à
semblables fautes. Pour moy, je sçay bien dire: il fait meschamment cela, et
vertueusement cecy. De mesmes, aux prognostiques ou evenements sinis-
tres des affaires, ils veulent que chacun, en son party, soit aveugle et hebeté;
que notre persuasion et jugement serve non à la verité mais au project de
notre désir. Je faudroy plustost vers l'autre extremité, tant je crains que mon
desir me suborne. Joint que je me deffie un peu tendrement des choses que
je souhaitte. (F 942–3, VS 1013)

Montaigne here extends his self-portrait as a free-thinker who is not
only able to protect his judgements from zeal, but also willing to denounce
the baleful influence of zeal on his contemporaries, and in particular on
the two extremist groups of contemporary French politics, the Huguenots
and the members of the hardline Catholic League. He pinpoints the same
two groups as offering examples of what he calls 'this bad form of arguing'.
He offers wider examples, in a satirical vein, to show how passion-fuelled
partisan thinking produces injustices as well as bad arguments: the case
of the woman thought to smell horrid just because she is a whore, of
the lawyer said to be halting of speech just because he is hated, and so
on. He then reveals the process whereby he moderates his desires, even
leans against them, for fear of enslaving his judgement to them. This
passage exemplifies 'Of husbanding your will' above all, perhaps, in that,
even as Montaigne offers a master-class in the art of free-thinking, the
civil-war context in which his master-class is visibly embedded shows
how formidable the obstacles are to the cultivation of that art. Yet the
more formidable those obstacles appear, the more uncompromising he
becomes in his advocacy, urging his readers to share his view that free-
thinking is vital to a good life and to a healthy body politic. The passage
does more, in this respect, than encapsulate 'Of husbanding your will': it
intensifies the commitment shown throughout the third and final Book
of the *Essais* to the principle of inward freedom of thought. It offers a
thought-experiment, conducted in the face of other people's passionate
certainties, but marked by a different form of engagement: the author
is equally committed to the qualifications and hesitations he expresses
in this passage as he is to the principle of unfettered thought by which
he claims to make judgements. I say equally committed, because those

qualifications and hesitations are not ornamental to his way of thinking, they are its life-blood. In this respect, the passage is characteristic of the seam running throughout Montaigne's work that I have sought to mine in this book, and it provides a fitting example with which to end.

It also presents characteristic challenges. It is, except for the opening sentence, part of a longer section added to the chapter after its first publication in 1588. What effect does the addition make on the chapter as a whole? That addition contains discreet allusions to several of Montaigne's own actions in the past. Which actions, and why the need for discretion? It sees the essayist, the 'I' ('je'), trying out his thoughts in the company of others, notably three groups, which he refers to respectively as 'one' ('on'), 'they' ('ils'), and 'we' ('nous'). Whom does he have in mind? How does the drama of personal pronouns animate the passage?

The Past in the Present

There is something irretrievably timebound about the form in which Montaigne states his commitment to inward freedom of thought in the passage just quoted. The tenses that he uses offer varying perspectives on the present and the past and, in so doing, firmly place Montaigne's preoccupations and commitments in the flood of time. They start and end the passage in a present tense whose aspect is 'iterative' in the sense that it describes Montaigne's customary ways of being and doing: his ever-moderate support of good causes, his self-protective distrust of the things he desires, and so on. This gives way, at the beginning of the passage added after 1588, to a present tense whose aspect is 'punctual' in the sense that it relates to a state of affairs at a particular point in time, when French politics was dominated by three parties, those of the Huguenots and of the League at either extreme, and, in the middle, the party of Henri III, to which Montaigne declares his firm adherence. Since Henri III was assassinated on 1 August 1589, throwing French politics into new upheaval, we can be sure that Montaigne composed this passage some time after June 1588, when Book III was first published, and before the assassination took place. The present tense in which Montaigne condemns the partisan arguments of his polarized contemporaries looks, in retrospect, all too punctually timebound: like a brief moment, suspended between political murders, in which a thought floated free.

The present tenses in which Montaigne states his commitment to free-thinking in this passage are counterbalanced, however, by the ability of his mind to travel through time. The idea of time-travel, which is powerfully at work in this passage as elsewhere in the *Essais*, carries Montaigne upstream as well as downstream through the temporal flood. His upstream time-travel takes him as far back as ancient Rome, which here embodies the wisdom of the free-thinking past, as so often for Montaigne. He refers in particular to the rise and fall, in around 390 BCE, of the legendary hero Marcus Manlius. Alerted to the arrival in the city of the marauding Gauls by the cackling geese on Rome's Capitol Hill, the story goes, Marcus Manlius earned his nickname 'Capitolinus' by promptly putting the enemy to flight. He fought that day to protect the freedom of the Roman Republic, as Montaigne puts it, but he later sought to steal the same freedom by bidding to seize tyrannical power. What makes the ancient Romans wise, in Montaigne's view, is that they – unlike most of his contemporaries – were able to judge actions each according to its merits and to praise Marcus Manlius' heroism even as they punished his treachery. When Montaigne declares himself to be capable of making judgements in the same unfettered way, a few sentences after he finishes telling the story of Marcus Manlius, he implicitly presents himself, as he explicitly does La Boétie in 'Of friendship' and elsewhere, as having a mind cast after the pattern of wiser ages than this one. He brings, in the time-travelling vehicle of his text, a remote past towards the present.

Between the remote past and the present, in this passage, lies the altogether nearer past of Montaigne's early compositions and their reception. The author, discreetly but unmistakably, refers to this past on two occasions in this passage to support his engagements in the present. The first is the sentence in which he claims to have made no concession even to the magistrate who condemned a book for praising a poet who was also a heretic. The second occasion is the sentence in which he says: 'I have elsewhere touched on the zeal that impels good men into similar faults' ('J'ay touché ailleurs le zele qui poussa des gens de bien à semblables fautes'). These two sentences play mutually supporting roles in the argument, for the first adds to the portrait of the artist as a free-thinker, whereas the second bolsters his criticisms of his mentally fettered contemporaries.

In different ways, Montaigne alludes in both sentences to the recent past of the *Essais*, thus implicating that past, too, in the present composition and its engagements.

Montaigne in Rome

To what, precisely, is he looking back? The allusion in the second of the two sentences mentioned above can be swiftly explained since we have already explored the 'elsewhere' to which Montaigne here refers: it is none other than 'Of freedom of conscience'. This is the only occasion in Book III on which Montaigne looks back to that chapter. He has good reason to recall its analysis of the zeal that vitiates judgements on both sides of a confessional divide, for zeal is the culprit in 'Of husbanding your will' too, the reason why we moderns – as opposed to the wiser ancients – cannot appreciate the beauties of a poet who is also a heretic nor the eloquence of a lawyer who happens to be on the opposing side of the argument. Montaigne then extends that analysis by introducing a personal tone that went unsounded in 'Of freedom of conscience'. He presents himself, no less, as free from zeal, the vice of the age, and therefore able to judge particular actions on their merits: 'For my part, I can perfectly well say: "He does this wickedly and that virtuously"' ('Pour moy, je sçay bien dire: il fait meschamment cela, et vertueusement cecy'). The repetition of first-person pronouns at the beginning of the sentence, combined with the absence throughout of qualifying or moderating expressions, sounds here an emphatic statement of the turn of mind that Montaigne brings to the art of making judgements. In 'Of freedom of conscience', it will be remembered, Montaigne echoes the chapter 'Of custom' (I.23) in suggesting indirectly that public freedom of conscience ought to be allowed in the exceptional circumstances of the French civil wars. In 'Of husbanding your will', he recalls 'Of freedom of conscience', but the argument has shifted: he is now offering, in his own name, an absolute advocacy, in the same circumstances, of personal freedom of thought.

The allusion in the first of the two sentences mentioned above will require more elucidation. That sentence refers to Montaigne's defence of 'a book' that was condemned by 'a magistrate' for praising the poetry of a heretic. The book in question is none other than the *Essais* of 1580, it turns out, and the magistrate a key figure in the process of Roman censorship that Montaigne's text underwent during its author's visit to the city in 1581.

Rome was the final destination of the fourteen-month journey on which Montaigne, surrounded by a dozen or so companions, embarked in September 1580, shortly after the publication of the first edition of the *Essais*, and which took him through France, Switzerland, Germany, and Austria as well as Italy. The most thoughtful account of why Montaigne, at the age of forty-seven, decided to undertake such a long and arduous journey, and of how he would respond to those who criticized his decision, is contained in 'Of vanity'. Montaigne ascribes his taste for travel, in that chapter, to two desires: to escape the cares of home and the woes of France, on the one hand, and, on the other, to make new friends abroad and see the world. This latter desire is deeply rooted in his cast of mind: back in 'Of the education of children' (I.26), after all, he described travel – whose purpose is, as he puts it, to rub and polish our brains against the brains of others (F 136, VS 153) – as inestimably valuable to an education in free-thinking. The time Montaigne spent in Rome between 30 November 1580 and 19 April 1581 was just such an education.

It took the form of an encounter with figures central to two of the period's most feared institutional curbs on freedom of thought and expression, namely, the Roman Inquisition and Index. The story was preserved for posterity in the *Travel Journal* (*Journal de Voyage*), a private account of Montaigne's European tour first discovered in 1770 and published four years later. The *Journal* is a work by several hands in several languages. It comes in four unequal parts, the first part (amounting to almost one half of the entire text) being the work of an anonymous secretary, and the rest that of Montaigne, who composed the second part, for the purposes of practice, in the vernacular dialect of Tuscany (what later became Italian). The *Journal* adds to the motives offered in 'Of vanity' a further, intimate, one for Montaigne's journey, namely, his desire to try the effect of mineral waters on the kidney stones from which, by the time he set out, he had been suffering for two long years. The *Journal* is, as a result, the record of a cure as well as of a journey. It is to that record that we must first turn if we are to learn how a magistrate condemned Montaigne for praising the poetry of a heretic.

The twinned themes of intellectual freedom and censorship provide the context for the story. Montaigne's secretary reports that customs men searched his master's baggage when he entered Rome and took away his books – among them a copy of the *Essais* that he planned to give the Pope – for examination by the theologians of the Inquisition. The secretary presents the episode as the example that Montaigne used to lean on most heavily when disagreeing with those who compared the freedom of Rome favourably to that of Venice (F 1142, G 190). That episode and the discussion it provokes in the *Journal* bear out my claim that Montaigne's freethinking, along with that of his Renaissance contemporaries, is embedded in a complex institutional history, as well as an intellectual one, and that our author, for all his status as a gentleman amateur in the world of letters, was no stranger to the policing of thought. Montaigne twice discussed his *Essais* with two Roman censors. The senior partner on both occasions was Sisto Fabri (1541–94), who as Master of the Sacred Palace served as the Pope's personal theologian and as an adviser both to the Congregation of the Inquisition and to the Congregation of the Index, the body that oversaw the censorship of all books printed in or brought to Rome and was charged with compiling the Pope's list of forbidden books. The junior partner was one Giovanni Battista Lancio (*d.* 1598), companion to the Master of the Sacred Palace and, since November 1580, secretary of the Congregation of the Index.

Montaigne tells the story of the first meeting in his *Journal* (F 1166, G 221–2). It took place on the evening of 20 March 1581. The censors returned to Montaigne his copy of the *Essais*, marked up according to a set of objections, and Montaigne answered each of the objections in turn. It seems unlikely that the censors themselves were the authors of these objections: Montaigne reports that, since Fabri had no French, 'some French friar' had read the *Essais* on his behalf; and there is no indication that Lancio had had a part in the drafting of the objections. Rather, it seems, Fabri and Lancio had the task of deciding what censorship, if any, to impose upon the author of the *Essais* on the basis of a preliminary report that they had commissioned – 'the opinion of the learned monks' ('l'opinion des docteurs moines'), as Montaigne puts it, one of whom was clearly the French friar – and the author's responses to their preliminary report.

Montaigne briefly lists six specific objections in the *Journal*. The first was that he had used the word 'fortune'; the chapter 'Fortune is often met in the path of reason' (I.34) contains significant occurrences, as does 'Let business wait till tomorrow' (II.4: 'A demain les affaires'), of a word that appears no fewer than 173 times in the course of the 1580 edition. The second objection, the one to which Montaigne alludes in 'Of husbanding your will', was that he had named heretic poets; this refers primarily to a passage in 'Of presumption' (II.17; F 609, VS 661) where Montaigne ranks among the best neo-Latin poets of the day the Scottish humanist George Buchanan (1506–82), who taught the young Montaigne at the Collège de Guyenne in Bordeaux, and the Calvinist theologian Theodore Beza. In 1564 the Council of Trent had prohibited the complete works of arch-heretics, including their non-religious publications, and by 1581 the names of Buchanan and Beza appeared in various lists of forbidden books across Europe (though they were not listed on the Roman Index until 1590). The third objection was that Montaigne had 'excused' Julian; his portrait of the non-Christian Roman emperor in 'Of freedom of conscience' (II.19) is the target here. The fourth was that he had suggested that one should be pure of evil impulses when one prays; this Montaigne does in 'Of prayers' (I.56: 'Des prières'). The fifth was that he had reckoned anything that goes beyond plain death to be cruelty; this refers to the condemnations of torture in the twinned chapters 'Of cruelty' (II.11) and 'Cowardice, mother of cruelty' (II.27). The sixth objection was to Montaigne's opinion that a child should be brought up to be able to do anything; this thought appears in 'Of the education of children' (I.26) when Montaigne stresses the need for a child to learn to adapt to different circumstances and customs: 'While the body is still supple, it should for that reason be bent to all fashions and customs [...] Let him be able to do all things, and love to do only the good' ('Le corps encore souple, on le doit, à cette cause, plier à toutes façons et coustumes [...] Qu'il puisse faire toutes choses, et n'ayme à faire que les bonnes'; F 150, VS 166–7). It is the first clause of that second sentence which drew from the correctors the sixth and final objection listed by Montaigne.

Montaigne's list of the objections made against his book is manifestly incomplete, ending as it does with an *et cetera*, but, since his *Journal* remained for over two hundred years the only primary source for this episode to which scholars had access, the matter rested there. The official opening in January 1998 of the archives of the Holy Roman and Universal Inquisition and of the Congregation for the Index of Prohibited Books changed all that. The historian Peter Godman unearthed in the archives of the Index a document, written in 1581 by two hands in a mixture of Latin and Italian, listing objections made against the *Essais*. This document – a transcript of which was first published by Godman in 2000 – appears to be none other than the preliminary report to which Montaigne was asked to respond at his first meeting with Fabri and Lancio. It contains some forty objections, eighteen of which are noted by a first corrector and the rest by a second corrector, who also adds comments on the points made by the other. The discovery of this document has made it possible, among other things, to reassess, in the light of the objections themselves, the passages in the *Journal* and the *Essais* in which Montaigne describes and considers the objections he was called upon to answer in front of the Roman censors. In recent years, Alain Legros and others have started to do just that, though it will take some time for the scholarly community to pursue all of the leads unearthed by the Godman discovery. The discovery certainly has, as I have indicated throughout, fascinating implications for some of the texts that have been analysed in the course of this book.

Of still greater interest is the account that Montaigne gives in his *Journal* of his first meeting with the two Roman censors, for it shifts the story away from the prospect of arbitrary censorship and towards the exercise of the art of free-thinking, an art that Montaigne and the senior censor, Fabri, turn out to share. Even censors, when they put their minds to it, can master the art! Montaigne seems to have been properly deferential towards the censors and the report they had commissioned while remaining discerning about the report's substance. He claims that some of its objections were based upon a misunderstanding of his text. But he does so only after he has conceded that other objections – the six points listed above in particular – do indeed represent his opinions and confessed that he had not thought them errors. The two papal representatives might well have chosen, on the strength of the report, to condemn the *Essais* outright or to impose deletions or revisions. Montaigne makes it clear that the more junior of the pair (Lancio) sided with the report against him (and this may well have been the part Lancio was meant to play in the proceedings). Fabri pursued a different course. He seems, if the *Journal* is to be believed on this score, to have reached the judgement early on in the first meeting that Montaigne was to be trusted. He made it clear that he had little sympathy for the report, accepted the replies he heard to each of its objections, and then produced against the other censor arguments of great ingenuity, as Montaigne puts it, in favour of his case.

The account of the first discussion ends, inconclusively, in disagreement between the censors about what is to be done.

By the time of the second meeting between the three men (on 15 April), Fabri appears to have prevailed over Lancio, and well-tempered free-thinking over ill-considered censorship. The two censors, having had the preliminary report read by 'some other Frenchmen', are now of one mind. Montaigne records the following entry in his *Journal*:

> On April 15th I went to say good-bye to the Master of the Sacred Palace and his colleague, who urged me not to make use of the censorship of my book, in which censorship some other Frenchmen had informed them there were many stupid things; saying that they honoured both my intention and affection for the Church and my ability, and thought so well of my frankness and conscience that they left it to myself to cut out of my book, when I wanted to republish it, whatever I found too licentious in it, and among other things the uses of the word 'fortune'. […] They urged me to help the Church by my eloquence (those are their courteous formulas) and to make my abode in this city, at peace and without interference from them. These are persons of great authority and potential cardinals.

> Le 15 avril, je fus prendre congé du maître *del Sacro Palazzo* et de son compagnon, qui me prièrent ne me servir point de la censure de mon livre, en laquelle autres Français les avaient avertis qu'il y avait plusieurs sottises; qu'ils honoraient et mon intention et mon affection envers l'Eglise et ma suffisance, et estimaient tant de ma franchise et conscience qu'ils remettaient à moi-même de retrancher en mon livre, quand je le voudrais réimprimer, ce que j'y trouverais trop licencieux et, entre autres choses, les mots de *fortune*. […] [Ils] me prièrent d'aider à l'Eglise par mon éloquence (ce sont leurs mots de courtoisie), et de faire demeure en cette ville paisible et hors de trouble avec eux. Ce sont personnes de grande autorité et cardinalables.
>
> (F 1178, G 237)

Along with the title of Roman citizen, which he had secured a few days earlier (F 1174, G 232), Montaigne was now being offered by the Pope's representatives the freedom of the universal city to write and think without fear of censorship. His fulsome praise of these representatives in the final sentence quoted above shows how pleased he was. The freedom on offer is of course surrounded by constraint, but it is a constraint to be exercised by Montaigne, not the censors. It requires him to use his frankness and conscience in excising anything from his own text that he judges to be 'too licentious' ('trop licencieux'). Licence, as we saw earlier, is the unbridled excess that gives the taking of liberties a bad name. The censors, in leaving Montaigne free to curb his own licentious excesses, were in effect treating him just as he, in one of the sentences of the *Essais* marked out for censorship in the preliminary report, calls for the child in 'Of the education of children' to be brought up: 'Let him be able to do all things, and love to do only the good' ('Qu'il puisse faire toutes choses, et n'ayme à faire que les bonnes'). They were enabling Montaigne to bring to the revisions of his text the well-tempered art of free-thinking.

He duly responded. The various revisions that may be traced to his encounters with the Roman censors are masterpieces in the art he shared with Sisto Fabri. He makes full use of the freedom invested in him by the censors to deal with the preliminary report as he sees fit. Only the six objections that he mentions in the *Journal* prompt him to any kind of response in the *Essais*; the others he ignores; and of the six, he responds directly to just two, meeting both with argued resistance.

The first objection – to Montaigne's uses of the word 'fortune', judged by the second corrector to be 'pagan' and 'Epicurean' – is the only one by which the censors set enough store to have referred to it in the second meeting. Montaigne's response comes in 'Of prayers' (I.56), the chapter he revises most extensively in the wake of his Roman adventure, emphasizing his submission to the absolute authority of the Church while also claiming the freedom to pursue in print his own thoughts on every sort of topic, including the religious topic of prayer, his thoughts being no more – and no less – than a layman's opinions. The chapter's opening sentences (F 278, VS 317–18), added on Montaigne's return from Rome in time for the 1582 edition of the *Essais* and extended again after 1588, may be seen as a response to the author's experience of Roman censorship as a whole. Montaigne makes it clear that his submission to the correction of the Church does not limit the freedom of the secular discourse to follow but, on the contrary, makes it possible. In a 1588 passage that occurs later in the same chapter, he turns to the objection made against his choice of language, taking the opportunity to reinforce what he sees as the proper distinction between the domain of theology (which he presents as the doctrinal and institutional preserve of the Church and its representatives) and that of philosophy (which he presents as open to his and others' merely human speculations). He relies on this distinction to defend his uses of 'fortune' and similar words. It is, he suggests, to the greater glory of theology that its divine lexicon is kept separate from the non-technical, unsanctioned vocabulary that befits the discourse of a layman such as he, a religious one, but a layman nonetheless. A sentence added at this point in the text after 1588 makes the argument relevant to Montaigne's project as a whole by connecting the secular character of the text to its essaying mode:

> I set forth notions that are human and my own, simply as human notions considered in themselves, not as determined and decreed by heavenly ordinance and permitting neither doubt nor dispute; matter of opinion, not matter of faith; what I reason out according to me, not what I believe according to God; as children set forth their essays, to be instructed, not to instruct; in a lay manner, not clerical, but always very religious.

> Je propose les fantasies humaines et miennes, simplement comme humaines fantasies, et separement considérées, non comme arrestees et reglées par l'ordonnance celeste, incapables de doubte et d'altercation: matiere d'opinion, non matiere de foy; ce que je discours selon moy, non ce que je croy selon Dieu, comme les enfans proposent leurs essais: instruisables, non instruisants; d'une maniere laïque, non clericale, mais tres-religieuse toujours.
> (F 284, VS 323)

Prompted by the censors, it seems, Montaigne here produces one of his clearest descriptions of the spirit that animates the *Essais*.

The second objection – that he had named heretic poets – draws a response on at least two occasions. One of these, a passage first added in 1588 to 'Of presumption' (II.17), occurs a page or two before the praise of Beza and Buchanan that first provoked the objection. Montaigne emphasizes the dispassionate generosity of spirit with which he attempts to treat his enemies in order jealously to preserve what he calls 'the liberty of my judgement' ('la liberté de mon jugement'; F 607, VS 659). The connection between this statement of his commitment to free-thinking and the monk's objection to his praise of heretic poets remains implicit. He responds directly to the monk's second objection, of course, in the passage from 'Of husbanding your will' analysed in this chapter. He does so there in a way that seems directly to emphasize the adherence to freedom of judgement voiced in 'Of presumption'. He reserves for the Roman censor the final, emphatic, place in the list of examples he gives of bad partisan thinking and of his opposition to it: 'And I did not concede even to the magistrate that he was right to condemn a book for having placed a heretic among the best poets of this century' ('Et ne conceday pas au magistrat mesme qu'il eust raison de condamner un livre pour avoir logé entre les meilleurs poëtes de ce siècle un heretique'). It is his view that the heretic and the poet lodged within Beza are two, marked by the same clear separation that exists between the divine wisdom of the Church and the merely human speculations of the *Essais*, and he stresses his refusal to yield to the censor who confused the one with the other. The adverb 'even' ('mesme') shows that the episode offers an emphatic statement of Montaigne's freedom of judgement.

To the report's first two objections, then, Montaigne responds directly in the later editions of the *Essais* – 1582 and 1588 – published during his lifetime. Notice, though, how discreetly he phrases those responses: in 'Of prayers' and 'Of presumption' alike he makes no reference either to the initial objection or to its author, and when he does so in 'Of husbanding your will', it is in a glancing allusion to a 'magistrate'. He wraps his encounter with the Roman censors in a discreet silence, and while he does not alter his intellectual commitment to independence of judgement, neither does he flaunt it. He practises, in other words, the well-tempered art of free-thinking that he shares with his principal censor.

He does not honour the four remaining objections with direct responses. He does respond indirectly, however, and almost always with a discreet defiance. He rarely contents himself with simply declining to excise the point that drew the initial objection; he usually finds some way of sharpening its point and purchase. This process takes time – some of his more pointed reactions are late additions that did not appear in print during his lifetime – but by the end of his life they were ready for inclusion in the text of the *Essais*.

His revision of the chapter 'Of freedom of conscience' (II.19) is a case in point, if a complex one, requiring further assessment in the light of the unearthed report. We now know that the second of Montaigne's Roman readers took him to task on three grounds: for 'praising Julian the Apostate exceedingly' ('mirifice laudat Julianum Apostatum'); for dismissing as apocryphal the story that Julian, at the moment of death, acknowledged that Christ had defeated him; and for 'calling into question whether or not freedom of conscience, which the heretics so avidly seek, should be allowed' ('facit dubium an debeat permitti libertas religionis illa, quam heretici tantopere requirunt, necne'). He meets the first and third points with the constancy of silence in later iterations of the *Essais*. The first point should, however, cause us to look afresh at the *Journal*, where Montaigne records merely that he was criticized for having 'excused' Julian, a word that hardly does justice to the force of 'mirifice laudat'! He does indeed, as Alain Legros has suggested, seem to have toned down the severity of the objection in his account of it. The third point made by his Roman reader concerns the passage, analysed in chapter 5 above, in which Montaigne offers his readers alternative ways of understanding freedom of conscience as a policy. The Roman reader's objection seems to be that Montaigne is opening up for debate an issue on which the Church had – firmly – pronounced (the Council of Trent, in 1562 and 1563, opposed the use of concessions in the search for religious concord). Montaigne may well have felt that, just as in 'Of prayers', here too he was essaying his lay judgement on an unresolved matter of political opinion, not pronouncing on a matter of faith, and that he had said enough in the earlier chapter to answer the Roman reader's third point. He responds to the second point, initially at least, with a good deal more deference: he removes the offending passage from the chapter in the 1582 and 1588 editions of the *Essais*. But he reinstates the passage in the Bordeaux copy at a more prominent moment in the text than it first occupied, now coming right at the end of his portrait of Julian and just before the chapter's closing sequence, and the 1595 edition reflects the same choice. He reveals his unconstrained turn of mind once again, that is, by quietly turning the screw a notch tighter.

He does the same in response to the sixth and final objection that he picks out from the report, namely, that it was his opinion, in 'Of the education of children' (I.26), that a child should be brought up to be able to do anything. Two passages are of particular interest here.

The first is an addition to 'Of the education of children' itself. It comes in the sentences directly preceding the passage analysed in chapter 2 above. Montaigne argues there for the value of an education in free-thinking by stressing how rare it is and how shackled our minds really are. In 1588, he adds the story of Girolamo Borro (1512–92), an Aristotelian natural philosopher strongly influenced by Pomponazzi whom, as he records in the *Journal* (F 1235, G 319), he himself met in

Pisa in July 1581. He criticizes Borro (without naming him) for his slavish conformity to Aristotelian doctrine before voicing his unease at the
censorship Borro's work suffered at the hands of the Roman Inquisition.
The pro-Aristotelian proposition of Borro and its censorship by the
Inquisition emerge, in other words, as equally far from the truth. The
sentence in question, when added in 1588, read as follows: 'That proposition of his, having been interpreted a little too broadly and damagingly,
put him once, and kept him too long, in great danger at Rome' ('Cette
sienne proposition, pour avoir esté un peu largement et injurieusement
interpretée, le mit autrefois et tint long temps en grand accessoire à
Rome'; F 134–5, VS 151). The Bordeaux copy and the 1595 edition agree
on two crucial revisions to this sentence: 'damagingly' ('injurieusement')
is replaced by 'unfairly' ('iniquement'), emphasizing the moral force of
the misinterpretation, and the name of the institution that inflicted this
injustice on Borro – the Inquisition – is added to the final clause of the
sentence. This addition may not have been intended as a response to the
report's sixth objection in particular, but as a reflection on Montaigne's
experience of censorship in general, although the fact that it appears in
'Of the education of children', the chapter targeted, connects it to that
specific objection. The effect of the addition, in any case, is clear: to
reiterate Montaigne's opposition to abuses of censorship and to point
out that he knows others to have been less fortunate than he in their
encounters with the representatives of the Inquisition.

The second passage of interest here comes in the final chapter of the
Essais, 'Of experience' (III.13), Montaigne's valedictory essay in the art of
making personal experience serve the aim of self-knowledge. He stresses
there that habit need not set us in our ways: it can, at its best, shape us
to remain flexible and adaptable to different circumstances. This is precisely the broader point he had made in the passage in 'Of the education
of children' that drew the fire of his Roman readers. In 'Of experience'
Montaigne personalizes the point by claiming to possess this kind of
flexibility and describing it as his best quality. He emphasizes, just as he
had done in 'Of the education of children', the importance of education
and upbringing to the acquisition of this quality:

> A young man should violate his own rules to arouse his vigour and keep
> it from growing mouldy and lax. And there is no way of life so stupid and
> feeble as that which is conducted by rules and discipline.

Un jeune homme doit troubler ses regles pour esveiller sa vigueur, la garder de moisir et s'apoltronir. Et n'est train de vie si sot et si debile que celuy qui se conduict par ordonnance et discipline. (F 1011, VS 1083)

The theme and tone of the earlier chapter, 'Of the education of children', return here, and the advice to the young man remains the same, despite the objection it provoked in Rome. The second sentence repeats the anti-authoritarian position from which, in the earlier chapter, Montaigne advocates an education in free-thinking. Here, though, the perspective has broadened: he is thinking not just of an education but of an unfettered and unconstrained approach throughout life. The notion of free-thinking, absorbed into the matter and manner of the *Essais* in Book III, resurfaces here in the book's final chapter. It appears there, as it does in 'Of husbanding your will', as a late expression of a thought by which Montaigne now recognizes, in retrospect, that he has lived his life and written his book.

We readers of Montaigne owe a considerable debt of gratitude in this respect to his Roman censors, and particularly to Sisto Fabri, who led the process of censorship. Such a figure is – and for good reason – an unlikely hero to emerge from any account of early modern free-thinking. The Inquisition and Index, in most cases, did not just police anti-comformist thought; it oppressed it. The case of Girolamo Borro is one among many to demonstrate this. But those cases do not tell the whole story, and if we were to assume that they did, we would have lapsed into the bad form of arguing that Montaigne opposes in our chosen passage. We need to liberate ourselves from partisan judgements, in our turn, if we are to bring the method of free-thinking to bear on its own history. We too need to learn the art of saying 'they did this wickedly and that virtuously'. We have already seen the stimulus that – thanks to Fabri's liberal handling of them – four of the preliminary report's six objections mentioned by Montaigne provided the author in his later work. The two remaining objections acted in the same way. The report's objection to the condemnation of torture in 'Of cruelty' (II.11) and 'Cowardice, mother of cruelty' (II.27) spurs Montaigne on to reiterate his condemnation with increasing eloquence in successive editions of those two chapters. The fact that torture was an occasional practice of the Inquisition makes the latitude that Fabri offered Montaigne on this point all the more remarkable. Malcolm Smith suggests that it represents an unusual case of a papal censor 'certainly condoning and probably encouraging a reasoned attack upon a practice of the Roman Inquisition'. He suggests, too, that the objection, occasioned by the idea in 'Of prayers' (I.56) that prayer properly requires a rejection of vicious impulses, prompted Montaigne both to stress the fallibility of his opinions in that chapter – while nonetheless maintaining them – and to apply his idea about prayer to the practice of repentance in order to explain his provocative claim, in 'Of repentance' (III.2), that he rarely repents. Here too, then, is further evidence that the manner in which the Roman censors reacted to the 1580 *Essais* proved a vital goad and stimulus to Montaigne not only in his revisions of Books I and II, but also in the 'extension' of his project into Book III, where at various important moments he looks back to his encounter with censorship and thinks again about the vexed questions – those of intellectual freedom and constraint chief among them – that the encounter raised.

A Message to the Future

We have hardly strayed from our theme, but it is time to return to the passage in 'Of husbanding your will' that sent us to late sixteenth-century Rome, for we can now see that its reflections on the art of free-thinking are embedded in a present – the time of writing – in which the past looms large: the remote past of ancient Rome and the recent past of Montaigne's early compositions and their reception in the Rome of Fabri and company. The present, however freighted with the past, is never any more than a moving point in the onward flow of time. Montaigne, who realizes this, knows also that his present is the past of the future in which he hopes to be read. He uses the time-travelling vehicle of his thought and his writing not only to bring the past into the present, but also to write downstream in the flow of time, towards that future. Montaigne did not claim to be able to read what the future held, and he distrusted those of his contemporaries who did make such claims, as he makes clear in the early chapter 'Of prognostications' (I.11: 'Des prognostications'). Yet he looks to the future at certain moments in the *Essais*, thinks and writes about it in distinctive ways, and even, it might be said, makes a place for the future in the text.

We saw in the previous chapter how, in 'Of vanity', he does so by spelling out both the freedoms and the companionship available to the deserving reader and the conditions in which the undeserving will meet with a rebuke from his ghost. The passage in 'Of husbanding your will' is altogether less confrontational in its treatment of the reader: there are no moments of direct address here, as there are in 'Of vanity', no promises or threats. Quietly but firmly, Montaigne makes room for a reader wishing to be a companion to him in the adventure of the text, a reader whom he calls upon – as Don Quixote calls upon Sancho Panza – to agree or disagree with him in their shared endeavour to make a friend of truth. The quietness with which he does so here makes this a less hermeneutically exciting passage than the one in 'Of vanity', perhaps, but also a more typical example of the way in which he sets about creating a relationship with the reader in page after page of the *Essais*.

How does he approach his task? The answer is to be found in the passage's subtle interplay of personal pronouns. I noted earlier that the essayist, the speaking 'I' ('je'), tries out his thoughts in the company of three groups, which he refers to respectively as 'one' ('on'), 'they' ('ils'), and 'we' ('nous'). Frame introduces potential confusion here by translating not only 'ils' but also the indefinite personal pronoun 'on' as 'they'. But Montaigne reserves 'ils' for those incapable of free-thinking who reveal their prejudice, as he puts it towards the end of the passage, by wanting us to replicate it: 'They want everyone to be blind and stupid in his own cause, and our conviction and judgement to serve, not the truth, but the aim of our desire' ('Ils veulent que chacun, en son party, soit aveugle et hebeté; que notre persuasion et jugement serve non à la verité mais au project de notre désir'). He mainly applies 'on' to those wise and historically remote ancient Romans whose difference from 'ils' is that they served the truth as faithful friends even when it was uncomfortable to do so (as in the case of Marcus Manlius). 'Nous', as Montaigne uses it here, is the most flexible and capacious of the three groups. In the first sentence of the passage, his use of the pronoun is timebound, referring as it does to those of his contemporaries with whom he sides in the present troubles. It next appears in the sentence following the one in which Montaigne alludes to his brush with the Roman censors: 'Should we not dare say of a thief that he has a fine leg?' ('N'oserions nous dire d'un voleur qu'il a belle greve?') 'Nous' here floats free of a particular time and place. It implicates not only the essayist, but also the reader, whom Montaigne, through his inclusive choice of pronoun, challenges to join the circle of those free enough of mind to praise the physical grace of a villain. The only alternative home for the reader in this passage is, of course, the zealous group, lurking under the banner of 'ils', whom Montaigne charges with trying to foist 'their' prejudice upon 'us'. On this, its final occurrence in the passage, the first person plural is part of a declaration at once timebound and for times to come, a message sent to the future, quietly challenging its readers to judge where we belong in the drama of personal pronouns that the passage stages: whether we are one of 'them' or one of a free-thinking 'us' among which Montaigne numbers himself.

The Future of the Essais

Montaigne writes his way towards the future, then, by making room for any number of responses to his text. And he challenges his readers to decide whether or not they – we – belong to the company of the free-thinking among whom he numbers himself. How have his readers responded to this challenge? What has become of the future he imagines and fashions in the *Essais*?

An adequate answer to either of these questions would fill many a book, of course, and this one is coming to an end. A few preliminary remarks will have to suffice here. We might wonder, in the first place, what exactly is meant by 'the future' of a text written in a steadily retreating past. We ought, in that case, to distinguish between two sets of futures: those that an author like Montaigne imagines for his text, on the one hand, and, on the other, the futures that the text has encountered – and continues to encounter – in its journey downstream: what might be called its 'afterlives'. No sooner has this distinction been made, however, than Montaigne's *Essais* upset it: the futures that the text has known – its afterlives – actually turn out in large part to correspond to the futures it imagines.

This is by no means, of course, always the case. Reading Montaigne's *Essais* with an eye for the futures that he speaks of or reaches towards takes you to parts of the text that other topics do not reach. Some of the futures appear, with the benefit of hindsight, actual and familiar; others dormant or moribund. The latter include his hope that the pistol, which he views as an ineffectual weapon, will one day disappear from use; his claim that it would be more reasonable, given the 'ordinary weakness' ('faiblesse ordinaire') of the female sex, for a man to leave the management of his estate to his grown-up sons rather than his wife; and the suggestion he voices along with the Aztecs that the destruction of their civilization by the Europeans may be a sign that the world is about to end. When viewed from the downstream perspective of a world in which the destructive power of firearms cannot be denied, in which equal rights for women have been widely recognized and enshrined in property law as elsewhere, and in which apocalypse remains an unrealized fear, these merely imagined futures look remote, to say the least. They need to be understood on their own terms as interventions into broader sixteenth-century debates about the relative merits of the ancient and the modern, about questions of succession and inheritance, and about the European conquest of the New World. They remind us, all the same, that Montaigne's prescience has its limits.

Those of Montaigne's futures to have been in some way realized down-stream are greater in number and of more significance. These realized futures include Montaigne's suggestion in 'A consideration upon Cicero' (I.40) – which I examined at the end of chapter 2 above – that he has left room for ingenious minds of the future to produce from the subject-matter of his book 'numberless essays' ('infinis essais'); his claim that his exercise in first-person introspection has produced the only book of its kind in the world; his description of himself as a new figure in the shape of an 'accidental philosopher' who presents his thoughts in the company of the texts he has read; his uneasy sense that the arguments of Pyrrhonist scepticism carry a disturbing, self-defeating power in debates about religion, even when used in its defence; his search for a reader who will prove to be a friend: all of these passages have played a vital role in the text's afterlives, and it is tempting to list them in this way, extracted from their internal context in the *Essais*. They need, of course, to be handled with just as much caution as the apparently dormant or moribund futures. I pointed out earlier that, in the immediate context of the chapter 'A consideration upon Cicero', Montaigne's suggestion that his book makes room for numberless essays of the future is a reply in advance to those of his readers who might choose to reflect his critique of Cicero's desire for literary renown back on to his own reasons for writing. This immediate context should not be ignored, but it hardly exhausts the sense of Montaigne's suggestion, and his other messages to the future function in the same way.

These messages have received varying responses. One need only cite the development, starting with Bacon, of the essay as a literary genre after Montaigne's death; the explosion of interest in autobiography and other forms of first-person narrative, since the eighteenth century, whose effects continue to this day; the appearance of a 'new philosopher', in Descartes, whose method requires him to clear away all the texts he has read (including, no doubt, the *Essais*); the characterization of Montaigne in the age of Pascal as the archetypical irreligious free-thinker; and the suggestion of Marie de Gournay, the first editor of the *Essais* after Montaigne's death, that she was the friend and the reader that he sought. All of these stories bring the past with them into the present, and all may be said to start with Montaigne, if you are looking for stories with beginnings.

I prefer to say that they start alongside him: that they are best seen, not as developments whose origins can be traced back to him, but as adventures on which his readers have embarked in his company. They are adventures, as I have tried to suggest throughout this book, that Montaigne makes possible through his art of free-thinking. That last suggestion holds even when those adventures take his readers in directions that he could never have foreseen, in fact it holds even more strongly in such cases, since Montaigne opens his text to the prospect that it will encounter divergence as well as convergence in the undiscovered and unpredictable country that is the future. This does not mean that he gives his readers unbridled licence. He invites them to join him in making a greater friend of truth, but only on condition that they first understand what he has to say, and he threatens any reader who fails to do so – whether by subjecting him to excessive blame or praise – with a visit from his ghost. That first task of understanding is the condition of free-thinking friendship that keeps Montaigne's readers alongside him, and haunted by him, even as they strike out on their own adventures in search of the truth.

The question of how to resolve the legacy of Montaigne's ghost has long preoccupied his readers. Jean-Jacques Rousseau (1712–78) and Denis Diderot (1713–84), for example, diverge in their approaches to this question – as they did on so many other matters – when writing autobiographical narratives of self-revelation in the late eighteenth century.

Rousseau tries to bury the ghost in his posthumously published *Confessions* (1782). His claim – that he is the first person ever to have composed a portrait of himself that is true in every way – calls to mind Montaigne's insistence, in 'To the Reader', on the truth of his own self-portrait. So how can Rousseau claim to be first? He deals with this question in his preface to the Neuchâtel manuscript of the *Confessions* by presenting Montaigne as a false precursor and an arch-dissembler who reveals only a part of the truth: 'Montaigne offers us a likeness, but in profile. Who knows if some scar on the cheek or a missing eye on the side he keeps hidden from us would not have totally changed his physiognomy?'

('Montaigne se peint ressemblant mais de profil. Qui sait si quelque balafre à la joue ou un œil crevé du coté qu'il nous a caché, n'eut pas totalement changé sa physionomie.') It is hard not to think that Rousseau says more about himself here than he does about Montaigne. No text, after all, is more haunted than the *Confessions* by the prospect of failing to persuade its readers of the perfect friendship it shares with the truth.

If Rousseau attempts to bury the ghost, Diderot attempts to befriend it in his *Salon de 1767*, writing about two painted portraits of himself in the manner of Montaigne. As Kate E. Tunstall has shown, when he criticizes both portraits for failing to capture their subject, he does so by adapting to his purposes a free-thinking saying – 'Michel is my friend but a greater friend is truth' ('J'aime Michel, mais j'aime mieux la vérité') – the Michel in question being not Michel de Montaigne, but Diderot's friend Louis-Michel Vanloo (1707–71), the painter of one of the two portraits. Diderot then offers a textual self-portrait in terms that parody Montaigne's 'To the Reader' even as they realize the fiction of naked self-revelation that, as we saw at the beginning of chapter 1 above, Montaigne places beyond the limits of what he could have achieved at the time and in the place of his own writing. Imitating Montaigne, Tunstall suggests, enables Diderot to take his precursor's art of self-portraiture over the threshold of history and into a new world.

While Diderot and Rousseau diverge in their attitudes towards Montaigne, then, both find themselves writing their narratives of self-revelation alongside, and haunted by, his ghost. Rousseau and Diderot typify the contrasting reactions to Montaigne, of hostility and enthusiasm, which characterize the long and continuing reception history of the *Essais*. What provokes these reactions, I submit, is something open and free about the writing, from the first sentences of Montaigne's opening note 'To the Reader' onwards, which makes intimate friends – or enemies – of its readers.

Friedrich Nietzsche was one such friend, and he remains an influential one, given his towering status as a prophet of the modern age. In a letter of 21 March 1885, Nietzsche told his mother that the only three people for whom he greatly cared had been dead a long time, and named Montaigne among those absent intimates. Throughout his published work, Nietzsche's affection for Montaigne surfaces, accompanied by admiration for his spirit of mischief, the bravery of his sceptical approach, and the contrarian qualities that make him a true free-thinker. He touches on those last qualities when comparing Montaigne with another of his exemplars, the philosopher of pessimism Arthur Schopenhauer (1788–1860), in an early essay entitled 'Schopenhauer as Educator' ('Schopenhauer als Erzieher'; 1874). Montaigne and Schopenhauer, he says, have two things in common: honesty ('Ehrlichkeit'), the kind earned by freedom from the desire to deceive others and oneself, and a cheerfulness that truly cheers ('eine wirkliche erheiternde Heiterkeit'), not the ersatz version peddled by mediocre writers and complacent thinkers, but that which is produced by the human insights of those who have triumphed over the monstrous truth. Nietzsche places Montaigne above Schopenhauer in his possession of that first quality of honesty and offers, in the process, what can only be described as a truly cheering testimony to an absent friend:

> I know of only one other writer whom, as regards his honesty, I would set equal to or even above Schopenhauer: Montaigne. The joy of living on this earth has truly been increased by the fact that such a person wrote. At any rate, since my first encounter with this freest, most energetic of spirits, I have found it necessary to say of him what he said of Plutarch: 'As soon as I cast a glance at him, I sprouted another leg or a wing.' I would take my example from him if I were set the task of making myself feel at home on this earth.

> Ich weiß nur noch einen Schriftsteller, den ich in Betreff der Ehrlichkeit Schopenhauer gleich, ja noch höher stelle: das ist Montaigne. Daß ein solcher Mensch geschrieben hat, dadurch ist wahrlich die Lust, auf dieser Erde zu leben, vermehrt worden. Mir wenigstens geht es seit dem Bekanntwerden mit dieser freiesten und kräftigsten Seele so, daß ich sagen muß, was er von Plutarch sagt: 'kaum habe ich einen Blick auf ihn geworfen, so ist mir ein Bein oder ein Flügel gewachsen.' Mit ihm würde ich es halten, wenn die Aufgabe gestellt wäre, es sich auf der Erde heimisch zu machen.

Montaigne is the freest and most energetic of thinkers, for Nietzsche, and this is what made the encounter with him a joy and liberation. Nietzsche goes on to liberate himself from Montaigne by a joyous accident in this passage. He misquotes a sentence added to 'On some verses of Virgil' (III.5) after 1588 in which Montaigne, paying homage to the inexhaustibly edible riches he feasts on in Plutarch, says of him: 'I cannot be with him even a little without taking out a drumstick or a wing' ('Je ne le puis si racointer que je n'en tire cuisse ou aile'; F 809, VS 875). Nietzsche, when translating this sentence into German, transforms Montaigne's feasting metaphor for literary imitation – Plutarch as roast chicken – into a fantasy of metamorphosis and flight. He noted in the margin of his own printed copy of this essay at this point that he had made an incorrect translation of Montaigne. But nothing illustrates better the liberation that Nietzsche finds in Montaigne than his free and fantastical imitation of his absent friend's sentence about Plutarch.

Montaigne has had no enemy more intimate than Blaise Pascal. Pascal was involved in the second major episode of Catholic censorship to have affected the *Essais*, an episode with profound implications for the interpretation of Montaigne's free-thinking, so he brings this book, if not full circle, then certainly to a moment of closure in the downstream flow of time. I specify Catholic censorship, because between Montaigne's encounter of 1581 with the Roman censors and the age of Pascal comes Simon Goulart's Genevan 1595 edition of the *Essais*, based on the text published by Abel L'Angelier in 1588 but expurgated for a Calvinist readership. Goulart excises passages and entire chapters, including 'Of freedom of conscience', which – given what we have have already seen of its reception at the hands of its Roman readers – manifestly satisfied neither side of the confessional conflict in the late sixteenth century. The early reception of Montaigne's work was bound to find itself enmeshed in that conflict. But the Edict of Nantes of 1598 fixed the country's dominant Catholic majority and Huguenot minority in a lasting, if uneasy, accommodation, and by the time Pascal was deciding to write in defence of the Christian religion, a new battle for the soul of France was engaged between devout Catholics and irreligious free-thinkers.

This, at least, is how the Pascal of the *Pensées* and the *Entretien avec Sacy* sees matters. That Pascal, as I suggested at the outset of this book, identifies Montaigne as the archetype of the irreligious free-thinker or *libertin* he has in his sights. The *Entretien*, which contains Pascal's most sustained reading of Montaigne, records discussions about secular philosophy that took place between Pascal and Louis-Isaac Le Maistre de Sacy (1613–84), then spiritual director of the Augustinian (or Jansenist) movement based at Port-Royal, with which Pascal was closely associated. In Pascal's contribution to the *Entretien*, probably composed in the mid-1650s, he characterizes Montaigne as an easygoing but self-centred sceptic. He sees Montaigne's practice of Pyrrhonist doubt as the source of the freedom with which he judges actions and events:

> In this thoroughly free spirit of his, it makes no difference to him whether he wins or loses arguments, since he invariably has, in either case, a means of revealing the weakness of any opinion whatsoever: he has stationed himself in universal doubt so advantageously that he draws equal strength from his triumphs and defeats.

> Dans ce génie tout libre, il lui est entièrement égal de l'emporter ou non dans la dispute; ayant toujours, par l'un ou l'autre exemple, un moyen de faire voir la faiblesse des opinions; étant posté avec tant d'avantage dans ce doute universel qu'il s'y fortifie également par son triomphe et par sa défaite.

Pascal delights in Montaigne's sceptical freedom of mind and, in the face of considerable resistance from Sacy, argues for its use in destroying the presumptuous self-possession of the Stoic philosopher Epictetus (50–120 CE). He goes on to argue, however, that, once it has dismantled Stoic presumption, Pyrrhonist scepticism fails disastrously, for its extreme doubt lures Montaigne into a lax ethic of despair about and indifference to his salvation. The intention behind this double deconstruction – of Stoicism and Pyrrhonist scepticism – is to show secular philosophy as a whole that it can resolve its inner contradictions only by accepting the revealed truth of the Christian religion. Pascal's reading of Montaigne, along the way, makes two decisive moves: it fastens his freedom of thought to one intellectual position, Pyrrhonist scepticism; and it equates that form of scepticism with religious indifference. It thereby turns Montaigne into the archetype of the irreligious free-thinkers whom Pascal, in the apology for the Christian religion that he left unfinished at his death in 1662 and which was first published in fragmentary form under the title *Pensées* in 1670, attempts to shake out of what he views as their criminal indifference to their salvation. Written when he was starting to plan his apology, the *Entretien* contains an early sketch of that project, in which an irreligious free-thinking Montaigne figures as an obstacle to faith.

Pascal was not alone in seeing Montaigne in this guise. Those on the opposite side of the debate about religion from Pascal – leading *libertins* such as François de La Mothe le Vayer (1588–1672), Gabriel Naudé (1600–53), and Cyrano de Bergerac (1619–55) – claim Montaigne and his 'disciple' Pierre Charron (1541–1603), whom they systematically associate, as precursors for their ventures in irreligious sceptical free-thinking. By no means did all seventeenth-century French readers agree with this reading of Montaigne, of course, but the opposing sides in this debate did. Their combined force helped to produce a major turn in the reception history of the *Essais*: where 'Of freedom of conscience' (II.19) had been the contentious 'middle' chapter of the *Essais* in the late sixteenth century, it was now replaced by the 'Apology for Raymond Sebond' (II.12), seen as the author's sceptical manifesto in an age when scepticism meant just one damnable thing. Pascal was instrumental in this interpretive turn. His reading of Montaigne was adopted by his erstwhile friends at Port-Royal, Antoine Arnauld (1612–94) and Pierre Nicole (1625–95), in the decade following his death. The second (1666) edition of their *Logic, or The Art of Thinking* (*La Logique ou l'art de penser*), first published in 1662, includes by way of a digression an attack on the author of the *Essais*. That attack ends, as Alan M. Boase puts it, 'with a direct invitation to put Montaigne on the Index'. The terms of that attack are borrowed from Pascal. The leading French bishop of the day, Jacques Bénigne Bossuet (1627–1704), and the Catholic theologian and Cartesian philosopher Nicolas Malebranche (1638–1715) also largely shared Pascal's view of Montaigne. The *Essais* escaped inclusion on the 1593 Roman Index, which was compiled after Montaigne had published revisions to his text in 1582 and 1588, and was the Index in which writings in the various European vernacular languages came under particular scrutiny. But the text did not survive the devout late seventeenth-century barrage against it in France and was placed on the Roman Index of 1676. The report prepared on this occasion has also been unearthed in the archives of the Index. It argues that Montaigne's book should be forbidden because it is full of suspected heresies and affronts to good morals. It detects in the *Essais*, just as Pascal had done, more than a whiff of *libertinage*. The report, unlike the one Sisto Fabri had commissioned back in 1581, was adopted by the Congregation of the Index.

History does not record whether or not Fabri's late seventeenth-century successor received a visitation in the Vatican from Montaigne's ghost. But the reception history of his text had, by this point, certainly crossed a threshold. Montaigne would have surely understood Pascal's reading of his text, but rejected it, arguing that it confused the unrestrained licence of Pascal's irreligious contemporaries with his own well-tempered liberty of thought – and that it was possible, in his day at least, to think about all kinds of questions in an unconstrained secular manner that was compatible with, because distinct from, the authority of the Church and its teachings in matters of faith. That kind of thinking carried within it the risk of transgression – that risk is inherent in freedom – but also the resources of self-restraint. That Pascal and his contemporaries could not make the distinction showed only that they lived in a zealous age in which it was not possible to give even two cheers for free-thinking.

Pascal, like so many before and since him, reads Montaigne in a way that says more about him than it does about Montaigne. It is an extraordinary feature of their troubled relationship that Pascal realizes this. He encapsulates his misreading of the *Essais* in a sentence that recalls one of Montaigne's late masterpieces of free-thinking imitation in the passage from 'Of the education of children' analysed in chapter 2 above: 'It is no more according to Plato than according to me, since he and I understand and see it in the same way' ('Ce n'est non plus selon Platon que selon moy, puis que luy et moi l'entendons et voyons de mesme'). This, Montaigne's adaptation of a Senecan sentence, Pascal picks up from him and recasts in his own way in the *Pensées*: 'It is not in Montaigne but in myself that I find everything that I see there' ('Ce n'est pas dans Montaigne mais dans moi que je trouve tout ce que j'y vois'). Pascal refers back to Montaigne in this sentence even as he removes him from the picture. The strange mixture here of companionship in the search for truth – and violent disagreement – is what makes Pascal the most intimate of Montaigne's enemies. Terence Cave, surveying the broader reception history of the *Essais*, says of Pascal's sentence: 'That, in its briefest form, is how to use Montaigne's book according to a rule it insistently formulates but with an outcome it never predicted.' I would want to add to Cave's observation, by way of a conclusion to the present book, that it is thanks to his literary art of free-thinking that Montaigne makes it possible for a reader like Pascal to use and abuse him in this way.

This book has advanced the argument that free-thinking is an important and, since the age of Pascal, much misunderstood literary and philosophical context for the venture – and adventure – of the *Essais*. It has tried, at the same time, to remain open to the excess of the *Essais*, the text's ability to connect contexts and to exceed them, leaving its readers searching for yet another path that will lead to the heart of the labyrinth. This approach is the result of a particular interpretative judgement – which I share with many of his readers – about the exceptionally mercurial and open-ended nature of the text that Montaigne wrote. I have undertaken no exercises in free-thinking of my own but attempted, instead, to meet the prior condition of dispassionate understanding. I hope that it will now be clear why. Seeking to understand what a ghost as thoughtful as Montaigne has to say is the first step that a reader who would be a companion – and a Sancho Panza in search of an island to govern – needs to take. It is a formidable challenge in its own right – only a foolish reader would claim otherwise – for it requires you to read and reread the text, keeping one eye on its intimate fabric and one eye on the bigger picture, with imaginative sympathy and an open mind alike. That is enough work for now.

A year after it was put on the Index in Rome, a condensed version of the *Essais* appeared in Paris, entitled *The Spirit of the* Essais *of Michael, Lord Montaigne* (*L'Esprit des Essais de Michel, Seigneur de Montaigne*; 1677). Its author, Charles de Sercy (1623–1700?), explains in a short preface how he has taken the liberty of removing from the text the various features – its digressions, its long stretches of discursive reflection, and its use of Latin quotations – that its critics have judged excessive. The intention is not to side with those critics but to keep the text alive by performing upon it what is described as 'a pleasing reduction' ('une agreable reduction'). Just two of the six passages from across the *Essais* analysed at close quarters in the present book appear in any form in the *Spirit*. The passage from 'Of freedom of conscience' is the only one to survive largely intact, and in this respect at least, Charles de Sercy proves more faithful to the spirit of the *Essais* than certain devout Catholics and Calvinists of the previous century would have liked. The passage from 'Of the education of children', the only other one to survive, fares less well. Where, as we saw, Montaigne in that passage takes the commonplace metaphor for literary imitation of bees travelling from flower to flower and applies it to the exercise of free-thinking, the *Spirit* reverses that move, making Montaigne's use of those wild bees entirely tame and commonplace. And the other passages, of course, have gone. With friends like Charles de Sercy, one cannot help feeling, Montaigne had no need of enemies in the late seventeenth century to see to it that his text would not trouble the printers of France for half a century thereafter. The reduction that the *Spirit* performs on the *Essais* is pleasing only if one prefers the ease and straight lines of conventional thought over the difficulty and indirections of an unusual mind on the move. It deals the text a mortal blow by stripping it of its freedom.

The title of Charles de Sercy's work suggests that its author was attempting to capture in reduced form the spirit of the original. The attempt, in that case, was no success. It is true of course that every attempt to grasp the mystery of a book as voluble and as volatile as the *Essais* must end in failure. But one can at least try to avoid certain kinds of failure. I have preferred – for my part – to suggest too many points of entry into the text, to point out too many of its directions and indirections, rather than too few. If the present book leaves its reader on the threshold of the *Essais*, intrigued by the freedom of the text but still a little disorientated, then it will have failed as best it could.

Notes

THE SPIRIT OF THE ESSAIS

3.   INSCRIPTION: see Montaigne, *Les Essais*, ed. Jean Balsamo, Michel Magnien, and Catherine Magnien-Simonin (Paris: Gallimard, 2007), p. 1315.

5–6.   TERENCE CAVE: *How to Read Montaigne* (London: Granta, 2007), p. 37.

6.   DAVID QUINT: *Montaigne and the Quality of Mercy: Ethical and Political Themes in the* Essais (Princeton, NJ: Princeton University Press, 1998), p. xiii.

6–7.   MARIE DE GOURNAY: *Les Essais*, ed. Balsamo, Magnien, and Magnien-Simonin, p. 10.

8.   THE 1948 UNITED NATIONS DECLARATION OF HUMAN RIGHTS: printed as an Appendix to Robert E. Asher et al., *The United Nations and the Promotion of the General Welfare* (Washington, DC: The Brookings Institution, 1957), pp. 1108–12 (esp. pp. 1109–10).

12.   JOHN O'BRIEN: 'Retrait', in *Montaigne politique*, ed. Philippe Desan (Paris: Champion, 2006), pp. 205–22 (pp. 206–7).

15.   TERENCE CAVE: *How to Read Montaigne*, p. 5.

16–17.   A. D. NUTTALL: *Shakespeare the Thinker* (New Haven, CT, and London: Yale University Press, 2007), pp. 380, 383.

17.   MIGUEL DE CERVANTES: *Don Quijote de la Mancha*, 2 vols, ed. Francisco Rico (Barcelona: Instituto Cervantes, 1998), I, p. 1050. The translation is that of Charles Jarvis, *Don Quixote de la Mancha*, intro. Milan Kundera (Oxford: Oxford World's Classics, 1999), p. 949.

1 OPENING MOVES

23. PEDRO MEXÍA: I consulted the 1577 edition of Claude Gruget's translation, entitled *Les Diverses leçons de Pierre Messie* (Paris: Nicolas Bonfons). The text was first published in Spanish under the title *Silva de varia lección* (1540).

28. 'THE CHILDREN OF OUR MIND': on this see Wes Williams, 'Back to the Future: "Les Enfantements de Nostre Esprit"', in *Pre-Histories and Afterlives: Studies in Critical Method*, ed. Anna Holland and Richard Scholar (London: Legenda, 2009), pp. 121–34.

31. CRITICAL SURVEY OF MEDICINE: see Jean Starobinski, *Montaigne en mouvement* (Paris: Gallimard, 1982), pp. 180–6.

37. CONVERSATION ... WITH THE FRIEND: on this see Starobinski, *Montaigne en mouvement*, pp. 52–71, and Gérard Defaux, *Montaigne et le travail de l'amitié: du lit de mort d'Etienne de La Boétie aux* Essais *de 1595* (Orléans: Paradigme, 2001).

    FRANCIS BACON: *The Essays*, ed. John Pitcher (Harmondsworth: Penguin, 1985), p. 239.

2 AN EDUCATION IN FREE-THINKING

44. *LIBERTIN* AND *LIBERTINAGE*: on the word history of *libertin* and its semantic field see Isabelle Moreau, *'Guérir du sot': les stratégies d'écriture des libertins à l'âge classique* (Paris: Champion, 2007), pp. 25–148.

45. *LIBERTAS PHILOSOPHANDI*: I have learnt most from Robert B. Sutton, 'The Phrase *Libertas Philosophandi*', *Journal of the History of Ideas*, 14 (1953), 10–16; M. A. Stewart, '*Libertas Philosophandi*: From Natural to Speculative Philosophy', *The Australian Journal of Politics and History*, 40 (1994), 29–46; Ian Maclean, *Logic, Signs and Nature in the Renaissance: The Case of Learned Medicine* (Cambridge: Cambridge University Press, 2002), pp. 191–3; and, by the same author, 'The "Sceptical Crisis" Reconsidered: Galen, Rational Medicine and the *Libertas Philosophandi*', *Early Science and Medicine*, 11 (2006), 247–74. I am indebted to these accounts in much of what follows.

46. SPINOZA'S RADICAL THESIS: on this see Jonathan Israel, *Radical Enlightenment: Philosophy and the Making of Modernity, 1650–1750* (Oxford: Oxford University Press, 2001), esp. pp. 265–70.

48. 'AMICUS PLATO …': see Henry Guerlac, '*Amicus Plato* and Other Friends', *Journal of the History of Ideas*, 39 (1978), 627–33, and Leonardo Tarán, '*Amicus Plato sed magis amica veritas*: From Plato and Aristotle to Cervantes', *Antike und Abendland*, 30 (1984), 93–125.

49. LODOVICO DOLCE: 'Dialogo della pittura intitolato L'Aretino', in Paola Barocchi (ed.), *Trattati d'arte del cinquecento: Fra manierismo e controriforma*, 3 vols (Bari: Laterza, 1960–2), I, p. 148.

50. ARGUMENTATION *IN UTRAMQUE PARTEM*: on this see Russ McDonald, *Shakespeare and the Arts of Language* (Oxford: Oxford University Press, 2001), pp. 48–50.

    PARADOX: see Ian Maclean's Introduction to *Heterodoxy in Early Modern Science and Theology*, ed. John Brook and Ian Maclean (Oxford: Oxford University Press, 2005), pp. xiv–xx. A further important contribution to the scholarship is to be found in Agnieszka Steczowicz's unpublished University of Oxford doctoral thesis of 2004, 'The Defence of Contraries: Paradox in the Late Renaissance Disciplines', esp. pp. 218–27.

59. LITERARY IMITATION: see Terence Cave, *The Cornucopian Text: Problems of Writing in the French Renaissance* (Oxford: Clarendon Press, 1979); Thomas M. Greene, *The Light in Troy: Imitation and Discovery in Renaissance Poetry* (New Haven, CT, and London: Yale University Press, 1982); and Martin McLaughlin, *Literary Imitation in the Italian Renaissance: The Theory and Practice of Literary Imitation in Italy from Dante to Bembo* (Oxford: Clarendon Press, 1995).

    COMMONPLACE BOOKS: see Ann Moss, *Printed Commonplace-Books and the Structuring of Renaissance Thought* (Oxford: Clarendon Press, 1996).

    'TO EXPRESS ONESELF': on this see Terence Cave, *Retrospectives: Essays in Literature, Poetics and Cultural History*, ed. Neil Kenny and Wes Williams (London: Legenda, 2009), pp. 139 and 144 n. 42.

60. ERASMUS: this sentence is from his *Ciceronianus* (1528), as quoted and translated by Moss, *Printed Commonplace-Books*, p. 105. Moss traces the bee metaphor as it roams its way through the debate about literary imitation.

63. TERENCE CAVE: *Pré-histoires: textes troublés au seuil de la modernité* (Geneva: Droz, 1999), p. 124.

3 AN INTRODUCTION TO ESSAYING

74. ESSAYS, AS MONTAIGNE UNDERSTANDS THE TERM: the classic study is E. V. Telle, 'A propos du mot "essai" chez Montaigne', *Bibliothèque d'Humanisme et Renaissance*, 30 (1968), 225–47.

HUGO FRIEDRICH: *Montaigne*, trans. into French by Robert Rovini (Paris: Gallimard, 1968), pp. 353–8.

75. ROBERT BOYLE: *The Works*, 6 vols, ed. Thomas Birch (Hildesheim: Georg Olas, 1965–6), I, p. 303.

75–6. THE ESSAYISTIC TRADITION: on the development and nature of the essay as a genre, see Claire De Obaldia, *The Essayistic Spirit: Literature, Modern Criticism, and the Essay* (Oxford: Clarendon Press, 1996). Anyone wishing to sample the similarities and differences between Montaigne and writers in the essayistic tradition might compare his composition on a particular topic with one of theirs: 'Of the affection of fathers for their children' (II.8), for example, with Bacon's 'Of Parents and Children' (1612); 'Of the education of children' (I.26) with parts I and II of Descartes's *Discourse on the Method* (*Discours de la méthode*; 1637); 'Of cripples' (III.11: 'Des boyteux') with Lamb's 'Witches, and Other Night-Fears' (1821) in his *Essays of Elia*; and 'Of friendship' (I.28) with Emerson's 'Friendship' (1841) in the first series of his *Essays*.

TERENCE CAVE: *How to Read Montaigne*, p. 3; M. A. Screech's remark is to be found in the Introduction to his translation and edition of *The Complete Essays* (London: Allen Lane, The Penguin Press, 1991), p. xv.

RICHARD SAYCE: *The Essays of Montaigne: A Critical Exploration* (London: Weidenfeld and Nicolson, 1972), p. 9.

77. JOHN O'BRIEN: 'Are We Reading What Montaigne Wrote?', *French Studies*, 58 (2004), 527–32. My sketch of the textual history owes much to O'Brien's article and to Sayce, *The Essays of Montaigne*, pp. 8–24.

81. ADAPTATIONS OF THE *ESSAIS*: these include the editions of Claude Pinganaud (Paris: Arléa, 2002 [1992]) and André Lanly (Paris: Gallimard, 2009).

83. DAVID MASKELL: 'Quel est le dernier état authentique des *Essais* de Montaigne?', *Bibliothèque d'Humanisme et Renaissance*, 40 (1978), 85–103 (p. 103).

MONTAIGNE'S OWN INTERVENTIONS: see David Maskell, 'Montaigne correcteur de l'exemplaire de Bordeaux', *Bulletin de la Société des Amis de Montaigne*, 25–6 (1978), 57–71 (p. 62).

84.   THE BORDEAUX COPY AND THE 1595 EDITION: on the differences of
punctuation see André Tournon, 'La Segmentation du texte: usages et
singularités', in *Editer les Essais de Montaigne*, ed. Claude Blum (Paris:
Champion, 1997), pp. 173–96.

INSTRUCTIONS TO THE PRINTER: these instructions are included in
André Tournon's edition, *Essais de Michel de Montaigne*, 3 vols (Paris:
Imprimerie nationale, 1998), I, pp. 663–4.

87.   NEW PLÉIADE EDITORS: *Les Essais*, ed. Balsamo, Magnien, and Magnien-
Simonin, p. 1481.

4 TWO CHEERS FOR FREE-THINKING

94.   SCREECH'S EDITION OF MONTAIGNE: see the Appendices,
pp. liv–lviii.

THE ROMAN INDEX: on this – and on Montaigne's motivations for writing
the 'Apology' – see Philippe Desan, 'Apologie de Sebond ou justification
de Montaigne?', in *'Dieu à nostre commerce et société': Montaigne et la
théologie*, ed. Philippe Desan (Geneva: Droz, 2008), pp. 175–200.

96.   A CATHOLIC PRINCESS AT THE PROTESTANT COURT OF NAVARRE:
the two apostrophes of Book II are further connected by the fact that
Montaigne's protectress Madame de Duras, whom he addresses in 'Of the
Resemblance of Children to their Fathers', was a member of Marguerite's
royal suite at the court of Navarre. On this see *Les Essais*, ed. Balsamo,
Magnien, and Magnien-Simonin, p. 1557.

CAVE: *Pré-histoires*, pp. 35–50; see also, for a revised English-language ver-
sion of the same analysis, his *Retrospectives*, pp. 109–29. I am indebted in
much of what follows to Cave's reading of the apostrophe to the princess.
Other important readings of the same passage include André Tournon,
'Images du pyrrhonisme selon quelques écrivains de la Renaissance', in
Les Humanistes et l'antiquité grecque, ed. Mitchiko Ishigami-Iagolnitzer
(Paris: Editions du CNRS, 1989), pp. 27–37, and François Rigolot, 'D'une
Théologie "pour les dames" à une *Apologie* "per le donne"', in *'Apologie
de Raimond Sebond': De la 'Theologia' à la 'Théologie'*, ed. Claude Blum
(Paris: Champion, 1990), pp. 261–90. The collective volume in which
Rigolot's article appears offers an excellent introduction to scholarship
on the 'Apology' as a whole.

98.   MONTAIGNE'S MEDAL: on the medal, Montaigne's motto, and the
        Pyrrhonians' keyword, see the article 'Jeton' by Marie-Luce Demonet
        in the *Dictionnaire de Michel de Montaigne*, ed. Philippe Desan (Paris:
        Champion, 2007), pp. 612–14.

101.   RICHARD POPKIN: *The History of Scepticism from Savonarola to Bayle*
        (New York, NY: Oxford University Press, 2003), pp. 55–6.

        POPKIN'S THESIS: on this see the collective volumes *Histoire du scep-
        ticisme: de Sextus Empiricus à Richard H. Popkin*, ed. Pierre-François
        Moreau, *Revue de Synthèse*, 119 (1998), nos 2–3, and *Skepticism in
        Renaissance and Post-Renaissance Thought: New Interpretations*, ed.
        José R. Maia Neto and Richard H. Popkin (Amherst, NY: Humanity
        Books, 2004). See also Maclean, 'The "Sceptical Crisis" Reconsidered'.

102.   MONTAIGNE'S ENCOUNTER WITH PYRRHONISM: among the vast bibili-
        ography on this topic, and in addition to the references given elsewhere in
        this chapter, the following may be of particular interest: Elaine Limbrick,
        'Was Montaigne Really a Pyrrhonian?', *Bibliothèque d'Humanisme et
        Renaissance*, 39 (1977), 67–80; Frédéric Brahami, *Le Scepticisme de
        Montaigne* (Paris: PUF, 1997); André Tournon, *Montaigne: la glose et
        l'essai* (Paris: Champion, 2000 [1983]), pp. 228–56; Marie-Luce Demonet
        and Alain Legros (eds), *L'Ecriture du scepticisme chez Montaigne* (Geneva:
        Droz, 2004); Ann Hartle, 'Montaigne and Skepticism', in *The Cambridge
        Companion to Montaigne*, ed. Ullrich Langer (Cambridge: Cambridge
        University Press, 2005), pp. 183–207.

        ACCIDENTAL PHILOSOPHER: on this phrase as a defining statement
        of Montaigne's attitude towards philosophy, see Ann Hartle, *Michel de
        Montaigne: Accidental Philosopher* (Cambridge: Cambridge University
        Press, 2003).

104.   CAVE: *Pré-histoires*, p. 40; *Retrospectives*, p. 121.

109.   ATHENS IN THE TIME OF PLATO: Robin Lane Fox, *The Classical World:
        An Epic History of Greece and Rome* (London: Penguin Books, 2006),
        provides a comprehensive and accessible account of ancient Greek demo-
        cracy and its Roman counterpart in relation to the issues of freedom
        and justice. See esp. pp. 25, 88–98, 201–11, and 282–3.

        QUENTIN SKINNER: *Hobbes and Republican Liberty* (Cambridge:
        Cambridge University Press, 2008), p. x.

5 TWO FREEDOMS

115. ATTITUDE OF THE FRENCH CROWN: on this see Quentin Skinner, *The Foundations of Modern Political Thought*, 2 vols (Cambridge: Cambridge University Press, 1978), II, pp. 239–301; Biancamaria Fontana, *Montaigne's Politics: Authority and Governance in the* Essais (Princeton, NJ, and Oxford: Princeton University Press, 2008), pp. 66–81.

116. MONTAIGNE'S POLITICAL POSITION: see Peter Burke, *Montaigne* (Oxford: Oxford University Press, 1981), pp. 28–35 (p. 28); the collective volume *Montaigne politique*, ed. Philippe Desan (Paris: Champion, 2006); and Fontana, *Montaigne's Politics*, esp. pp. 1–25 and 81–4.

117. EDICT OF BEAULIEU: on this see Géralde Nakam, *Montaigne: la manière et la matière* (Paris: Champion, 2006), pp. 119–49 (p. 124).

118. JULIAN THE APOSTATE: see G. W. Bowersock, *Julian the Apostate* (London: Duckworth, 1978).

119. A DIFFERENT JULIAN: see Nakam, *Montaigne*, pp. 121–3.
       JEAN BODIN: *La Méthode de l'Histoire*, trans. Pierre Mesnard (Paris: Les Belles Lettres, 1941), pp. 65–6.

121. EUTROPIUS: *Breviarium*, trans. and ed. H. W. Bird (Liverpool: Liverpool University Press, 1993).
       AMMIANUS MARCELLINUS: *Rerum gestarum libri*, Latin text with English transl. by John C. Rolfe, 3 vols (Cambridge, MA, and London: Loeb Classical Library, 1935–71).

122. AMMIANUS' REMARKS ABOUT CHRISTIANS: on the conflicting interpretations of these, see Timothy Barnes, *Ammianus Marcellinus and the Representation of Historical Reality* (Ithaca, NY, and London: Cornell University Press, 1998), pp. 79–94 (p. 80). I am grateful to David Maskell for providing me with this reference.
       PROBABLE TRUTH: on this see Ian Maclean, *Montaigne philosophe* (Paris: PUF, 1996), pp. 23–9.

126. ANDRÉ TOURNON: *'Route par ailleurs': le 'nouveau langage' des* Essais (Paris: Champion, 2006), pp. 299–300.
       A THIRD OPTION: Bowersock sees Julian's policy as the expression neither of a disinterested and just ruler nor of a Machiavel driven by anti-Christian fear and loathing but, instead, of an active supporter of paganism: 'Julian envisaged a pagan empire, not merely in which pagans were free to practise their religion but in which paganism was the state religion [...] The amnesty was proclaimed so that the power

of Constantius's Christians might be weakened. Thus paganism could flourish again' (*Julian the Apostate*, p. 71).

130.　FREEDOM OF CONSCIENCE AS A PRINCIPLE: on Postel, Castellio, and Bodin as advocates of this principle, see Skinner, *The Foundations of Modern Political Thought*, II, pp. 244–9.

　　THE RELIGIONS IN UTOPIA: in *Three Early Modern Utopias*, ed. Susan Bruce (Oxford: Oxford World's Classics, 1999), pp. 106–19.

　　STEPHEN GREENBLATT: *Renaissance Self-Fashioning* (Chicago, IL, and London: The University of Chicago Press, 1980), p. 41.

131.　TERENCE: on the fortunes of his formula in the sixteenth-century French debate about the crown see *Les Essais*, ed. Balsamo, Magnien, and Magnien-Simonin, p. 1660.

133.　NAKAM: *Montaigne*, pp. 125–31.

134.　AN ARCHITECTURAL ORGANIZATION: on this see David Lewis Schaefer (ed.), *Freedom over Servitude: Montaigne, La Boétie and 'On Voluntary Servitude'* (Westport, CT, and London: Greenwood Press, 1998).

6 OF FREE-THINKING AND FRIENDSHIP

136.　'KNOW THYSELF': see Agnieszka Steczowicz, '"Au rebours des autres": The "Know Thyself" Motif in "De la vanité"', in *'Revelations of Character': Ethos, Rhetoric and Moral Philosophy in Montaigne*, ed. Corinne Noirot-Maguire with Valérie M. Dionne (Newcastle: Cambridge Scholars Publishing, 2007), pp. 121–32.

142.　RECENT SCHOLARSHIP: examples include Ullrich Langer, *Perfect Friendship: Studies in Literature and Moral Philosophy from Boccaccio to Corneille* (Geneva: Droz, 1994), and 'Ethics in Context: Fortitude (I.12) and Justice (I.23)', in *Montaigne and Ethics*, ed. Patrick Henry, *Montaigne Studies*, 14 (2002), 7–18; Quint, *Montaigne and the Quality of Mercy*; and Jerome Schwartz, 'Reflections on Montaigne's Ethical Thinking', *Philosophy and Literature*, 24 (2000), 154–64.

　　LANGER: 'Ethics in Context', p. 18.

143.　JACQUES DERRIDA: *Politiques de l'amitié; suivi de L'Oreille de Heidegger* (Paris: Galilée, 1994); this has been translated into English by George Collins under the title *Politics of Friendship* (London: Verso, 1997).

　　FRIEDRICH: *Montaigne*, p. 258.

143.   TIMOTHY J. REISS: 'Montaigne and the Subject of Polity', in *Literary Theory / Renaissance Texts*, ed. Patricia Parker and David Quint (Baltimore, MD: The Johns Hopkins University Press, 1986), pp. 115–50 (p. 143).

ERIC MACPHAIL: 'Friendship as a Political Ideal in Montaigne's *Essais*', *Montaigne Studies*, 1 (1989), 177–87 (p. 187).

QUINT: *Montaigne and the Quality of Mercy*, pp. 120–2.

144.   LANGER: *Perfect Friendship*, pp. 166–7.

DERRIDA: *Politiques de l'amitié*, pp. 203–15.

147.   THE *JE-NE-SAIS-QUOI*: on this phrase see my study *The* Je-Ne-Sais-Quoi *in Early Modern Europe: Encounters with a Certain Something* (Oxford: Oxford University Press, 2005).

150.   THE 'GREAT-SOULED MAN': see Hartle, *Michel de Montaigne*, pp. 171–91.

151.   DERRIDA: *Politiques de l'amitié*, pp. 210–11; Cicero discusses the case in *Laelius de amicitia*, XI–XII.

7 OF KEEPING YOUR FREEDOM ALIVE

165.   TIME-TRAVEL […] DOWNSTREAM: on the theme of time-travel and the 'downstream' metaphor, see Holland and Scholar (eds), *Pre-Histories and Afterlives*.

MARCUS MANLIUS: Montaigne's sources for his story are Livy's history of Rome, V.47 and VI.11, and Cicero, *On the Republic* (*De republica*), II.27.49.

167.   AN ENCOUNTER WITH […] THE ROMAN INQUISITION AND INDEX: the classic work on this episode by Malcolm Smith, *Montaigne and the Roman Censors* (Geneva: Droz, 1981), now needs to be updated with reference to the studies listed below.

169.   HERETIC POETS: The objection may also refer to Clément Marot, or 'our good Marot', as Montaigne calls him in 'A Custom of the Island of Cea' (II.3: 'Coustume de l'isle de Cea'; F 312, VS 357).

170.   PUBLISHED BY GODMAN: Peter Godman, *The Saint as Censor: Robert Bellarmine Between Inquisition and Index* (Leiden, Boston, and Cologne: Brill, 2000), pp. 339–42.

LEGROS AND OTHERS: see Alain Legros, 'Montaigne face à ses censeurs romains de 1581 (mise à jour)', *Bibliothèque d'Humanisme et Renaissance*, 71 (2009), 7–33; see also the contributions of Jean-Robert Armogathe,

Vincent Carraud, and Philippe Desan to the collective volume, ed. Desan, *'Dieu à nostre commerce et société'*. In that volume, Desan reproduces Godman's transcription of the preliminary report as an appendix to his article (pp. 197–200), and it is to that appendix that I refer in what follows.

172.   'OF PRAYERS': on this chapter see Montaigne, *Essais, I, 56: 'Des prières'*, ed. Alain Legros (Geneva: Droz, 2003).

174.   THE SECOND OF MONTAIGNE'S ROMAN READERS: see Desan (ed.), *'Dieu à nostre commerce et société'*, pp. 199–200.

175.   AS ALAIN LEGROS HAS SUGGESTED: in 'Montaigne face à ses censeurs romains', p. 28.
        COUNCIL OF TRENT: on this see Smith, *Montaigne and the Roman Censors*, pp. 83 and 86.

177–8.   SMITH: *Montaigne and the Roman Censors*, pp. 86 and 67–9.

178.   TOWARDS THAT FUTURE: on Montaigne's writing for the future, see Cave, *How to Read Montaigne*, pp. 106–16, and my essay 'Montaigne's Forays into the Undiscovered Country', in *The Uses of the Future in Early Modern Europe*, ed. Andrea Brady and Emily Butterworth (New York, NY, and London: Routledge, 2010), pp. 39–53.

THE FUTURE OF THE ESSAIS

181.   MANY A BOOK: the existing studies on the reception history of the *Essais* include Alan M. Boase, *The Fortunes of Montaigne: A History of the Essays in France, 1580–1669* (London: Methuen, 1935); Olivier Millet, *La Première réception des* Essais *de Montaigne (1580–1640)* (Paris: Champion, 1995); Maturin Dréano, *La Renommée de Montaigne en France au XVIIIe siècle, 1677–1802* (Angers: Editions de l'Ouest, 1952); Donald Frame, *Montaigne in France, 1812–1852* (New York, NY: Columbia University Press, 1940); and Dudley M. Marchi, *Montaigne Among the Moderns: Receptions of the* Essais (Providence, RI, and Oxford: Berghahn Books, 1994).
        FUTURES […] DORMANT OR MORIBUND: see 'Of war horses' (I.48; F 257, VS 290); 'Of the affection of fathers for their children' (II.8; F 350, VS 397); and 'Of coaches' (III.6; F 847, VS 913–14). Montaigne's dislike of modern firearms is shared by Ludovico Ariosto: see his *Orlando furioso*,

XI, 21–8. The difference between them is that Ariosto does not doubt of their effectiveness and accepts that they are here to stay.

182. FUTURES […] REALIZED: see 'A consideration upon Cicero' (I.40; F 224, VS 251); 'Of the affection of fathers for their children' (II.8; F 338, VS 385); 'Apology for Raymond Sebond' (II.12; F 497, VS 546; and F 508, VS 558); and 'Of vanity' (III.9; F 911–12, VS 981).

A REPLY IN ADVANCE: This reply is further complicated by the following chapter, 'Of not communicating one's glory' (I.41), in which Montaigne remarks that the desire for worldly renown is so powerful in us all as to leave him wondering whether *anyone* is entirely exempt from it.

182–3. VARYING RESPONSES: on the essay see De Obaldia, *The Essayistic Spirit*; and, for Marie de Gournay's suggestion, see her preface to the 1595 edition of the *Essais*, ed. Balsamo, Magnien, and Magnien-Simonin, p. 23.

183–4. THE NEUCHÂTEL MANUSCRIPT: in Rousseau, *Œuvres complètes*, 5 vols, ed. Bernard Gagnebin and Marcel Raymond (Paris: Gallimard, 1959–95), I, p. 1150. The English translation is by Angela Scholar, *Confessions*, ed. Patrick Coleman (Oxford: Oxford World's Classics, 2000), p. 644.

184. KATE E. TUNSTALL: 'Diderot and Montaigne: Portraits and Afterlives', in *Pre-Histories and Afterlives*, ed. Holland and Scholar, pp. 95–105. The quotation from Diderot is to be found in his *Œuvres*, 5 vols, ed. Laurent Versini (Paris: Robert Laffont, 1994–97), IV, p. 531.

ABSENT INTIMATES: on this see J. P. Stern, *A Study of Nietzsche* (Cambridge: Cambridge University Press, 1979), pp. 21, 50.

185. NIETZSCHE['S …] TRULY CHEERING TESTIMONY: Friedrich Nietzsche, *Werke*, 3 vols, ed. Karl Schlechta (Munich: Carl Hanser, 1966), I, p. 296. See also II, p. 1088 (on Montaigne's mischief) and III, p. 460 (on his sceptical approach). The English translation is by Richard T. Gray, *Unfashionable Observations* (Stanford, CA: Stanford University Press, 1995), p. 181. On Nietzsche's attitude towards Montaigne, see Nicola Panichi's article 'Nietzsche' in the *Dictionnaire de Michel de Montaigne*, pp. 818–19, and, by the same author, *Picta historia: lettura di Montaigne e Nietzsche* (Urbino: Quattro Venti, 1995).

186. SIMON GOULART: though it appeared in Geneva, the title page of this edition states that it was published by François le Febvre of Lyons in 1595. On Goulart, see Boase, *The Fortunes of Montaigne*, pp. 8–9.

187. PASCAL: *Entretien avec Sacy sur la philosophie*, ed. Richard Scholar (Arles: Actes Sud, 2003), p. 32.

187. LEADING *LIBERTINS*: on these figures and their work, see Jean-Pierre Cavaillé, *Dis/simulations: religion, morale et politique au XVIIᵉ siècle* (Paris: Champion, 2002), and Moreau, *'Guérir du sot'*. On their reception of Montaigne, see Giovanni Dotoli, *Montaigne et les libertins* (Paris: Champion, 2006), and the collection *Les libertins et Montaigne*, ed. Giovanni Dotoli, *Montaigne Studies*, 19 (2007).

188. ANTOINE ARNAULD AND PIERRE NICOLE: *La Logique ou l'Art de Penser*, ed. Pierre Clair and François Girbal (Paris: PUF, 1965), pp. 267–9.
    BOASE: *The Fortunes of Montaigne*, p. 411.
    THE ROMAN INDEX OF 1676: see Jean-Robert Armogathe and Vincent Carraud, 'Les *Essais* de Montaigne dans les archives du Saint-Office', in *Papes, princes et savants dans l'Europe moderne: mélanges à la mémoire de Bruno Neveu*, ed. Jean-Louis Quantin and Jean-Claude Waquet (Geneva: Droz, 2007), pp. 79–96.

189. PASCAL: *Pensées*, ed. Philippe Sellier (Paris: Bordas, 1991), frag. 568.
    CAVE: *How to Read Montaigne*, p. 115.

190. 'A PLEASING REDUCTION': *L'Esprit des Essais de Michel, Seigneur de Montaigne* (Paris: Charles de Sercy, 1677), Preface, A5ʳ. On the *Esprit*, see Dréano, *La Renommée de Montaigne*, pp. 13–20.

Further Reading

One possibility would be to read in their entirety the chapters principally discussed in the course of this book: 'Au lecteur', I.8, I.26, I.28, I.50, I.56, II.12, II.19, II.37, III.2, III.9, and III.10, adding in I.31, II.6, II.17, III.5, III.6, and III.13 for good measure. But the *Essais*, in truth, contain riches around every corner. Those wishing to further and deepen their acquaintance of the text could therefore do no better, perhaps, than adopt Orson Welles's practice and read a page or two from anywhere in Montaigne's work, at least once a week, 'for the pleasure of his company'. They may well find themselves, as a result, moved to read the classical and Renaissance authors that Montaigne admires and cites.

Only a narrow selection of the vast and ever-growing body of scholarship devoted to the study of Montaigne appears in the Bibliography. I shall confine my suggestions here to a still more limited number of accessible works in English.

The best short introductions to Montaigne in English are Burke (1981) and Cave (2007). Cave, to whom I am indebted, presents a conception of the *Essais* that is similar, in many respects, to the one adopted here. The two books, for that reason, may be regarded as companion studies. Useful works by several hands include the collections of essays edited by McFarlane and Maclean (1982) and Langer (2005): these offer brief treatments by major specialists of a range of major topics. General critical accounts by a single author have produced some of the best work done on Montaigne: the classic studies of Frame (1955), Sayce (1972), Regosin (1977), Screech (1983), Starobinski (1985), and Friedrich (1991) may be of particular interest.

The only full biography in English is Frame (1965). Hoffmann (1998) offers a fascinating revisionist account of Montaigne's writing career. Bakewell (2010) is a well-informed double biography (of the man and his book) written in the idiom of a self-help guide.

The reception history of the *Essais* from the late sixteenth century onwards reveals much about the text itself as well as about the receiving culture: the major studies in English to date are Boase (1935), Frame (1940), and Marchi (1994).

Warren Boutcher's *The School of Montaigne: Enfranchising the Reader-Writer in Early Modern Europe* (Oxford: Oxford University Press, forthcoming) was in preparation when this book went to press. While I have read no part of Boutcher's manuscript at the time of writing, I have discussed it with the author on several occasions, and the indications are that it will offer arguments complementary to those presented here while developing the theme of free-thinking in ways I have not explored. *The School of Montaigne* promises, in particular, to make a contribution to the broader contexts of European book and cultural history. Any reader who wants to see those matters dealt with in full should read Boutcher.

I suggest further reading on various other aspects of the *Essais* in the Notes above.

Bibliography

PRIMARY SOURCES

Alcinous (1993). *The Handbook of Platonism*, ed. and trans. John Dillon (Oxford: Clarendon Press).

Ammianus Marcellinus (1935–71). *Rerum gestarum libri*, 3 vols, Latin text with English transl. by John C. Rolfe (Cambridge, MA, and London: Loeb Classical Library).

Arnauld, Antoine, and Pierre Nicole (1965). *La Logique ou l'Art de Penser*, ed. Pierre Clair and François Girbal (Paris: Presses universitaires de France).

Bacon, Francis (1985). *The Essays*, ed. John Pitcher (Harmondsworth: Penguin).

Bodin, Jean (1941). *La Méthode de l'Histoire*, trans. Pierre Mesnard (Paris: Les Belles Lettres).

Boyle, Robert (1965–6). *The Works*, 6 vols, ed. Thomas Birch (Hildesheim: Georg Olas).

Cervantes, Miguel de (1998). *Don Quijote de la Mancha*, 2 vols, ed. Francisco Rico (Barcelona: Instituto Cervantes).

——(1999). *Don Quixote de la Mancha*, intro. Milan Kundera, trans. Charles Jarvis (Oxford: Oxford World's Classics). [Eng. transl. of Cervantes (1998)]

Descartes, René (1992). *Discours de la méthode*, ed. Geneviève Rodis-Lewis (Paris: Flammarion).

——(2006). *A Discourse on the Method of Correctly Conducting One's Reason and Seeking Truth in the Sciences*, trans. Ian Maclean (Oxford: Oxford's World Classics). [Eng. transl. of Descartes (1992)]

Diderot, Denis (1994–7). *Œuvres*, 5 vols, ed. Laurent Versini (Paris: Robert Laffont).

Dolce, Lodovico (1960–2). 'Dialogo della pittura intitolato L'Aretino', in *Trattati d'arte del cinquecento: Fra manierismo e controriforma*, 3 vols, ed. Paola Barocchi (Bari: Laterza), vol. I.

Emerson, Ralph Waldo (1971). *Essays: First Series*, vol. II of *The Collected Works*, ed. Alfred R. Ferguson and Robert E. Spiller (Cambridge, MA, and London: The Belknap Press of Harvard University Press).

Eutropius (1993). *Breviarium*, trans. and ed. H. W. Bird (Liverpool: Liverpool University Press).

Lamb, Charles (2003). *Essays of Elia* (Iowa City, IA: University of Iowa Press).

Mexía, Pedro (1577). *Les Diverses leçons de Pierre Messie*, trans. Claude Gruget (Paris: Nicolas Bonfons).

Montaigne, Michel de (1983). *Journal de Voyage*, ed. Fausta Garavini (Paris: Gallimard).

—— (1991). *The Complete Essays*, trans. M. A. Screech (London: Allen Lane, The Penguin Press [1965]).

—— (1992). *Les Essais*, ed. Pierre Villey and V.-L. Saulnier (Paris: Presses universitaires de France [1965]).

—— (1998). *Essais de Michel de Montaigne*, 3 vols, ed. André Tournon (Paris: Imprimerie nationale).

—— (2002). *Les Essais*, ed. Claude Pinganaud (Paris: Arléa [1992]).

—— (2003). *The Complete Works*, trans. Donald M. Frame (London: Everyman's Library).

—— (2003). *Essais, I, 56: 'Des prières'*, ed. Alain Legros (Geneva: Droz).

—— (2007). *Les Essais*, ed. Jean Balsamo, Michel Magnien, and Catherine Magnien-Simonin (Paris: Gallimard, Bibliothèque de la Pléiade).

—— (2009). *Les Essais en français moderne*, ed. and adapt. André Lanly (Paris: Gallimard).

More, Thomas (1999). *Utopia*, in *Three Early Modern Utopias*, ed. Susan Bruce (Oxford: Oxford World's Classics).

Nietzsche, Friedrich (1966). *Werke*, 3 vols, ed. Karl Schlechta (Munich: Carl Hanser).

—— (1995). *Unfashionable Observations*, trans. Richard T. Gray (Stanford, CA: Stanford University Press).

Pascal, Blaise (1991). *Pensées*, ed. Philippe Sellier (Paris: Bordas).

—— (2003). *Entretien avec Sacy sur la philosophie*, ed. Richard Scholar (Arles: Actes Sud).

Rousseau, Jean-Jacques (1959–95). *Œuvres complètes*, 5 vols, ed. Bernard Gagnebin and Marcel Raymond (Paris: Gallimard).

—— (2000). *Confessions*, ed. Patrick Coleman, trans. Angela Scholar (Oxford: Oxford World's Classics).

Sercy, Charles de (1677). *L'Esprit des Essais de Michel, Seigneur de Montaigne* (Paris: Charles de Sercy).

Spinoza, Benedict de (1925). *Opera*, 4 vols, ed. Carl Gebhardt (Heidelberg: C. Winter).

—— (1989). *Tractatus Theologico-Politicus*, trans. Samuel Shirley (Leiden: Brill).

SECONDARY SOURCES

Armogathe, Jean-Robert, and Vincent Carraud (2007). 'Les *Essais* de Montaigne dans les archives du Saint-Office', in *Papes, princes et savants dans l'Europe moderne: mélanges à la mémoire de Bruno Neveu*, ed. Jean-Louis Quantin and Jean-Claude Waquet (Geneva: Droz), pp. 79–96.

Asher, Robert E., et al. (1957). *The United Nations and the Promotion of the General Welfare* (Washington, DC: The Brookings Institution).

Bakewell, Sarah (2010). *How To Live, or, A Life of Montaigne in One Question and Twenty Attempts at an Answer* (London: Chatto and Windus).

Barnes, Timothy (1998). *Ammianus Marcellinus and the Representation of Historical Reality* (Ithaca, NY, and London: Cornell University Press).

Blum, Claude, ed. (1990). *'Apologie de Raimond Sebond': De la 'Theologia' à la 'Théologie'* (Paris: Champion).

Boase, Alan M. (1935). *The Fortunes of Montaigne: A History of the Essays in France, 1580–1669* (London: Methuen).

Boutcher, Warren (2004). 'Marginal Commentaries: The Cultural Transmission of Montaigne's *Essais* in Shakespeare's England', in *Shakespeare et Montaigne: vers un nouvel humanisme*, ed. Pierre Kapitaniak and Jean-Marie Maguin (Montpellier: Société Française Shakespeare), pp. 13–29.

—— (2006). 'Unoriginal Authors: How to Do Things with Texts in the Renaissance', in *Rethinking the Foundations of Modern Political Thought*, ed. Annabel Brett and James Tully with Holly Hamilton-Bleakley (Cambridge: Cambridge University Press), pp. 73–92.

Bowersock, G. W. (1978). *Julian the Apostate* (London: Duckworth).

Brahami, Frédéric (1997). *Le Scepticisme de Montaigne* (Paris: Presses universitaires de France).

Brook, John, and Ian Maclean, eds (2005). *Heterodoxy in Early Modern Science and Theology* (Oxford: Oxford University Press).

Buck, August (1963). 'Democritus ridens et Heraclitus flens', in *Wort und Text: Festschrift für Fritz Schalk*, ed. Harri Meier and Hans Sckommodan (Frankfurt am Main: Vittorio Klostermann), pp. 167–86.

Burke, Peter (1981). *Montaigne* (Oxford: Oxford University Press).

Burrow, Colin (2003). 'Friskes, Skips, and Jumps', *London Review of Books*, 25 (no. 21), p. 22. [Review of Hartle (2003)]

Cavaillé, Jean-Pierre (2002). *Dis/simulations: religion, morale et politique au XVIIᵉ siècle* (Paris: Champion).

Cave, Terence (1979). *The Cornucopian Text: Problems of Writing in the French Renaissance* (Oxford: Clarendon Press).

——— (1982). 'Problems of Reading in the *Essais*', in *Montaigne*, ed. McFarlane and Maclean, pp. 133–66.

——— (1999). *Pré-histoires: textes troublés au seuil de la modernité* (Geneva: Droz).

——— (2007). *How to Read Montaigne* (London: Granta).

——— (2009). *Retrospectives: Essays in Literature, Poetics and Cultural History*, ed. Neil Kenny and Wes Williams (London: Legenda).

Colclough, David (2005). *Freedom of Speech in Early Stuart England* (Cambridge: Cambridge University Press).

Conche, Marcel (1993). *Montaigne et la philosophie* (Paris: Presses universitaires de France).

Defaux, Gérard (2001). *Montaigne et le travail de l'amitié: du lit de mort d'Etienne de La Boétie aux Essais de 1595* (Orléans: Paradigme).

Demonet, Marie-Luce, ed. (1999). *Montaigne et la question de l'homme* (Paris: Presses universitaires de France).

Demonet, Marie-Luce, and Alain Legros, eds (2004). *L'Ecriture du scepticisme chez Montaigne* (Geneva: Droz).

De Obaldia, Claire (1996). *The Essayistic Spirit: Literature, Modern Criticism, and the Essay* (Oxford: Clarendon Press).

Derrida, Jacques (1994). *Politiques de l'amitié; suivi de L'Oreille de Heidegger* (Paris: Galilée).

——— (1997). *Politics of Friendship*, trans. George Collins (London: Verso). [English transl. of Derrida (1994)]

Desan, Philippe (2008a). 'Apologie de Sebond ou justification de Montaigne?', in *'Dieu à nostre commerce et société'*, ed. Desan, pp. 175–200.

Desan, Philippe, ed. (2006). *Montaigne politique* (Paris: Champion).

——— (2007). *Dictionnaire de Michel de Montaigne* (Paris: Champion).

—— (2008b). *'Dieu à nostre commerce et société': Montaigne et la théologie* (Geneva: Droz).

Dotoli, Giovanni (2006). *Montaigne et les libertins* (Paris: Champion).

Dotoli, Giovanni, ed. (2007). *Les libertins et Montaigne, Montaigne Studies* (19).

Dréano, Maturin (1952). *La Renommée de Montaigne en France au XVIIIe siècle, 1677–1802* (Angers: Editions de l'Ouest).

Fontana, Biancamaria (2008). *Montaigne's Politics: Authority and Governance in the* Essais (Princeton, NJ, and Oxford: Princeton University Press).

Frame, Donald M. (1940). *Montaigne in France, 1812–1852* (New York, NY: Columbia University Press).

—— (1955). *Montaigne's Discovery of Man: The Humanization of a Humanist* (New York, NY: Columbia Press).

—— (1965). *Montaigne: A Biography* (London: Hamish Hamilton).

Friedrich, Hugo (1949). *Montaigne* (Bern: A. Francke).

—— (1968). *Montaigne*, trans. Robert Rovini (Paris: Gallimard). [French transl. of Friedrich (1949)]

—— (1991). *Montaigne*, ed. Philippe Desan, trans. Dawn Eng (Berkeley, CA: University of California Press). [Eng. transl. of Friedrich (1949)]

Giocanti, Sylvia (2001). *Penser l'irrésolution: Montaigne, Pascal, La Mothe le Vayer – trois itinéraires sceptiques* (Paris: Champion).

Godman, Peter (2000). *The Saint as Censor: Robert Bellarmine Between Inquisition and Index* (Leiden, Boston, and Cologne: Brill).

Greenblatt, Stephen (1980). *Renaissance Self-Fashioning* (Chicago, IL, and London: The University of Chicago Press).

Greene, Thomas M. (1982). *The Light in Troy: Imitation and Discovery in Renaissance Poetry* (New Haven, CT, and London: Yale University Press).

Guerlac, Henry (1978). *'Amicus Plato* and Other Friends', *Journal of the History of Ideas* (39), 627–33.

Hampton, Timothy (1990). *Writing from History: The Rhetoric of Exemplarity in Renaissance Literature* (Ithaca, NY, and London: Cornell University Press).

Hartle, Ann (2003). *Michel de Montaigne: Accidental Philosopher* (Cambridge: Cambridge University Press).

Hoffmann, George (1998). *Montaigne's Career* (Oxford: Clarendon Press).

Holland, Anna, and Richard Scholar, eds (2009). *Pre-Histories and Afterlives: Studies in Critical Method* (London: Legenda).

Israel, Jonathan (2001). *Radical Enlightenment: Philosophy and the Making of Modernity, 1650–1750* (Oxford: Oxford University Press).

Jeanneret, Michel (1997). *Perpetuum mobile: métamorphoses des corps et des œuvres, de Vinci à Montaigne* (Paris: Macula).

—— (2001). *Perpetual Motion: Transforming Shapes in the Renaissance, from da Vinci to Montaigne*, trans. Nidra Poller (Baltimore, MD, and London: Johns Hopkins University Press). [Eng. transl. of Jeanneret (1997)]

Lane Fox, Robin (2006). *The Classical World: An Epic History of Greece and Rome* (London: Penguin Books).

Langer, Ullrich (1994). *Perfect Friendship: Studies in Literature and Moral Philosophy from Boccaccio to Corneille* (Geneva: Droz).

—— (2002). 'Ethics in Context: Fortitude (I.12) and Justice (I.23)', in *Montaigne and Ethics*, ed. Patrick Henry, *Montaigne Studies* (14), 7–18.

Langer, Ullrich, ed. (2005). *The Cambridge Companion to Montaigne* (Cambridge: Cambridge University Press).

Legros, Alain (2009). 'Montaigne face à ses censeurs romains de 1581 (mise à jour)', *Bibliothèque d'Humanisme et Renaissance* (71), 7–33.

Limbrick, Elaine (1977). 'Was Montaigne Really a Pyrrhonian?', *Bibliothèque d'Humanisme et Renaissance* (39), 67–80.

Lyons, John D. (2005). *Before Imagination: Embodied Thought from Montaigne to Rousseau* (Stanford, CA: Stanford University Press).

Maclean, Ian (1982). '"Le Païs au Delà": Montaigne and Philosophical Speculation', in *Montaigne*, ed. McFarlane and Maclean, pp. 101–32.

—— (1983). 'Montaigne, Cardano: The Reading of Subtlety / the Subtlety of Reading', *French Studies* (37), 143–57.

—— (1996). *Montaigne philosophe* (Paris: Presses universitaires de France).

—— (2002). *Logic, Signs and Nature in the Renaissance: The Case of Learned Medicine* (Cambridge: Cambridge University Press).

—— (2006). 'The "Sceptical Crisis" Reconsidered: Galen, Rational Medicine and the *Libertas Philosophandi*', *Early Science and Medicine* (11), 247–74.

MacPhail, Eric (1989). 'Friendship as a Political Ideal in Montaigne's *Essais*', *Montaigne Studies* (1), 177–87.

Maia Neto, José R., and Richard H. Popkin, eds (2004). *Skepticism in Renaissance and Post-Renaissance Thought: New Interpretations* (Amherst, NY: Humanity Books).

Marchi, Dudley M. (1994). *Montaigne Among the Moderns: Receptions of the Essais* (Providence, RI, and Oxford: Berghahn Books).

Maskell, David (1978a). 'Quel est le dernier état authentique des *Essais* de Montaigne?', *Bibliothèque d'Humanisme et Renaissance* (40), 85–103.

—— (1978b). 'Montaigne correcteur de l'exemplaire de Bordeaux', *Bulletin de la Société des Amis de Montaigne* (25–6), 57–71.

McDonald, Russ (2001). *Shakespeare and the Arts of Language* (Oxford: Oxford University Press).

McFarlane, I. D., and Ian Maclean (1982). *Montaigne: Essays in Memory of Richard Sayce* (Oxford: Clarendon Press).

McKinley, Mary B. (1981). *Words in a Corner: Studies in Montaigne's Latin Quotations* (Lexington, KY: French Forum).

—— (1996). *Les Terrains vagues des* Essais: *itinéraires et intertextes* (Paris: Champion).

McLaughlin, Martin (1995). *Literary Imitation in the Italian Renaissance: The Theory and Practice of Literary Imitation in Italy from Dante to Bembo* (Oxford: Clarendon Press).

Millet, Olivier (1995). *La Première réception des* Essais *de Montaigne (1580–1640)* (Paris: Champion).

Moreau, Isabelle (2007). *'Guérir du sot': les stratégies d'écriture des libertins à l'âge classique* (Paris: Champion).

Moreau, Pierre-François, ed. (1998). *Histoire du scepticisme: de Sextus Empiricus à Richard H. Popkin, Revue de Synthèse* (119), nos 2–3.

Moss, Ann (1996). *Printed Commonplace-Books and the Structuring of Renaissance Thought* (Oxford: Clarendon Press).

Nakam, Géralde (1993). *Montaigne et son temps: les événements et les* Essais (Paris: Gallimard [1982]).

—— (2006). *Montaigne: la manière et la matière* (Paris: Champion).

Noirot-Maguire, Corinne, ed., with Valérie M. Dionne (2007). *'Revelations of Character':* Ethos, *Rhetoric and Moral Philosophy in Montaigne* (Newcastle: Cambridge Scholars Publishing).

Nuttall, A. D. (2007). *Shakespeare the Thinker* (New Haven, CT, and London: Yale University Press).

O'Brien, John (2004). 'Are We Reading What Montaigne Wrote?', *French Studies* (58), 527–32.

—— (2006). 'Retrait', in *Montaigne politique*, ed. Desan, pp. 205–22.

Panichi, Nicola (1995). *Picta historia: lettura di Montaigne e Nietzsche* (Urbino: Quattro Venti).

Popkin, Richard H. (2003). *The History of Scepticism from Savonarola to Bayle* (New York, NY: Oxford University Press).

Pouilloux, Jean-Yves (1994). *Montaigne: l'éveil de la pensée* (Paris: Champion).

Quint, David (1998). *Montaigne and the Quality of Mercy: Ethical and Political Themes in the* Essais (Princeton, NJ: Princeton University Press).

Regosin, Richard L. (1977). *The Matter of My Book: Montaigne's* Essais *as the Book of the Self* (Berkeley, CA: University of California Press).

Reiss, Timothy J. (1986). 'Montaigne and the Subject of Polity', in *Literary Theory / Renaissance Texts*, ed. Patricia Parker and David Quint (Baltimore, MD: The Johns Hopkins University Press), pp. 115–50.

Rigolot, François (1988). *Les Métamorphoses de Montaigne* (Paris: Presses universitaires de France).

——(1990). 'D'une *Théologie* "pour les dames" à une *Apologie* "per le donne"', in *'Apologie de Raimond Sebond'*, ed. Blum, pp. 261–90.

Sayce, Richard (1972). *The Essays of Montaigne: A Critical Exploration* (London: Weidenfeld and Nicolson).

Schaefer, David Lewis, ed. (1998). *Freedom over Servitude: Montaigne, La Boétie and 'On Voluntary Servitude'* (Westport, CT, and London: Greenwood Press).

Scholar, Richard (2005). *The Je-Ne-Sais-Quoi in Early Modern Europe: Encounters with a Certain Something* (Oxford: Oxford University Press).

——(2006). 'Two Cheers for Free-Thinking', in *Theory and the Early Modern*, ed. Michael Moriarty and John O'Brien, *Paragraph* (29), 40–53.

——(2007). 'Friendship and Free-Thinking in Montaigne', in *'Revelations of Character'*, ed. Noirot-Maguire, pp. 31–46.

——(2010). 'Montaigne's Forays into the Undiscovered Country', in *The Uses of the Future in Early Modern Europe*, ed. Andrea Brady and Emily Butterworth (New York, NY, and London: Routledge), pp. 39–53.

Schwartz, Jerome (2000). 'Reflections on Montaigne's Ethical Thinking', *Philosophy and Literature* (24), 154–64.

Screech, M. A. (1983). *Montaigne and Melancholy: The Wisdom of the Essays* (London: Duckworth).

Skinner, Quentin (1978). *The Foundations of Modern Political Thought*, 2 vols (Cambridge: Cambridge University Press).

——(2008). *Hobbes and Republican Liberty* (Cambridge: Cambridge University Press).

Smith, Malcolm (1981). *Montaigne and the Roman Censors* (Geneva: Droz).

——(1991). *Montaigne and Religious Freedom: The Dawn of Pluralism* (Geneva: Droz).

Starobinski, Jean (1982). *Montaigne en mouvement* (Paris: Gallimard).

——(1985). *Montaigne in Motion*, trans. Arthur Goldhammer (Chicago, IL: Chicago University Press). [Eng. transl. of Starobinski (1982)]

Steczowicz, Agnieszka (2004). 'The Defence of Contraries: Paradox in the Late Renaissance Disciplines', unpublished University of Oxford doctoral thesis.

—— (2007). '"Au rebours des autres": The "Know Thyself" Motif in "De la vanité"', in *'Revelations of Character'*, ed. Noirot-Maguire, pp. 121–32.

Stern, J. P. (1979). *A Study of Nietzsche* (Cambridge: Cambridge University Press).

Stewart, M. A. (1994). '*Libertas Philosophandi*: From Natural to Speculative Philosophy', *The Australian Journal of Politics and History* (40), 29–46.

Supple, James J. (1984). *Arms versus Letters: The Military and Literary Ideals in the* Essais *of Montaigne* (Oxford: Clarendon Press).

—— (2000). *Les* Essais *de Montaigne: méthode(s) et méthodologies* (Paris: Champion).

Sutton, Robert B. (1953). 'The Phrase *Libertas Philosophandi*', *Journal of the History of Ideas* (14), 10–16.

Tarán, Leonardo (1984). '*Amicus Plato sed magis amica veritas*: From Plato and Aristotle to Cervantes', *Antike und Abendland* (30), 93–125.

Telle, E. V. (1968). 'A propos du mot "essai" chez Montaigne', *Bibliothèque d'Humanisme et Renaissance* (30), 225–47.

Toulmin, Stephen (1989). *Cosmopolis: The Hidden Agenda of Modernity* (New York, NY: The Free Press).

Tournon, André (1989). 'Images du pyrrhonisme selon quelques écrivains de la Renaissance', in *Les Humanistes et l'antiquité grecque*, ed. Mitchiko Ishigami-Iagolnitzer (Paris: Editions du CNRS), pp. 27–37.

—— (1997). 'La Segmentation du texte: usages et singularités', in *Editer les Essais de Montaigne*, ed. Claude Blum (Paris: Champion), pp. 173–96.

—— (2000). *Montaigne: la glose et l'essai* (Paris: Champion [revised edn; first published 1983])

—— (2006). *'Route par ailleurs': le 'nouveau langage' des* Essais (Paris: Champion).

Tunstall, Kate E. (2009). 'Diderot and Montaigne: Portraits and Afterlives', in *Pre-Histories and Afterlives*, ed. Holland and Scholar, pp. 95–105.

Villey, Pierre (1933). *Les Sources et l'évolution des* Essais *de Montaigne* (Paris: Hachette [1908]).

—— (1935). *Montaigne devant la postérité* (Paris: Boivin).

Williams, Wes (2009). 'Back to the Future: "Les Enfantements de Nostre Esprit"', in *Pre-Histories and Afterlives*, ed. Holland and Scholar, pp. 121–34.

Acknowledgements

This book was written during my tenure of a Research Fellowship funded by the Leverhulme Trust and it was completed with the help of a Philip Leverhulme Prize. I should like to express my gratitude to the Trust for its support of my work. I thank, for theirs, my colleagues at Oriel College, Oxford, and in the Faculty of Medieval and Modern Languages and the Humanities Division of the University of Oxford. I would like to mention in particular my colleague and friend Liz Nash, who passed away shortly before this book went to press, and whom I count myself as fortunate to have known and worked alongside at Oriel.

Four sections of this book have appeared in partial, earlier versions elsewhere: chapters 2 and 4 in *Theory and the Early Modern*, ed. Michael Moriarty and John O'Brien, *Paragraph*, 29 (2006), pp. 40–53 (pp. 46–50); chapter 6 in *'Revelations of Character': Ethos, Rhetoric, and Moral Philosophy in Montaigne*, ed. Corinne Noirot-Maguire with Valérie M. Dionne (Newcastle: Cambridge Scholars Publishing, 2007), pp. 31–46; and 'The Future of the *Essais*' in *The Uses of the Future in Early Modern Europe*, ed. Andrea Brady and Emily Butterworth (New York, NY, and London: Routledge, 2010), pp. 39–53 (pp. 47–51). These excerpts are published with the permission of, respectively, Edinburgh University Press, Cambridge Scholars Publishing, and Routledge. Quotations from *The Complete Works of Montaigne*, translated by Donald M. Frame, are copyright © 1943 by Donald M. Frame, renewed 1971; © 1948, 1957, 1958 by the Board of Trustees of the Leland Stanford University Press. All rights reserved. Used with the permission of Stanford University Press, www.sup.org.

I am grateful to Professor Philippe Desan of *Montaigne Studies* for granting me permission to reproduce two plates showing pages of the Bordeaux copy from the *Reproduction en quadrichromie de l'Exemplaire de Bordeaux des* Essais *de Montaigne*, ed. Philippe Desan (Fasano-Chicago: Schena Editore, Montaigne Studies, 2002).

I presented outlines of the book's ideas at departmental seminars and colloquia in the following institutions: the University of Durham; the University of Minnesota, where in 2007 I was fortunate to spend a week as a guest of the Theorizing Early Modern Studies Collaborative and the Department of French and Italian; Royal Holloway, University of London; Queen Mary, University of London; the University of Nottingham; and the Maison Française d'Oxford. I have also regularly tried out my ideas on students in Durham and Oxford. I am grateful to them and to my interlocutors in the seminars and colloquia mentioned above for their questions and remarks. My debts to other writers on Montaigne, which are many, will be clear to anyone familiar with the secondary literature. In an introductory book aimed principally at a wider readership, I have not listed my debts in detail, but I acknowledge them gratefully here.

Alexis Kirschbaum at Peter Lang commissioned this book for the Past in the Present series, and Nick Reynolds saw the project through to completion: both have my thanks, as does my pleasant and efficient copy-editor, Jennifer Speake. At a trying time for us both, Will Poole proved worthy of the old adage about a friend in need, for which I thank him. I am indebted to those people who read this book in the making for their invaluable comments and suggestions. In addition to Peter Lang's two anonymous readers, I should like to mention in particular Terence Cave, Ita Mac Carthy, Ian Maclean, David Maskell, and John Scholar. I have also received various kinds of encouragement and help, in the writing of this book, from Frédérique Aït-Touati, Chimène Bateman, Christian Belin, Warren Boutcher, Kathryn Banks, Andrea Brady, Jerry Brotton, Colin Burrow, Emily Butterworth, Ben and Julia Cairns, Tim Chesters, Thomas Constantinesco, Richard Cooper, Patrick Declerck, Kathy Eden, Jon Elek, Tanya Filer, James Helgeson, Emma Herdman, Anna Holland, Michel Jeanneret, Neil Kenny, Reidar Maliks, Charlie and Melissa Marshall, Thibaut Maus de Rolley, Donal McCarthy, Alice and James McConnachie, Mary McKinley, Michael Montgomery, Isabelle Moreau, Michael Moriarty, Neela Mukherjee, Kathryn Murphy, Corinne Noirot, John O'Brien, Richard Parish, Roger Pearson, Pierre Ronzeaud, Charlotte Scott, Agnieszka Steczowicz, Alexis Tadié, Rowan Tomlinson, Kate Tunstall, Alain Viala, Bill and Penny Warrell, Caroline Warman, and Wes Williams. They, too, have my thanks.

Index

Dates are given (where known) of the people mentioned in this book. For most, dates are those of birth and death, but for some they mark the period during which the person is presumed to have been active (indicated by *fl.*). Modern scholars are listed only insofar as they impinge directly on the editorial history of the *Essais*. Works, where listed, are to be found under the names of their authors.